PUBLIC ARCHEOLOGY

STUDIES IN ARCHEOLOGY

Consulting Editor: Stuart Struever

Department of Anthropology
Northwestern University
Evanston, Illinois

PUBLIC ARCHEOLOGY

CHARLES R. McGIMSEY III
Director
Arkansas Archeological Survey
and
University of Arkansas Museum

ʃP

SEMINAR PRESS   New York and London   1972

SEMINAR PRESS, INC.
111 Fifth Avenue, New York, New York 10003

United Kingdom Edition published by
SEMINAR PRESS LIMITED
24/28 Oval Road, London NW1 7DD

LIBRARY OF CONGRESS CATALOG CARD NUMBER: 70-182662

PRINTED IN THE UNITED STATES OF AMERICA

TO

The people of Arkansas and their elected representatives, who together have had the foresight and determination to blaze new trails in archeological legislation and public support, and by so doing have provided Arkansas with a potential for the best state program of archeological research, preservation, and development in the country.

Contents

Designing a State Antiquities Act

One Example—Arkansas

A SUMMARY OF CURRENT STATE AND FEDERAL SUPPORT

THE STATUS OF PUBLIC SUPPORT FOR ARCHEOLOGY IN EACH STATE

Introduction

EXAMPLES OF ARCHEOLOGICAL LEGISLATION

Examples of State and Local Archeological Legislation

Principal Federal Legislation Affecting Archeological Preservation

Preface

In 1958 I was asked to assist the Legislative Council of the Arkansas Legislature in making a study of state-supported programs of archeological research. The results of this study were reported briefly in a paper given at the 1958 meeting of the Society for American Archaeology in Norman, Oklahoma. Mimeographed copies of excerpts from typical state antiquities acts were distributed at that time, but no further public report was made. This initial study resulted in the legislative establishment of a state program of archeological research at the University of Arkansas (Act 82 of 1959, Acts of Arkansas—see page 63), but, unfortunately, no funds were made available to implement this program either then or subsequently.

In an attempt to remedy that situation the Legislature requested that I make a second study in 1966. This resulted in a rather complete compilation of data on state-supported archeological research programs in each of the fifty states. During the compilation of this report it became evident that interest in this type of information was widespread and that legislatures other than that of Arkansas desired this type of background information when considering programs of their own.

The 1966 study resulted in the legislative establishment and, even more important, the funding of the Arkansas Archeological Survey, and I was named as its Director. Despite several abortive attempts to bring the 1966 study up-to-date and make it available to a wider audience than the Arkansas Legislature, the duties attendant upon establishment and operation of the Survey have been such that this did not prove possible until now.

This publication was prepared with two audiences in mind: my colleagues in the archeological profession who are or may be about to become engaged in developing programs in their own states, and the growing number of legislators and other interested citizens who are becoming increasingly concerned with preserving their states' archeological heritage. My colleagues may find some sections somewhat elementary in nature while others may feel that I have not provided enought basic data. I have tried to steer a middle course in order to make the information desired by both audiences available in a single publication.

Hopefully, this publication will provide a base for discussion as well as encourage the development of well-thought-out state-supported archeological programs in each state. If it is a factor leading to such a development in only one or two states, however, I believe all who have taken the time to provide and coordinate the data will feel that their time was well invested.

The state which *really* matters is your own. It is to those persons in each state who are determined to insure development of an archeological program or who may be inspired and helped to do so by more complete information that this publication is particularly directed.

I am deeply indebted to my many professorial colleagues and others in each of the fifty states for supplying the data for the initial legislative reports and for this publication. I hope this information will be of as much assistance to other states as it was to us in Arkansas in developing an adequate state-supported program of archeological research, preservation, and development. I would be remiss if I did not take note that the text of the first sections benefited greatly from the critical comments of Louis Brennan, Hester A. Davis, E. Mott Davis, Henry Hamilton, the late Dan Josselyn, and a number of the archeologists associated with the Arkansas Archeological Survey.

While the data reported herein was basically supplied by my colleagues and others in each state and generally was revised by them in draft in late 1969, I want to make it clear that I, alone, am responsible for the final selection and interpretation of that data. Every effort was made to insure accuracy and completeness, but any errors or misinterpretations present are my responsibility. I have made an attempt to keep in touch with developments during 1970, and insofar as possible have brought the state summaries up to date as of early 1971. No doubt I was not totally successful in this attempt and will appreciate receiving additions and corrections.

Charles R. McGimsey III

ARCHEOLOGY AND THE PUBLIC

A Challenge

The next fifty years—some would say twenty-five—are going to be the most critical in the history of American archeology. What is recovered, what is preserved, and how these goals are accomplished during this period will largely determine *for all time* the knowledge available to subsequent generations of Americans concerning their heritage from the past. It is incumbent upon all persons knowledgeable about or interested in archeology, to whatever degree, to do their utmost *now* to insure that the maximum amount of critical data is preserved. Our generation cannot postpone the decision to work toward this preservation, for the forces of destruction are multiplying and gaining momentum. The next generation cannot study or preserve what already has been destroyed.

Perhaps you feel I am exaggerating the danger. Archeologists are accustomed to working slowly and sometimes are inclined to ignore what is going on around them. We all are inured, to some extent at least, to the constant destruction of sites. Is there now a really critical cause for alarm? I can cite facts and figures for Arkansas, and I know that they reflect a situation found throughout the Mississippi Alluvial Valley. I have reason to believe that similar, equally destructive circumstances prevail throughout the country.

Spot checks in Arkansas indicate that twenty-five percent of the known sites have been destroyed within the past ten years. In a five-year period (1960-1964) an estimated 703,000 acres in Arkansas were newly cleared. Not only are sites destroyed during clearing but also, once cleared, these sites are subject to modern but archeologically destructive practices such as chisel plowing, subsoiling, and land leveling. In Arkansas, leveling in particular is an urgent problem. The United States Soil Conservation Service confidently expresses the opinion that within twenty-five years all levelable land in Arkansas will have been leveled. That constitutes over one-third of the total land surface in the state and includes a major portion of the heartland of the Mississippi and Caddo archeological culture areas. Once an area has been leveled, perhaps ninety percent of the archeological information is destroyed.

I believe that a little effort would reveal similar, perhaps even graver, figures for every state, if not in connection with land leveling, then with chisel plowing, subsoiling, strip mining, urban expansion, highway and reservoir construction, or some combination of these and other factors. To these "necessary" destructive agencies must be added the host of collectors who can be almost equally destructive, unless they are provided with and accept the leadership which can make their interest constructive and rewarding to all.

Archeologists and other concerned citizens of today who fail to act quickly and positively must share the blame for the loss of our heritage equally with those forces which are actively, even if unwittingly, destroying the past. Indeed, those who understand the problem are even more to blame, for the forces destroying the past can usually justify their actions by showing that at least to some degree they are building for the future. The only justifications the archeologist and the interested citizen can put forward for their equally destructive inactivity are preoccupation with other areas of responsibility, a disinclination to become personally involved, or simple laziness. In view of the nature, scope, and immediacy of this problem, these now are unsatisfactory excuses at best. Archeologists, amateur and professional, cannot expect others to preserve the nation's heritage if we, who by interest or training are best qualified in the field, do not assume a role of positive leadership and public education. If, in another two generations, our archeological successors are reduced to doing little more than restudying museum collections, they can point the finger of blame directly at the trained archeologists and other knowledgeable citizens of today.

This report is one step, long overdue, designed to provide some of the basic data necessary to the further development of effective, publicly supported programs of archeological research and development. The next step is up to you.

The Practice of Archeology:
A Principle and Some Problems

Statement of a Principle

There is no such thing as "private archeology."

We are none of us born in a vacuum. We all are products and recipients of tens of thousands of years of biological and cultural history. This history, working with our present-day surroundings, affects our every thought, our every action. Knowledge of this past, just as knowledge about our environment, is essential to our survival, and the right to that knowledge is and must be considered a human birthright. Archeology, the recovery and study of the past, thus is a proper concern of everyone. It follows that *no individual may act in a manner such that the public right to knowledge of the past is unduly endangered or destroyed.* This principle is crystal clear. Unfortunately, however, attempts to place it in practice are often thwarted by misunderstanding, by conflicts with more immediate and better understood if not more basic rights, or by impossible situations brought about through lack of funds and inadequately trained personnel.

Despite these very real problems, it remains valid to assert that all archeological data, including the archeological objects themselves, falls into the domain of public interest and concern. How then does this affect the practice of archeology?

The Public and Archeology

Even though private funds may finance archeological research and private citizens may collect relics using their own resources, *no one owns exclusive rights to an archeological object or, even more important, to archeological data* any more than the owner of a Rembrandt has exclusive rights to that painting. An individual or a corporate body may be the legal owner or repository of such data or such an object, but in a certain undefined, perhaps undefinable but nonetheless very real sense, objects of art and scientific information belong to and are rightfully a part of the heritage of everyone. Legal possession does not automatically carry with it the right of destruction, and no individual or corporate body possesses the right permanently to deprive the public of any significant part of that heritage.

In the field of archeology, two points are paramount in the public concern: the completeness of the data recovered and the ultimate and continued public availability of the artifacts, properly and permanently identified and with adequate accompanying data permanently preserved. At least three factors, all with almost infinite variations, affect these two points: the training and experience of the excavator involved; the material resources at his command which affect the degree of recovery and the fullness and promptness of the published report; and the ultimate disposition of the artifacts, including their continued security, the proper association of the objects with the necessary data, and their availability for public inspection.

By now, many readers may have the impression that I feel that no one may possess a prehistoric pot without a twinge of conscience and that only those with a Ph.D. in anthropology should pick up an arrowhead or touch a trowel to the ground. Nothing could be farther from the truth.

The prehistoric record of our human past is written in the soil. In this age of rapid transformation of the earth's landscape, our only hope for recovery of any major portion of this history is by nearly total involvement of the public. The trained archeologist or knowledgeable amateur who totally ignores this fact and fails to assume a position of leadership must shoulder a responsibility at least equal to that of the pothunter who spends every weekend digging through sites without making any record, and the trained individual who shirks his public responsibility is more responsible for loss of data than the individual who through ignorance simply could not care less. Knowledge is meaningless and generally destructive unless it carries with it responsibility. The greater one's knowledge of archeology, regardless of formal training in the subject, the greater the responsibility to take the initiative, to lead, to teach, and to persuade others to do likewise.

Some professional archeologists evidently still believe that extensive involvement of the nonprofessional and the public is a mistake, that amateur societies or public lectures simply increase pothunting. On the contrary, any such attitude is mistaken. By its very nature it is self-defeating.

If there was ever a time when archeologists could afford to operate as in a vacuum it has long since passed. Without public involvement there has not been and there cannot be effective public support of archeology, and without public support there cannot be legislative founding and funding of adequate programs to recover and protect a state's or the nation's archeological heritage. Without public appreciation of the importance of archeological sites and information there can be no effective protection of sites, or of the information contained within them, through well-written, enforceable antiquities legislation and through the willing effective cooperation of those who control the use of the land.

However, by emphasizing this need for total involvement I would not want anyone to gain the impression that I am suggesting that everyone should grab a shovel and go out and dig. Involvement has many facets, and each individual has an obligation to determine how he best can contribute and how his actions will affect the total picture. Here, too, knowledge carries with it equivalent responsibility, but lack of knowledge does not in any sense free one from responsibility. Irresponsible actions are never to be condoned, and they are even less tolerable in the field of archeology, where every record is unique, every loss irreplaceable.

The Practitioners of Archeology

Having stated that the proper practice of archeology entails total involvement of all interested parties and the public, the question now arises as to the degree and nature of this involvement with respect to individuals. Obviously, the vast majority of the public is not going to become involved beyond appreciating the need for proper archeological recovery and preservation and perhaps taking some interest in the results. There is, at the other extreme, a relatively small number of persons with graduate degrees in anthropology who teach and do research in archeology on a full-time basis. In between, there are a surprising number of individuals who, for whatever reasons, have not attempted or completed graduate work in archeology but who desire and intend to become actively involved in archeology, or who are already involved on a part-time basis in one way or another. It is the active practitioners of archeology, both full-time and part-time, who hold the key to future success or failure of the endeavor to educate the remainder of the public and to preserve our archeological heritage.

It is the responsibility of each individual who handles or affects archeological materials to examine his knowledge, his conscience, and his actions to determine if his activities are detrimental to the public good. The failure of persons to understand or recognize this individual responsibility and to accept the legitimate right of the public to the knowledge contained in archeological sites has been and will continue to be the greatest cause of friction and misunderstanding between those dedicated and determined to recover and protect that knowledge and those inclined to place private gain above the public good.

Professionally trained archeologists once burned by contact with individuals who do not understand or accept their individual responsibility are apt to be particularly cautious about further contact of any nature, and in some instances, they have tended to paint the entire public with the same black brush. Likewise, concerned amateurs or would-be archeological participants have been alienated or discouraged by experiences with preemptive or superior attitudes on the part of professionals who do not know how to or do not care to be bothered with developing public participation in and support for archeology.

There is ample evidence today that interested and concerned amateur archeologists are the professional's greatest source of assistance and support and, given the opportunity, can become immeasurably more so. On the one hand, irresponsible individuals (and at times and in some places they seem numerous indeed) must be viewed and handled as individuals. On the other hand, the really concerned amateur also must recognize his own limitations. (Is his archeological knowledge and background really adequate to accomplish the job without destroying more data than he is recovering?) The amateur must also recognize the limited resources available to the average professional and consequently the professional's constant and acute frustration that he cannot be everywhere at once and be "all things to all people." No one can investigate, much less save, sixty sites while carrying a full teaching load! The concerned amateur has a responsibility not only to hold his own archeological activity within the bounds of his knowledge, but he must also help insure that those with professional training in his state or area are provided with the funds and facilities necessary to enable them to work with maximum effectiveness.

Before proceeding further we must face briefly, if directly, the question: Just who or what is an archeologist? If the public is to be asked to support the field of archeology, it has a right to a practical as well as an academic answer to this question. There are some who would restrict the term solely to those who hold advanced academic degrees in the subject and are practicing archeology on a full-time basis. This is too narrow a definition. At the other extreme, not everyone who collects arrowheads or digs into an archeological site is an archeologist.

The professionally trained archeologist is interested almost entirely in the data. The objects themselves are simply one form of that data and have no intrinsic interest or value. They have "value" only because of what they can tell. At the other end of the spectrum, the pothunter is interested almost entirely in the objects as intrinsically and ofttimes materially valuable. The data, if considered by the pothunter at all, definitely is of secondary importance. Do these extremes help us reach a definition of an archeologist that is more flexible and realistic? I believe, as a rule of thumb, it can be said that anyone who is at least as interested in preserving archeological data as in recovering archeological objects, and who works with equal effectiveness to achieve both goals, should pass muster as an archeologist, amateur or professional—the distinction between amateur and professional being not a line but a gradation based solely upon the individual's training, experience, and degree of involvement.

It should be emphasized here that the vast majority of the practitioners of archeology do not fit into either extreme. They are neither fully trained professional archeologists nor out-and-out pothunters. While many may be strongly oriented toward objects and collections, a majority are well-intentioned capable individuals who are interested in establishing and maintaining the scientific integrity of those objects (or would be willing to learn how to achieve this).

Archeology is exceptional among the professions in the degree to which persons without advanced degrees can and do contribute to the accumulation and interpretation of knowledge in the subject. It is, thus, one of the best and most effective scientific activities for amateurs. This fact has been both a major source of strength to archeology and the source of some of its major headaches. The presence or absence of an advanced degree is assumed by all to have a certain significance. It does. It means that the holder has spent a certain amount of time working in and thinking about the subject and has demonstrated his competence to his professional colleagues. He can obtain a position working full-time in archeology, thereby increasing his experience. It means that he has a broad theoretical and factual background which should enable him to evaluate and interpret a wide variety of data and place it in its proper context. It does not mean he is fully competent in *all* phases of archeology or that he has the time or interest to become so.

The archeological participant who does not hold a degree in the subject does not start out with as thorough a background, nor does he normally have the opportunity to accumulate equivalent broad practical experience or theoretical knowledge. He often does have the opportunity to become extremely knowledgeable about one or more topics or regions, on not infrequent occasions equaling or surpassing in knowledge the degree-holding archeologist with respect to that particular region or topic. There seems little reason to belabor the point that an advanced degree in archeology, even one gained in an excellent department, does not alone provide absolute assurance that an individual will perform with complete competence or that the absence of such a degree precludes such competence. We all can think of examples where such assumptions have not proved to be totally valid. At best, an advanced degree suggests that competence should be assumed until the reverse is proved, while its absence carries with it the implication that the individual must prove himself by other means concerning the professional caliber of his work.

In passing it might be noted that the formal background and the breadth of experience of the proponent of an idea or theory will, or at least should, always be factors taken into account by others when considering the acceptance of that idea or theory—and properly so. Thus, the amateur archeologist must accept the fact that he is going to have to work harder and accumulate more supporting data in order to get a point of view generally accepted. Furthermore, he must disabuse himself of the notion that there is an "establishment" which passes upon or rejects each theory advanced in archeology. There is no group which can dictate what any individual scientist is to believe—he either accepts a theory or rejects it in light of his own competence and experience and in the light of his evaluation of the experience and competence of the proponents and opponents of that view, for no one could possibly review and evaluate personally all of the data relevant to every theory. Any competent investigator, whatever his background, must be willing and able to weigh all of the facts before reaching a conclusion, and, once having reached it, he must be able (and willing) to consider changing that conclusion should new facts be brought to light.

But if we accept the definition of an archeologist just given, how can equal effectiveness be determined? By each practitioner's deeds and attitudes. No degree, no certificate testifying to proper training, can suffice.

Each individual must demonstrate this equal concern by consistently placing the public's right to archeological knowledge above any personal wishes he might have to obtain or possess individual objects. He must endeavor to insure that the relevant data accompanying each object remains permanently associated with it. He must make every effort to recover *all* of the data which is disturbed by his work, not just a portion of it along with a portion of the objects. He must make some provision for public access to the objects recovered and their associated data, preferably including publication (and rare is the amateur or professional whose record is completely unblemished on this score). To the degree that he can and does do these things and restricts his activities to those within the limits of his training and competence, he can be considered a useful and needed practitioner of archeology.

It should be evident from this discussion that private collecting and private collections are not to be universally condemned. It *does* follow that *any* collecting activity, by whomever conducted, which needlessly destroys or fails to make publicly available the accompanying data is to be condemned. Persons or institutions responsible for such activity either directly (by making such collections) or indirectly (by purchasing or accepting collections so made) cannot be considered to be furthering the cause of archeology.

Further, any collection which does not maintain the integrity of the objects and their associated data is to be condemned. A difficulty with private collections is that generally they are more subject to loss of both objects and data, or to total dispersion, than are collections placed in public or private institutions. Regrettably, the record of such institutions in this same regard all too frequently has not been what it should be. But nothing is to be gained by hurling blanket charges against either individuals or institutions. Collections by individuals, which are properly made, with adequate provision for permanent preservation and public availability, can be of inestimable value. Efforts to guide and encourage such practices are far to be preferred to any shortsighted (and impossible) effort to ban any such individual activity. Institutions which contain valuable collections require not condemnation for their shortcomings but rather the active involvement of concerned individuals in their funding and operation. Only by such approaches can the public's interests best be served.

Those who go so far as to excavate must have the discretion and judgment to restrict their activities to sites and to a scale which their background and training enables them to handle without needlessly destroying data. There is more to being an accomplished field archeologist than good intentions or reading a book. It is because of this that the trained archeologist tends to look askance at the amateur's efforts in the field.

Proper determination of what to record, and in how much detail, when to excavate rapidly and when with painful slowness is essential to obtaining adequate records, yet this knowledge comes only with a broad theoretical background and extensive experience under proper supervision. This is often precisely what the amateur does not have, and sometimes he does not appreciate the need for it. If he does, and can recognize his own limitations, there is no reason why he should not be encouraged to proceed within those limitations and to expand them. Every excavator must remember, however, that no one can follow behind and correct his errors. Adequate records are the sole responsibility of the excavator. When in doubt, anyone excavating should ask for guidance from those who do know, and if this is not available, he should, if possible, cease and desist until it does become available. Finally, it is not enough to make adequate records. Those records must be made available to the public. This means that if you retain objects in a private or a public collection, the records which give those objects their scientific value likewise must be retained permanently and be capable of correlation with the relevant objects. An object without adequate accompanying data showing exactly where it was found, in what circumstances, and with what it was associated has little, if any, scientific value. It has passed from the scientific domain to become a curio, whether it resides on a mantelpiece or on a shelf in a museum. No one who contributes materially to this process can consider himself an archeologist.

The pothunter who excavates with no thought of the data obviously cannot be considered an archeologist. But neither can the collector who does not dig himself but encourages indiscriminate digging by offering high prices for choice items. The fact that some or even all of the data accompanying those particular choice items may be retained is no compensation to the public for the wealth of other data which is lost in the process of obtaining those particular pieces.

Shamefully, public museums and institutions, as well as private collectors, often are equally guilty of this practice, which is so patently contrary to the public good.

It may be true that it sometimes is in the public good for a public institution or a private individual to purchase an object solely to preserve the object itself. But the full circumstances surrounding that particular action, as well as the total ramifications of such activity, must be examined very carefully. It is of small comfort to the world if one or a dozen objects are saved, if such action leads indirectly but ultimately to the destruction of untold quantities of scientific data by demonstrating once again that there are financial or status rewards available regardless of the conditions under which the object was originally obtained.

Sites, Rights, and Responsibilities

While it is all very well to say that all persons interested in archeology must work together in order to obtain adequate public support, there are many factors which can lead to misunderstanding and dissension. While some of these factors can be laid at the door of such locally vital elements as individual personalities, the most significant source of potential misunderstanding, nation-wide, is in the area of ownership of artifacts and the nature of individual rights and unrealized responsibilities regarding archeological sites.

What rights, moral and/or legal, does a person have relative to a site he finds, collects from, digs, or perhaps simply knows about? That is, what actions and attitudes does he have a right to expect from others or, to look at the reverse side of the coin, what obligations and responsibilities does he have toward others—what do they have a right to expect from him?

The professional archeologist who finds a site is working both for the benefit of the public and because it is his job. His only excuse for not publicly reporting the location of a site is to protect it from destruction by nonarcheologists. This danger all too frequently provides just and sufficient cause for such reticence, for to reveal the location may well lead to the complete destruction of the very information and artifacts which, as an archeologist, he is trying to preserve. There can be no hard and fast answer here. He must decide for himself in each instance whether the public is better served by revelation and faith or by concealment and circumlocution.

What does a professional have a right to expect from others relative to sites he records? Certainly, there are no implied restrictions about visiting a site known to have been recorded or excavated by another, even though not yet published formally and in detail. Scientific surface collections can be made without it being felt necessary to contact the original recorder, but one professional more or less expects that another professional will have the courtesy at least to tell him that he plans to dig an unpublished site recorded or excavated (at least recently) by the first man. Further, it is expected that the second man would not plan to dig or otherwise disturb the site unless he understands that the discoverer does not plan to continue work there or that their work will not be at cross-purposes, and the first man will not attempt to discourage the second for reasons of "possessiveness" or simply because he *hopes* to dig the site *someday*. Of course, the same situation would pertain with relation to any qualified amateur who desires to dig the site. In all these circumstances the loss of valuable information and/or specimens to science does not enter in; it is simply a question of who obtains it. The pertinent factors are those of personal respect and courtesy.

What is the situation with respect to the rights of the discoverer and/or reporter among amateur archeologists or between them and the professional archeologists and institutions to whom the amateurs report sites? The situation is basically the same, of course, but we must approach it with the realization that some amateurs sometimes feel that they can obtain personal rewards and satisfaction from their archeological endeavors only through actual possession of the artifacts themselves. No amount of recording and reporting of information is likely to get the amateur a higher salary or a better position. However, he should have the opportunity to obtain personal satisfaction and professional recognition from seeing his name in print and through knowing that he is contributing to the public store of knowledge. I think the conscientious amateur often experiences this more legitimate satisfaction to an even greater degree than does the professional. Unfortunately, the opportunities for attaining this type of satisfaction are not always as readily available as they should be, and for this the professionals can largely blame themselves. Wholehearted cooperation between professional and amateur archeologists cannot be legislated; it must be won through work and understanding on the part of both.

In other words, the scientific results in terms of information gained and the degree of individual satisfaction achieved can be identical among professionals and amateurs, but some of the motivations, viewpoints, and even the shortcomings of the professional and the amateur may differ. The person who has not thought about the relationship in this light undoubtedly finds it difficult to understand why the amateur occasionally is so interested in the points and pots themselves or, conversely, why the average professional can be so cavalier in his personal unconcern about them.

Does the great range of archeological knowledge and competence among amateurs and their sometimes greater interest in the artifacts themselves affect the nature of "site rights" to the extent that, in fact, the situation often differs significantly from that just discussed with respect to sites found and reported by a professional? I think probably they do, but the extent undoubtedly varies with each individual occasion.

Because the amateur may often feel a certain vested interest in the material which potentially can be recovered from a site, his communications to other amateurs regarding its location will be determined on a personal basis. But what of sites reported by amateurs to professionals representing scientific institutions? What actions and attitudes do the respective parties have a right to expect? I feel that such institutions should recognize the somewhat personal nature of the site information reported and should make such information available to others only on the basis of a scientific need to know. If site locations are made available to the public indiscriminately, it will inevitably lead not only to indiscriminate destruction of those sites but also to a breakdown in communication between the institution and its most important source of information—the amateur. In turn, it must be recognized by the amateur that the institution has a duty to see that the site information is used to the best scientific advantage.

It can be argued correctly that such reticence is not the way things should be, but, until such time as a larger proportion of the public is aware of the value and the uniqueness of the data contained within each archeological site, it is a policy which must be adopted, though followed with discretion rather than as an ironclad rule.

To carry the discussion a step further, what rights and responsibilities pertain between an amateur and the institution to which he has reported a site when one or the other desires to carry out an extensive excavation of that site? A pothunter probably digs a site because he wants material to sell or display; an amateur archeologist may dig because he wants to acquire a "collection" and at the same time make a scientific contribution or, occasionally, because a particular site needs to be dug. The professional almost without exception digs a site because he or his supervisor feels it needs to be dug. In twenty years of excavation, I do not recall ever having dug a site for the simple reason that I wanted to dig it. It was always because the information which I hoped would be present was needed or else because the site was in danger of being destroyed. For all that, I am sure professionals enjoy digging just as much as amateurs. Certainly, there gets to be a personal identification between a site and the excavator (and this occasionally causes problems), but by and large the relationship for the professional tends to be a businesslike one rather than a personal one. I know of one particular site in New Mexico and several in Arkansas that I would give a very great deal to be able to dig, yet if someone else dug them, I could accept this without much pain *so long as they were dug properly*.

The amateur often feels a much closer personal attachment to a site. It is *his* site, and often he may not want *anyone* else to dig it. This tendency probably follows in part from the amateur's generally more restricted viewpoint or experience. For example, I have been concerned with sites all over Arkansas and thus am less likely to identify myself closely with any one particular site or group of sites. The amateur who goes out repeatedly over a period of years to only a few sites naturally feels a much closer identification with them. This tendency may also stem partially from the slightly different emphasis on goals already mentioned. If someone else digs "my" site but digs it properly and publishes his results, I still will have the information and therefore my primary goal will have been achieved. I will have lost the fun of digging the site and the credit for being the excavator, but these are (or should be) secondary. The materials from the site would not have been mine in any case. The amateur, even if he recognizes that information is of greatest importance, is more likely also to be interested in the associated material. It therefore follows that if anyone else digs his site and removes artifacts, the loss felt may be greater. Here, obviously, is a rich area for misunderstandings between institutions (and the professionals representing them) and amateurs.

If it is the amateur who wishes to dig, and he is a competent field archeologist who will report upon his work, or if the amateur has no intention of digging the site in which the institution is interested, then no problem is likely to arise. The problems stem from those situations where the amateur excavator is not adequately trained or for some reason is unlikely to excavate properly or where the institution feels it necessary to excavate extensively at a site an amateur is digging or actively plans to dig.

Here, though the elements of personal respect and courtesy still pertain, they, on occasion, may not be applied, and the archeologist is (or should be) much more concerned with seeing that valuable information is not lost than in standing on his own dignity or in protecting any personal "rights" he might feel he or anyone else possesses. From the archeologist's point of view, when the problem shifts to one of excavation by persons unlikely to preserve information, it ceases to be a question of individual rights and becomes one of the right of the public to the information threatened. The archeologist's actions, if any, must be based on that concern, irrespective of any presumed personal rights, either his own or those of the digger. Ideally, every archeologist should discourage excavation of any site (regardless of who found or reported it) by persons not qualified to dig it properly. Practically, of course, this cannot be done arbitrarily. The importance of the site, the relative competence of the digger, the amount and nature of potential destruction by the digger and/or other forces, public relations, and other factors all enter into any decision as to the proper course of action. When and how the archeologist should attempt to exercise this public and scientific obligation of protecting history is one of the most difficult questions he faces. The professional or amateur who attempts to make decisions as to when and how to take action on this question does so at his peril. But take action he must.

In the case of the reasonably competent amateur who wishes to excavate occasionally at a site he has reported, one has only to consider what the feelings of such an individual must be when he finds a good site, and dutifully reports it, only to have the university, the survey, or the professionals step in, excavate it entirely, and disappear with "his" artifacts. Unless his interests happen truly to center on information and not artifacts, this result of having reported a site is apt to give even the scientifically oriented amateur pause, particularly when you also consider the time it often takes the resultant information to appear in published form. When scientific necessity justifies the institution in taking over the work, the reporter has a right to expect the institution to explain the necessity, and the institution in turn has a right to expect the reporter to attempt to understand the situation. The only comfort is that such a circumstance is not likely to occur frequently. Unless unusual circumstances impart a special urgency, any institution would rather expend its limited funds excavating sites other than those already being excavated, however slowly, by competent amateurs who will eventually report on their work.

Two final points should be mentioned briefly. The first is the attitude typified by the comment: "Dams, highways, contractors, and farmers destroy lots more material than I do, so why shouldn't I dig? At least by so doing I save some of the pots or other material." This argument can be readily refuted. The material is not the important thing to save; in fact, scientifically, the material has almost no value at all unless the digger also preserves the related information (if he does, then, of course, these comments do not apply). Furthermore, the public cannot afford the attitude that because a lot of information is being unavoidably lost, a little more intentionally destroyed does not matter. Loss of information through construction and farming is a matter of very great concern, but at least the farmers, contractors, and others are doing their jobs and not intentionally destroying archeological information. What is the justification or excuse of the pothunter? Furthermore, intentional destruction is highly contagious! The public has a right to expect that every excavator will respect the public's welfare by obtaining information along with the artifacts, just as the public has a right to expect that an individual who buys a piece of property in a residential district will not erect a rendering plant on it.

Reporting a site to an institution certainly does not mean that excavation rights to that site thereby become transferred solely to the institution. But, to emphasize the second point needing wide public recognition, the fact that an institution does not excavate a site known to it does not bestow upon anyone else a right to destroy the site Yet some apparently do reach just such a conclusion. In a number of instances I have heard a comment to the effect that "the museum has known about this site for years and has done nothing about it, therefore what right has the museum to complain if I or anyone digs it?" The museum's right to complain, of course, is that of any public institution with an obligation to protect the rights of the public. Every archeological institution knows of hundreds of sites which for one reason or another it has had no opportunity to investigate. Lack of activity by the public institution, rather than bestowing on individuals a right· to dig and destroy, actually increases the responsibility of the individual to protect that information. If the public institution cannot operate as it would like to because of lack of funds, then it is up to any interested individual citizens to fill the gap either by helping protect the site or by helping secure funds in order that it may be excavated properly.

What it really comes to in resolving questions concerning an individual's rights with respect to a particular site is that all individuals involved—the professionals (representing institutions) and the amateurs—must be willing to act in a manner which best protects the right of the public to the archeological information contained within that site. And, as the parties most actively concerned, archeologists of all varieties must work together to protect the information from pothunters or other persons who would needlessly destroy it. Further, insofar as is possible, everyone concerned must operate from a position of mutual respect and trust, and each must justify this by exhibiting a willingness to discuss honest differences of opinion in a calm, candid manner. In no other way will it be possible for the professional to stand back with equanimity and watch an important site being dug by only partially trained persons (in such circumstances the professional often must feel like a parent whose daughter has just started to date), nor will it be possible for the amateur occasionally to stand aside with good will while a public institution accumulates artifacts (which otherwise might have accrued to him) in the course of recovering information essential to the reconstruction of prehistory. Nonetheless, in the overwhelming majority of instances, it *is* possible for all archeologists (professional and amateur) to work in close harmony, respecting the rights of all.

In concluding this section one important point must again be stressed. *No individual or organization (public or private) has the right to act in a manner such that those actions adversely affect the public weal*, in this case, specifically, archeological materials and data. Any possible adverse effect a particular course of action might have on this archeological heritage must be placed in the balance when the ultimate course of action is determined. When an individual or an agency determines that incidental rather than intentional destruction of archeological data is necessary, then the individuals or agencies responsible for this destruction have an obligation to endeavor to provide for the recovery of the essential archeological data. No other course of action can be justified.

This nation's past is contained in its soil. That soil is being disturbed and redistributed at an ever-increasing rate. *Those of us alive today will be the last ever to see any significant portion· of it in an undisturbed state.* This fact must form the basis for assessing the nature of everyone's rights and his responsibilities—to archeology—to the public—to the past—to the future.

Archeology Today

Anyone fully aware of the archeological situation in a particular state is aware that archeology today is in dire straits. Only a little of what one reads in the pages which follow is likely to hearten him or convince him that problems are restricted to his state alone.

There are, however, positive elements of hope. Federal legislation is providing some leadership and is encouraging implementation of archeological programs on the state level even though funding assistance still is at a minimum. In those states where everyone interested in archeology is working together there is a decided increase in public support of archeology.

This increased public support, if it is to achieve maximum effectiveness, is going to require a reorientation by all practitioners of archeology. New techniques for increasing communication among professionals and amateurs and for coordinating their efforts are going to have to be explored and developed. A greater effort is going to have to be made to educate those controling the land and its use to protect, insofar as practical, the sites on that land and to notify proper authorities well in advance of any necessary destruction. The general public needs to be better informed of the needs of archeology and the results of archeologists' efforts.

As more funds become available, freeing the archeologist from the restriction of digging only where salvage archeology is required, the archeologists themselves must develop a broader view of their problems. There never will be adequate funds to recover data from all the sites being destroyed. If we are to hope to recover a coherent story of the past and preserve appropriate examples for the future, we must determine where we are going to dig with the funds available to us on the basis of a broadly drawn problem-oriented plan. Emergency salvage will always be a factor to consider, but it must never again be *the* factor. The archeologist cannot afford to continue to let the engineer, the farmer, and the urban developer determine where he is to utilize the limited resources at his command.

It is up to the practitioners of archeology to develop these critically needed state, regional, and national programs of research and development and to prepare and execute a coordinated broadly based plan of procedure in accomplishing this research. No one else will or can do this for them.

The public as a group must recognize and be willing to support financially the needs of archeology, and as individuals they must cooperate in preserving to the maximum extent possible sites on their property or under their influence or control. Accomplishment of this, too, requires the coordinated efforts of all the practitioners of archeology.

A major portion of this report is concerned with the nature of the tools, legislative and financial, currently being supplied to the professional archeologist by the public. In no case are these resources enough to do what needs to be done, and only in a few scattered instances do they approach or attain a level which could be considered reasonable (or even rational) when viewed against the total context of social and scientific needs.

This fact serves to underscore again the necessity for the full-time practicing professional to cultivate and enlist the aid of the part-time amateur in arousing the general public. Not only can the amateur himself make a valuable scientific contribution but he provides as well the sole sure route to effective public and financial support. Failure of the professional archeologists to enlist this aid with maximum effectiveness has been one of archeology's most serious faults. Nor are the amateurs entirely blameless in this regard. When they fail to exercise the responsibility of their numbers as the most effective mechanism possible for generating public support for archeological research, they deprive the professional archeologists of the tools—money and time—to do the work they want to see done and to publish it. Thus, any failure to accomplish adequate field research in a state and to report upon it in sufficient detail to the public is a failure for which every archeologist—professional, amateur, and armchair alike—must accept some measure of responsibility.

Archeology presents the public with a problem which, unlike so many, will disappear completely if they continue to ignore it. But if this route is chosen, we and all succeeding generations will be infinitely poorer, and there will be no one to blame but ourselves.

THE STATE-SUPPORTED ARCHEOLOGICAL PROGRAM

Designing a State Program

The Need for a Program

Why should a state support archeological research with its public funds? What should a state-supported program of archeological research and development be designed to provide?

These two questions are crucial, but there is an even more basic question which underlies them: Why be concerned at all with recovering knowledge about the past? A brief answer to this question can be derived from several areas. In one area there is the scientist's need for information about man's past experience, the "laboratory" of human behavior. Only with this knowledge does he have a base against which he can compare man's present actions, thus providing the information necessary to enable some measure of prediction concerning how men will act and react in the future under given conditions. Our knowledge of the physical world has increased manyfold during the past several generations, but our understanding of our fellowman has not kept pace. This imbalance has reached a critical stage. It is true that the immediate results of archeological research can rarely be applied directly to such problems as international relations or population control, but the results do contribute extensively to our knowledge of man's use of and adaptation to his environment, the development of cultures, and to the gradual buildup of basic data that is essential if any measure of real understanding of ourselves and our fellowman is ever to be achieved. To a certain degree it is a part of the so-called pure science upon which "applied" science must always depend. The need for comprehending what makes human beings the way they are is so great that we can ill afford not to exploit every possible source of that information. Archeological research provides a rich body of just such data.

There also seems to be a deep-seated human "need to know" about the past. The day-to-day proof of this need is provided by the tremendous popular appeal ot problems such as determining De Soto's route through the Southeast, publications such as *American Heritage*, and preserved or reconstructed sites such as Mesa Verde National Park or Colonial Williamsburg. The "whys" of this "need to know" about our past need not concern us here. It is evident, however, that a state that has lost its past is as poor as an individual who has lost his memory.

On a completely practical level, archeological sites and materials represent a part of a state's nonrenewable resources. Archeological research and development can relate directly to problems of local and state economic development, for the practical value of developing a particular archeological site as a public attraction can be readily demonstrated. But more is required than the development of one or two sites as tourist attractions. Adequate conservation requires foresight to conserve as many of these resources as possible, for as each site is destroyed, a fragment of a state's history is irrevocably lost. Without preservation, future investigation is impossible, and we will have deprived ourselves and our children of an opportunity to participate in and learn from the past. The past belongs to the future, but only the present can preserve it.

Why State Supported

As mentioned, archeological sites are one of a state's nonrenewable resources, and since proper conservation of resources is a public concern, this conservation is the responsibility of each state. It is, of course, true that many of a state's archeological sites, like much of its wildlife, are on private land, but private individuals can act to preserve these resources most effectively through their state government and with active state leadership. In fact, without state leadership it is doubtful that any effective program of conservation will develop.

The results of archeological research are potentially of interest and concern to all citizens of the state, directly or indirectly. It is, therefore, both proper and logical that public funds be used to conserve and develop these resources. Private individuals and institutions should be encouraged, of course, to participate actively in the financing of archeological research and development, but the average citizen can best provide his measure of support via the state government, by means of which all participate. This also serves to reduce the cost to the individual to a reasonable and equitable amount while yet providing for an adequate program.

A properly established state program assures the state of an adequate level of scientific research, one that will result in maximum benefit at minimum cost to all its citizens. Only by means of a well-staffed state program is the public provided with a means for insuring proper protection and development.

Failure to develop a state's archeological resources will mean failure to develop one of the state's principal "natural" attractions. The cultural appetite of the tourist, from both in-state and out-of-state, is now being stimulated more than ever before, and it can be demonstrated that his interests center strongly on things of tradition and antiquity. For example, a recent study showed that Chicago's museums are the city's greatest tourist attraction, drawing more than twice as many people as the next most popular attraction, sporting events. The public is interested in archeology, and preservation of the past pays—in cold, hard cash.

A developed state program of archeological research encourages and develops additional financial support from both federal agencies and private sources. Without a state program full participation in federal programs is impossible, and grants of funds from federal and private sources are most likely to be made to those programs which can demonstrate the presence of a stable, qualified staff and a history of successful completion of projects. State funds, properly invested, can prime the pump and result in support and development which will greatly supplement the state's initial investment.

In sum, the state which does not actively support an adequate program of archeological research also fails to avail itself of a means of obtaining outside resources for the program itself and, in even larger measure, loses a rich source of direct and indirect income for its citizens, which can develop because of the program's results. Of greatest importance, it deprives its present and future citizens of knowledge and enjoyment which are rightfully theirs, and of the enriched cultural atmosphere upon which history has shown time and again the quality of a civilization depends.

What a State Program Should Provide

Leadership. The state program should set an example of archeological research and development which can be followed by others doing similar work in the state. In addition to leading by example, the program must be in a position to lead through instruction and assistance when institutions, organizations, or individuals request such aid. Archeological societies can be of inestimable assistance with this second form of leadership, but for them to be effective (and not a hindrance, which can happen) requires a great deal of the time of the archeologists connected with the state program. If these archeologists are few in number, hampered by lack of funds, or overburdened with emergency salvage projects, they cannot hope to provide the leadership necessary to engage hundreds of enthusiastic citizens in constructive archeological activities.

Coordination. The state program should be the coordinating agent for all state-supported archeological research, and its facilities should provide a repository for all the basic data concerning the archeology of the state. This is not to say that it should necessarily control all archeological research. On the contrary, it should encourage such work by others. But individuals and institutions can properly program their own work with respect to the total needs of the state only if they are aware of what others are doing and have access to all basic records via the state program. The program should also be in a position to coordinate state utilization of federal assistance available through the National Park Service, the Bureau of Public Roads, and other agencies. It should be the primary clearing house for the recommendation of archeological sites to be included on the National Register.

Such coordination of all state-supported archeological research is essential if the greatest return is to be expected from the state funds invested. In states where individual institutions have proceeded independently, without statewide coordination and guidance, duplication and competition have been the inevitable result.

Information. While leadership and coordination are vital, a state program which does not itself produce results in the form of information concerning the state's earliest history could hardly be considered adequate. The past brought alive can have both immediate and long-range benefits. This information should take many forms, including talks to interested groups and service organizations such as Lions, Kiwanis, parent-teacher associations, and chambers of commerce, exhibits designed to instruct students, museums to attract and inform tourists and local residents, and publications aimed at the general public, as well as the more technical reports required for scientific purposes. Furthermore, the program should have the capacity for prompt dissemination of its results. There is nothing more discouraging to an individual who has aided the program than to have to wait years to see the fruit of his cooperation. The artifacts gathered should also be readily available to other institutions or agencies for both scientific and general educational purposes through loans or by other means. Artifacts should be protected, but not all of them should be placed in cold storage. When they are in circulation and viewed by the public, they can become meaningful symbols of the past and the means of transmitting an understanding of and identification with the past. It is often in this manner that they can make their greatest contribution, educationally, culturally, and by promoting understanding and support of the state program itself.

Requisites of a State Program

The particular agency which is most appropriate to the administration and execution of a statewide program of archeological research and development will vary from state to state, just as organizational and administrative details will differ. However, the experience of those states which have evolved programs or partial programs or have attempted them suggests that whatever administrative route is followed, a number of aspects should be carefully considered if the program is to achieve maximum effectiveness and efficiency.

Administrative Structure. Recognition of the program as a separate budgetary entity either by direct legislative appropriation or as a separate department within a university, museum, or other state agency is a nearly universal trait of those programs which are adequately funded and which have shown any continued significant growth over the last ten years. Of course, the essential element here is proper recognition of the program and its responsibilities by both the basic funding authority and the organization (if any) to which the program is attached. No program can hope to obtain adequate funds if it has an unrecognized or peripheral position in the total organization of which it is a part. The establishment of a separate budget is one significant indication of the recognition necessary to the development of an adequate program.

Basic Facilities. The state program must have the facilities to carry out a well-rounded program of research over the state. Only in this manner can adequate information and materials be gained concerning the early history of the entire state. To achieve this overall orientation, the state program must have the capacity to handle three types of operations. (1) *Salvage archeology:* Federal and private funds often are available to permit the salvage of important sites being destroyed by federal or large-scale private construction projects. The state program must make provisions for the salvage of equally important sites being lost daily through urban expansion, individual farming operations, and many other losses for which no nonstate funds are or ever have been available. (2) *Problem-oriented research:* While it is important to recover information about to be lost, it is also necessary to obtain information from geographic areas, time periods, or particular phases of activity about which we know too little. If archeologists are restricted in their investigations to those sites chosen for them by construction engineers or farmers who are about to destroy the sites, they cannot hope to achieve a complete picture of history. The lack of resources to develop a broad problem-oriented research program is one of the great tragedies of American archeology. Creation of state programs that will make the development of such a plan possible is alone adequate justification for such programs. (3) *Cooperation with interested persons:* If any real progress is to be made, the assistance of interested and concerned citizens must be enlisted, and any fully effective program must develop, encourage, and permit wide interest and concern. This means that a proper state program must provide for facilities and personnel to work with these citizens. If an individual or a group of interested persons is desirous of saving an archeological site or of developing local archeological resources, the state should be in a position to render the assistance necessary for their efforts to attain a worthwhile scientific and public goal.

Auxiliary Facilities. A complete list of auxiliary facilities for archeological research would attain impressive proportions. For this reason it is highly desirable that the state program be in some way associated with a research-oriented organization such as a museum, or with an institution such as a college or university, which can help provide these auxiliary facilities at minimum expense. Necessary facilities include: permanent storage for the material recovered, a cataloging staff, an adequate library, ready availability of scientists in other fields (geologists, zoologists, malacologists, physicists, botanists) and the specialized equipment that each of them requires, a convenient source of short-term casual labor, type collections of archeological specimens, a vehicle pool, exhibit space and staff to maintain the exhibits, and so on. Most of these auxiliary resources, though essential, are required on only a part-time basis. If they can be pooled with other programs, maximum efficiency and economy will result.

Personnel. Organization and execution of an archeological research program is not a part-time activity. Though part-time personnel should be used, there must be at least one and, in a state with any significant amount of archeological resources, more than one archeologist who devotes full time to the task. Furthermore, the administrative organization must insure that these persons will be fully trained, competent, and reasonably free from unnecessary activities or pressures. How many may be required for an adequate program depends upon the size of the state and the richness of its archeological resources. As the Arkansas program gets into full swing, we are finding that ten full-time archeologists (including two who function primarily as administrative coordinators) are not going to be enough to do all that should be done, but they do give us a measure of basic coverage of the state. I do not believe that any state is so poor archeologically that the state program is a one-man job. Establishing the post of state archeologist is a step in the right direction, but, even if the post is adequately funded, a single archeologist can expect to do little more than keep a partial record of what is being destroyed. He will not be in a position to take more than minor positive action toward recovering and preserving the state's heritage.

The program should be provided with funds to hire auxiliary help—field crews to excavate, a laboratory staff to process the material, and secretarial help to maintain the necessary records. It makes little economic or scientific sense to hire a trained professional at $12,000 or more per year and then force him to spend a major portion of his time washing potsherds, which any untrained high school student can do, or to type up records, which could be more rapidly handled by a secretary at half the salary. The archeologists should be provided with a maximum opportunity to do what they and they alone can do—plan and develop a statewide research program, direct excavation, analyze the collections, prepare publications, and otherwise make the results of the program scientifically effective and available to the public.

The experience in Arkansas indicates that two administrative archeologists have ample work to occupy their time when there is a staff of eight research archeologists and the office and field personnel that must be available if the program is to operate smoothly and effectively. Furthermore, as any program grows beyond one or two research archeologists, definite provision must be made for second-level professional staff such as an editor, a registrar, a photographer, a draftsman, and adequate full-time secretarial personnel.

Budget. The size of the budget is directly related to the number of archeologists employed. A fairly accurate rule of thumb (in terms of the economic situation in 1971) would appear to be a minimum maintenance budget (for example, vehicle mileage, auxiliary help, supplies, equipment) of from $10,000 to $15,000 (allowing for some regional variation) for each full-time research archeologist. Another way to express this would be to say that the maintenance budget should at least equal the total salaries devoted to research. For programs large enough for a coordinating staff (and there should be one coordinating staff member for every four or five full-time research archeologists) it would appear that a figure of from $30,000 to $50,000 for maintenance for each professional coordinating staff member is by no means excessive. This last figure provides for centralized data processing equipment, bookkeeping, persons to handle photography and registration of the artifacts recovered, and auxiliary staff members such as temporary or part-time help and secretarial assistance. Actually, these figures probably represent an absolute minimum and, even so, are predicated on the program having free housing and building maintenance and the loan of at least some major items of equipment from other agencies.

One point should be emphasized to those designing a state program. Do not be bashful. The work and public support required for a truly adequate program is not significantly greater than for a completely inadequate program. Besides, an adequate program is easier to "sell" because you are convinced of its worth.

Development of a Program

Study of the various state programs, as well as my own experience, leads me to suggest that two elements are vital to the inception, growth, and development of adequate state support for archeological research. The varied histories of archeological research in the states that do have developed programs is adequate evidence that there is no single road to success, yet I am confident that no adequate program will develop unless one or the other of these elements is present to serve actively as a catalytic agent. There are also other, subsidiary elements, and the more elements present, the more likely it is that a state will develop and maintain an effective program.

The first essential element is one or more individuals dedicated to the development of a state program. This person need not be, but most logically and often is, an archeologist already employed by the state. In the past and doubtless in the future, nonanthropologically trained personnel of state museums or historical societies, legislators, and other interested individuals (amateur archeologists all, to one or another degree) have performed this function. But it is the state-employed archeologist who can best serve in this capacity. In my opinion, he is under professional obligation to do so. This opinion, I suspect, will not be received with unanimous agreement by all of my colleagues. That they do not all agree or do not feel in a position to undertake the task is perhaps one of the reasons that there still is so little state support for archeological research. However, it should be emphasized that there is no one-to-one correlation between archeologists who do practice or have tried to practice this philosophy and the presence of developed state programs. Many have tried and failed and grown tired of trying because of the absence of at least one additional element. The archeologist can and should serve as a catalyst, but a catalyst cannot function in a vacuum. It is true that in many instances the logical person to perform this role has not done so, but before anyone is too hasty with criticism of an individual for such failure, it should be pointed out that successful performance in this role requires a personal and professional orientation and capability quite different from those which normally lead the archeologist to become an archeologist in the first place. He must enjoy or at least be capable of dealing with people, he must be a capable politician (in the best sense of that much-abused term), an adequate administrator, an imaginative developer, a good communicator, and almost immune to discouragement. More often than not, an archeologist is an archeologist because he prefers potsherds to politics (or he would have gone into social anthropology or even into politics!); although archeologists have become capable administrators, few really set out to do so. Rare is the individual in any field who is an imaginative developer and immune to discouragement. Further, proper performance in this capacity more often than not requires of the archeologist that he postpone the research he desires to do and, generally, that he must assume these responsibilities over and above the teaching, departmental, or research duties for which he was hired. The archeologist who is in a position to assume the role of developer of state support but who decides that he will not do so can find numerous justifiable personal, professional, and financial reasons for his decision. However, prehistory will continue to suffer unnecessary wholesale destruction so long as archeologists continue to fall back on these reasons, for the profession will thereby be failing to meet one of its most important obligations.

The second vital element in the development of an adequate state program is an active, interested, and coordinated body of citizenry. Sometimes this element assumes the form of a state archeological society. In fact, some such organization is highly desirable, for without it statewide coordination and communication become so difficult and time consuming as to be impractical. No one person can know or be able to talk or write to everyone who needs to be contacted if a program is to be developed successfully. Often the catalyzing individual, if he is a state employee, is not in a position to go to members of the state legislature to discuss new programs. To be effective, a great many people need to be active, but they need to be selling a coherent sensible program. This necessitates proper leadership and effective communication, and that in turn implies an organization of some sort. A state archeological society is the most logical such organization.

I can conceive of a state program being developed without one or the other of these two catalytic agents—although if both are present and they are working together, it is infinitely easier—but I cannot conceive of the development of an adequate program where neither of these two agents is present and operative.

While these two elements are crucial, there are a number of other factors which can play a decisive role in the development of a state program. These include a cooperative state-supported museum or a state university with a liberal policy toward research and development, an essentially separate appropriation for the program, one or more interested or concerned legislators, and development of a program which successfully involves and coordinates all of the state agencies concerned with archeological research and development. There may well be other factors which could be critical in individual states, and recently an increasing number of states have begun actively exploring various avenues of approach.

Not only is a state-supported museum or a research-oriented university in a position to provide the program with needed personnel and facilities for processing, storage, display, and distribution of the materials collected by the program but also a program budget attached to a functioning institution is perhaps more likely to receive active support. Most larger museums are accustomed to budgeting for research, and while universities, historical societies, or other agencies may also do this, research is less likely to take precedence in their budget discussions. Anyone who has attempted to compete for funds for an archeological research budget against increased enrollment figures in a university's department of English, for example, will appreciate this point. Certainly, a university or college which requires a heavy teaching load and makes little or no provision for research is unlikely to spawn an archeologist with the resources and time to aid in the development of a state program.

Separate recognition of the program's budget by the funding authority is likely to be a crucial factor in the continued growth and development of a program and, depending upon circumstances, may be critical in its creation. In Arkansas, for example, despite legislative authority and a sympathetic university administration, it proved impossible to fund a program until a procedure for an essentially separate appropriation was worked out.

One of the trickier elements in states in which several organizations already are active in archeological research may be in developing a coordinated program which enables all of these organizations to participate. The Arkansas system would be successful in states where only one or two organizations are already active but where there are others which wish to be. In other circumstances, doubtless, other systems must be developed. The system must fit the circumstances, and thus is best designed by the local expert, but success or failure in the area of coordination and total participation is likely to be crucial.

The Catalyst at Work

Experience with the successful establishment of the Arkansas Archeological Survey and with its abortive predecessors in Arkansas leads me to offer several suggestions to others. Most are obvious but bear repeating.

You will become discouraged, but do not remain that way long. I suggest no longer than overnight. Accept the situation as it is, in the sense of attempting to understand the basis for the attitude of others and, when necessary, adjust to that situation.

Design a program in which you have complete faith and then sell it. If someone raises what appears to be a legitimate question (legitimate from his point of view even if not from yours), be able to answer it to his satisfaction. If you cannot do so immediately, be sure to work out a mutually satisfactory answer before proceeding much further. Review any substantial changes with those with whom you have already conferred. Sell the same program to everybody. Realize that everybody has his own concerns and interests just as you do. Your program has got to benefit him in some way, however indirectly, or he is not going to be overly interested. If it affects him, it should benefit him. In some instances, the direct results of the program may appear—and actually be—deleterious from an individual's point of view. In this case you must sell the long-range benefits.

Generate a wide base of public, institutional, and legislative support. Arkansas was extremely fortunate from the beginning in having several legislators who were very interested and concerned. This meant that normally the archeologists were responding to legislative requests for action rather than the other way around. This obviously is a great help. If the archeologists in a state cannot generate initiative in at least one legislator to preserve the state's archeological heritage, they must start with the public, who eventually can elicit legislative action.

If legislative enthusiasm develops for protecting the state's archeological resources, then I advise strongly against directing the main effort toward an antiquities act. This by nature is a negative approach and should be viewed only as an adjunct to what is really needed—a positive program for state support of archeological research and development. No antiquities act can substitute for such a program, and it is unlikely to be able to serve even as a satisfactory first step. You cannot stop or slow down destruction by fiat. You can accomplish that only through a program of educating the public. To educate the public you must have archeologists available, and that does not mean archeologists who are employed to teach or do administrative tasks and who are expected to work with the public in their spare time. There simply is not that much spare time available to anyone, even if the person is completely dedicated and unmarried!

When you undertake to design a state program, do not be timid. Design a program you think will do the job well. There are two good reasons for this. Whatever program you design you are going to have to sell—to the public, to the legislature, and to the institutions which are involved. The best way to sell a program (or anything) is to be sold on it yourself. If you have designed a half-baked program, you are not going to be able to sell it with enthusiasm. Anybody can become an effective salesman if he really believes in what he is selling. I know, for no one could be less desirous or less qualified by inclination or experience to sell anything than I was. The second reason for going ahead and designing a first-rate program is that it does not take much (if any) more organization or effort to sell a good big program than an inadequate little one. Do not make the mistake of underestimating what the people are willing to pay if they are convinced that what they are paying for is worthwhile.

All institutions and groups (including the archeological societies) basically affected by the Arkansas legislation participated in the formulation of the legislation from the beginning. Differing points of view were thrashed out, but someone first had to take the initiative in providing a plan of operation or initial draft to form the basis for these discussions. The approval of the final draft of the bills by *all* affected organizations was gained prior to introduction of the bills to the legislature. This meant that when the bills came before the legislature, there was no source of organized opposition. The archeological societies saw to it that neither was there any possibility of failure because of inertia. Nearly every legislator on every legislative committee that studied the legislation was thoroughly briefed by a knowledgeable society member, normally one from his home district. In fact, almost every legislator heard favorable comments at one time or another from one or more constituents, and all received at least two mailings from the state archeological society, one containing a two-color illustrated brochure explaining the program and the other containing Xerox copies of several editorials from newspapers published over the state favoring the legislation. (The brochure with a covering letter had been mailed to every newspaper editor in the state.) These mailings were timed to arrive on the legislators' desks the day before or the day of the vote on the bill. The Arkansas program came into being because a great many amateur archeologists, legislators, other interested people, and the few professionals present worked hard and together. None of us is likely to forget that fact.

Probably the most useful approach for selling the program is the imminence of near-total destruction of archeological resources. A strong case for this can be developed in every state. The development of a state's ability to protect and retain its own archeological resources—rather than having them all disappear out of state—also can be a valuable argument, but when the chips are down, more people can be sold on the basis of the fact that we must either act now or not have any resources left to develop than can be convinced by any other argument.

Action cannot be postponed any longer. Nearly every legislator can be reminded of a site, known to him personally, that has been destroyed without record, and the archeologist who tries can readily summon impressive facts and figures to support his argument that the state's resources are rapidly disappearing. In short, the point is so valid, so vital, and so obvious, it is easy to get across.

One of the most important lessons on mechanics which we had to learn in Arkansas was that after the program is actually designed and legislation introduced, the work has only begun. Legislation does not just happen. I am not referring here to lobbying, at least not as I had understood the term—that is, buttonholing legislators and convincing them to vote for or against a certain bill. Legislative contacts of that nature can best be made by constituents. What I have reference to is the task of shepherding the bill through the various necessary steps and stages until it is finally signed into law. The "shepherd" must be on the spot or readily available to the legislature most of the time and he must understand or learn the legislative process as well as or better than the legislators themselves. On occasion he must be fast on his feet, able to compromise or improvise on a moment's notice. This last requirement implies that he must be thoroughly familiar with every aspect of the program and the total ramifications of each facet or approach.

To fully understand why a shepherd is so essential, it is necessary to remember that every legislator must determine how to vote on a dozen or more bills a day and must study hundreds of others at least cursorily, as well as talk to numerous lobbyists and constituents about bills already in process, coming up for consideration, or even those already voted upon, while he is at the same time trying to stay on top of the immediate business taking place on the floor of the chamber. It is a demanding task which, if done well, requires every resource at the legislator's command. He cannot possibly be expected to keep track of any single piece of legislation and all of the factors affecting it, even if he is the official sponsor and vitally concerned personally. Indeed, he should not attempt to do so, for this would necessitate shirking other duties and, as important as we all believe archeological legislation to be, a state legislator does have other demanding responsibilities. That is where the shepherd comes in.

I could not possibly even outline all of the duties that fall to the shepherd, but perhaps I can cite a few examples which will convey the idea.

The bills in their final form for introduction must be carefully checked over for typing errors, inadvertent omissions, word or phrase changes which purposely or accidentally change the meaning, and so on. This may mean sitting down with whoever does the actual drafting for the legislator, or at least getting a copy before it is introduced. Before the bill is introduced changes are easy to effect. No legislator can be expected to proofread every bill before introduction, and the official drafters cannot always be aware of all the implications of each word or phrase and so might, for example, use a "standard" phrase at a time when it was inappropriate. If somebody is not there to catch any such errors and get a change made immediately, the final legislation could be faulty. It may be that a copy of the bill cannot be or is not obtained until after introduction. Better late than never. But now even a single letter or word change requires seeing that an amendment is drafted, proofread, and introduced. This could cause a delay of days which might in itself endanger passage of the basic legislation. The longer the introduction of necessary amendments is delayed, the further the original bill will have progressed, the harder it becomes to amend it, and the greater the probable delay in the progress of the entire legislation. The shepherd not only needs to be on his toes but needs to know how (or if) amendments can be accomplished at every stage as well.

The shepherd also needs to see to it that things and people are where they need to be when they need to be there. I can remember one instance when a sponsoring legislator needed a promised letter from the governor indicating the governor's support of the appropriation bill in order that the legislator might have it for his appearance before the Joint Budget Committee, which in Arkansas has to approve all appropriations. The time of the meeting was changed. Someone had to be available to see that the governor's staff was made aware of this and that his letter actually reached the legislator's hands before the meeting. If this had not been done and the governor's letter had been late, the governor would have been embarrassed, the legislator (who was from another party) would have been thoroughly annoyed, the Committee would not have been able to act effectively without knowing the governor's position, and the entire legislation could have been seriously imperiled. All that was needed was an hour or more of rather frantic running around by one person to keep everything on the track. The Budget Committee which had made the time change had no one to do this, the legislator was caught up in other business, and the governor and his staff had no reason even to be aware of the fact that the minor time change seriously affected one of the hundreds of letters they were preparing. In short, without a shepherd there could have been a disaster; with one there not only was no serious problem but considerable gain—the governor was able to fulfill a promise, the legislator was able to make a strong case for one of "his" bills, the Committee was able to act positively, knowing that it was not going to be subjected to cross fire from the governor's office or the legislative chambers, and, coincidentally, the archeological program got its appropriation!

After experience with seven legislative sessions I consider the occasional, and sometimes almost constant, presence of a shepherd absolutely essential to the successful passage of any major legislation—unless you are luckier than any archeologist has a right to be. (See page 181 for an apparent example of what *can* happen without one.) The more legislation there is or the more difficult it is, the longer he has to be there. The shepherd does not need to be a professional archeologist. He does need to be someone who is able to work with people and who has the confidence of everyone who is closely involved. He must be thoroughly familiar with the archeological program, with the proposed legislation, with the legislative process, and, finally, he needs to be readily available to the legislature at all times when the bills are in process.

Let me offer two concluding suggestions. The first is directed to those active in organizing, coordinating, and selling the program. *Never lose your cool*, regardless of the circumstances or provocation. No one single factor is more important. Remember, almost without exception you are dealing with sincere men with major responsibilities in their own areas. If an individual does not see things your way (for example, if he exhibits lack of concern or even antagonism), remember it is either because he has what is to him a valid reason for his attitude (and it may be completely unrelated to the merits of your proposal) or because you have been unsuccessful in making him see how your program fits into his area of responsibility. You can only hurt yourself and your program if you give vent to your feelings and say what you think or feel at the moment. Go home, cool off for a day, then sit down and write out the reasons why you feel this individual should change his stand in the light of what your program does relative to his responsibilities as you know them. It may be that you will find shortcomings in your program by so doing. A carefully worded logical explanation arriving in the mail a day or two later followed up by another personal discussion will do more to convince the doubting administrator or legislator than will any amount of emotional expostulation.

While it is necessary that you be totally committed personally to the program, it is even more necessary that you never permit yourself, whatever the provocation, to give vent to your feelings as an individual. Giving vent to your personal feelings or reactions either to a person or to a situation always must remain secondary to whatever action or reaction will best serve the program and its development. Suppress any feelings of irritation, insult, outrage, or disappointment you may have. Then, without compromising principles, carefully and calmly determine what course of action will make the greatest headway against whatever obstacles have been raised.

The second suggestion is, be lucky. But remember, "luck" benefits only those who recognize it when it occurs and who have a plan and an organization to capitalize rapidly upon it. As someone has said, "Luck is the residence of design."

Public Participation

From earliest times the public has evinced an interest in participating in activities concerning the archeological record of even earlier periods. Archeologists, who make a profession of studying and learning from the past, somehow have tended to overlook or ignore the implications of that repeatedly demonstrated fact. Nevertheless, the public is going to participate, and no amount of legal action or moral suasion is going to discourage them. It thus behooves professional archeologists to utilize this inescapable fact to archeology's advantage rather than to condemn such participation, or to pretend it will go away, or simply to wring their hands in horror.

A great deal more is involved than simply bowing to the inevitable or facing up to the dictum "If you can't beat'em, join'em." Public participation provides the potential for archeology's salvation. There is too much to do and too little time to do it in for the professionals to hope that they can accomplish everything themselves with their present or any forseeable resources. There is only one place to look for the assistance that is essential to success—the public. Public participation can provide the four key elements that must be called into play if there is to be any hope for preserving any meaningful portion of this nation's past before it is destroyed. These four elements are: (1) adequate financial support for professional efforts, (2) an effective medium for increasing understanding of archeology on the part of that portion of the public which controls the land, (3) local resources that can be called upon readily in cases of emergency, and (4) experienced auxiliary forces that can carry an increasingly significant part of the investigative load.

Development of these elements requires a full and continuing dialogue among interested parties. If this, in turn, is to prove possible, the professional archeologists must not make the mistake of being condescending. Rather they must remember that, almost to a man, the amateurs are *volunteering* time, resources, and expertise. It is the responsibility of the professionals to see to it that others have an opportunity to develop and participate to the limit of their time, ability, and desire. Amateurs should not be forced, or even encouraged, to limit their "approved" activities to surface collecting or the reporting of sites.

This may remain a major area of contribution for many or even most, but opportunities to do more should be afforded.

For their own part the amateurs must recognize their own limitations as well as the severe (but different) limitations under which most professional archeologists operate. They must recognize the intense concern the professionals feel for preservation of data and understand their concern over any practices which tend to endanger that data.

It is the true amateur archeologist, not the professional, who can and must assume the most forceful and effective role in assuring that a state's archeological resources are not pillaged and lost through the actions of unthinking persons, persons unaware of the public's legitimate interest in and concern for those archeological resources, or by persons acting for their private benefit in such a manner that the public's rights are grievously transgressed.

If, for whatever reason, the professional archeologists present in an area are not willing or do not feel in a position to initiate the development of a comprehensive program, then it is the responsibility of the amateurs to do so. If they succeed, other professionals will thereby become available to develop and continue the dialogue.

If the professional archeologists in an area do not develop a coordinated program of amateur-professional activity, the amateurs, rather than blaming the professionals, may well need to look to themselves for the blame. No adequate program is possible if there are not sufficient funds. Funds for publicly supported programs are available only through state and federal legislation, and legislators provide funds for programs that their constituents demand be supported. The professional cannot do this. He can initiate, he can provide information, but he himself cannot carry the entire burden. Often he is prohibited from even approaching the legislature. The real burden of providing a state with an adequate program must be borne by the amateur archeologists of that state. Once the crucial role of amateurs in archeological development is understood by all participants, the intensity of the dialogue among them should increase with mutual profit. As a program develops, the amateurs will be joined by additional professional archeologists who will have an opportunity to provide increasing leadership and guidance, while the professional will be increasingly freed from the bondage of too little, too late. Arkansas' experience demonstrates that with only minimal professional resources available it is possible for coordinated cooperative efforts to achieve a viable state program.

With respect to alerting the general public to the need for protecting archeological sites, it should be a responsibility of the professional archeologist to provide the initiative and the documentation necessary to establish the importance of recovering and preserving the state's archeological resources. Nonetheless, it falls to all participants, and particularly to the amateurs, to make this information available to other citizens so that it will do the most good. A professor from the state university can lecture to members of chambers of commerce and Kiwanis clubs about the value of preserving a site until he is blue in the face, with only minimal discernible results. Landowners, like legislators, respond more readily to pressure from their friends and neighbors than to exhortations by outlanders from a college, university, or a state agency. Amateurs must make increased efforts to contact clubs, schools, large landowners, and corporations to explain the current national crisis facing our archeological resources. Unless and until *all* archeological participants can cooperate in an effort to make the nonparticipating public aware of the value of protecting and preserving archeological resources, the future of the entire field of archeology will remain in peril. Amateur participants, working on their own, might possibly enable citizens of an area to achieve a full appreciation of the archeological crisis. Professional participants could not possibly do so. If they work together, there is real hope.

The third critical element is the ability of the amateur participants to provide the professional with the interested, concerned, and largely volunteer forces so often necessary to carry out survey and excavation when public funds or the time to raise such funds are not available. From no other source can the professional hope to gain such a large body of dedicated assistance at short notice. To say that it is shortsighted for archeology not to make maximum use of this resource is a vast understatement.

The real heart of the problem, however, is the provision of maximum opportunities for the continued development of the auxiliary forces available. This is the fourth essential element. If the amateur participant in archeology is to be expected to make a meaningful contribution, he must be able to achieve personal satisfaction thereby. The professional, after all, is being paid to do proper archeology. The amateur is doing it solely because he wants to do so. If he ceases to want to do so, he stops, either entirely or by ceasing to use proper methods; either course results in an irreparable loss to archeology.

If we accept the assertion that archeology needs all the help it can get, it behooves us to discuss and, if possible, determine how best to enlist and maintain increased public involvement at every level. This is not likely to be achieved by informing the amateur that his only proper function is to find sites and tell the professional about them so that the latter may excavate them—someday, maybe.

Archeology is an increasingly complex science, but there is nothing mystical about it. Actually, the increased complexity may be a boon, for it is making each professional increasingly aware of how many subareas (geographic as well as topical) there are within the field, about which he may be only vaguely aware. Given this recognition of his personal limitations, perhaps it will be much easier for him to view the amateur, who likewise is likely to be knowledgeable in some areas and ignorant in others, with increased understanding. But the professional normally can, and knows he can, obtain additional information and expertise about any of these other areas. The same or at least similar opportunities must be available to the amateur if his interest is to be maintained and if he is to make maximum contributions.

In the section on the archeological catalyst I was speaking almost entirely from personal experience. In what follows I am, on occasion, speaking from experience, but to an even greater degree I am putting forth ideas which the Arkansas Archeological Society and the Arkansas Archeological Survey are in the process of devising and developing. Experience with implementing these ideas doubtless will suggest modifications. Hopefully, others will join the experiment.

The basic idea upon which the Survey and the Society are agreed is that the information and the opportunity should be available to amateur participants to become as knowledgeable and competent in field, laboratory, and analytical theories and techniques as their time, interests, and abilities permit.

Formation of the Society was itself the first step in this process. This not only made for improved communication among the state's archeologists but also made it possible for the most efficient interchange between the amateurs and the few professionals then present (only two in the entire state in 1960, when the Society was organized, and neither of whom was employed to do research or "public" education). The principal objective of the Society was and has remained *communication*. Because this has been its primary consideration, the Society has never attempted to equate Society membership with any particular set of attitudes. Membership currently includes the state archeologist and some of the more intense pothunters in the state. The Society constitution provides for expelling members, but the approach of the officers and board of advisors always has been that, however much of the membership as a whole might disagree with the practices of a few, it was better by far to remain in communication with those few than to alienate and thereby inhibit communication with anyone who could affect the state's archeological resources.

There is no possibility of influencing a person's ideas or his approach to a subject if you are not in effective communication with him. Even if attitudes are not changed, communication increases knowledge of each other, and such knowledge tends to inspire mutual trust and understanding. Some extremely valuable assistance and scientific information has been forthcoming from some avid pothunters as a result of this policy. A few have changed their outlook. What would have been gained by casting these members out? Nothing, and much would have been lost.

The Society, like most such organizations, immediately began to publish a newsletter which includes articles by both professionals and amateurs. These articles are of the educational ("how to") variety, or are reports on investigations accomplished. The emphasis during at least the first two years was on educational articles. Since that time, the emphasis has been on reports. Thus, if you were a charter member, you have a good file of both types of articles. Unfortunately, although an amazing portion of the charter members still belong, there is, nonetheless, considerable annual turnover so that these individuals make up only a relatively small portion of the Society's seven-hundred or more current members. Thus the majority of the current members have reports, but are sadly lacking in any direction or assistance by the Society in learning how to do more themselves. To correct this, the Society's board of advisors for several years has been urging that the earlier articles be revised and made available. As a consequence, the Society is now producing both revised and new educational articles which are being mailed to each current member. New members, when they join, will get a complete up-to-date file of these articles. In this manner each current member of the Society will have at his disposal a handbook of basic archeological techniques and procedures, which will constantly be updated and revised.

The Arkansas Society early extended its activities beyond meetings and the production of a newsletter. In the past six years there has been one or more Society digs each year, each of four to nine days duration. These are designed basically to be training exercises, although scientific work also is accomplished. Each person participating must first attend a full morning lecture on the nature of archeology, the background of the particular site being investigated, and the reason it was chosen, as well as the details of archeological record keeping and field procedures. After he has participated in this orientation lecture he is free to take part in the excavations for as much time as his schedule will permit. Two or more professional archeologists are available at all times to answer questions and provide instruction and guidance in the actual field operations. Lectures on one or another aspect of archeological theory or practice are given each evening. Some attempt has been made also during these digs to include processing and analytical techniques and procedures for those interested in these aspects of the work. All artifacts recovered are retained by the Society and are turned over to the Survey following analysis and publication. In the past this analysis has been accomplished either by the amateurs themselves, by some of the professionals, or by both. Publication is in the Society bulletin.

In the recent past the feeling has grown increasingly that provision of publications and the Society dig do not provide a really adequate means of individual growth for the more interested or experienced members of the Society. With this problem in mind, the Society and the Survey currently are attempting to design a program of education which will extend from indoctrinating the rankest newcomer to what archeology is all about to providing opportunities for Society members to become field archeologists on a fully professional level. In other words, we intend to make every effort to develop fully competent auxiliary forces which, together with the professional staff of the Survey, will be able to make a maximum effort to preserve Arkansas' archeological resources.

As it presently is envisioned, this educational program will supplement what already is being done. Also, it will be subdivided in a number of ways, for it is recognized that not all Society members are interested in achieving a professional level of competence, or of achieving one in all or the same areas.

One program will be designed for the individual whose primary interest, at least at this point, is toward becoming an expert at locating, recording, and, on the basis of surface evidence, interpreting archeological sites. This would entail designing a survey project and turning in to the Survey a specified number of survey reports, prepared in detail and including an analysis of the material recovered. At least half of these would subsequently be checked out for accuracy and completeness by one of the Survey archeologists. It also would entail completion of various assigned readings in the handbook and in other publications. The individual would then be designated a certified archeological surveyor by the Archeological Survey. The materials obtained would not necessarily belong to the Survey, unless the individual so desired. A complete report on them would be made to the Survey with the understanding that they would remain publicly available for further scientific studies as necessary.

Once a Society member has become certified, the Survey would be in a position publicly to sponsor him to carry out necessary surveys in delimited areas, and also would be in a position to sponsor surveys by this individual on state and federal lands, confident that he is fully competent to carry out the necessary reconnaissance and the subsequent evaluation and interpretation. Of course, with regard to projects on state and federal land it is beyond the legal powers of the Survey to permit anyone to become the legal possessor of materials gained thereby, but when desirable it would seem possible to work out an arrangement whereby at least some of the material recovered could be placed with the individual on a long-term loan basis.

A second program will be oriented toward the person who, while not particularly interested in surface collecting or locating sites, does wish to participate in archeological excavations. By doing assigned reading and attending Society digs, which would be partially restructured for this purpose, such individuals could become trained in all phases of archeological field excavation, including laying out grids with simple instruments, excavating various types of sites, and maintaining adequate field records under all circumstances. He would then become a certified archeological crew member. It would not be intended that he would thereby be qualified to initiate and carry out independent excavations. Rather he would be a more-than-welcome volunteer or paid addition to archeological excavations carried out by the Survey, and the Survey would be happy to recommend him to archeologists elsewhere. Thus this certification would permit such persons to participate in archeological excavations as crew members whenever their own schedules permitted them to be free and under a wide variety of archeological circumstances both in Arkansas and, hopefully, elsewhere. At the present time at a normal Survey field project it is not possible for the Survey Archeologist to spend an extensive amount of time working with any amateurs who might appear and wish to help. The archeologist in charge of the dig has sufficient responsibilities already. However, institution of the program described here would make it perfectly feasible for any certified crew member to present himself to an archeologist and be welcomed as an addition to the crew, perhaps enabling the archeologist to carry out far more work than his resources might otherwise have permitted, and enabling the Society member to participate to the maximum degree he wishes in a variety of archeological field experiences.

A third program will be directed toward members interested in participating in laboratory analysis. Here we will attempt to work out a program which will enable these persons to gain experience and competence in all normal phases of laboratory processing and in one or more specialized aspects of laboratory analysis.

It is planned that any individual participating in any of these three programs will be provided with a log book similar to a pilot's flight log where times, places, topics covered, experience gained, and the instructor's name will be noted. The instructor or supervisor will sign the log book. This should provide the individual with an interesting record of his archeological activities as well as providing the basic documentation necessary for certification by the Survey.

Hopefully, some individuals will be interested and able to continue beyond these basic programs to become a certified field archeologist. Such an individual would be certified as a surveyor, crew member, and laboratory technician but would proceed beyond that by individual instruction from one or more Survey archeologists so that, in addition, he would become knowledgeable about the procedures necessary to test archeological sites independently and to describe, report upon, and evaluate adequately the material and features resulting from this work. Once this was accomplished, it would become possible for the Survey, or other archeological agencies, to publicly support independent work by these individuals in connection with independent small-scale excavations. Such persons also would be eligible and available to serve as crew chiefs on Society digs or other investigations.

In time it may be possible to establish an additional stage of publicly recognized competence. Any individual already a certified field archeologist would work in close association and under the direct guidance of one or more Survey archeologists in order to become sufficiently competent to organize and supervise a full-scale archeological field operation and be responsible for the subsequent descriptive and analytical report. Such a master field archeologist would be, in all likelihood, equal or superior in field experience and the archeological knowledge of a given small region to the average new Ph.D.-holding archeologist. He might well, of course, lack the broad theoretical and factual background in the total geographical and topical range of archeological data and its correlation into the whole field of anthropology which marks the professional archeologist. However, if an individual is interested in obtaining this broader background as well, there is ample opportunity to do so at almost any major university.

In short, the various approaches just outlined should enable Society members in Arkansas to become professionally competent in one or as many aspects as they wish of archeological field, laboratory, and analytical procedures and should provide a means whereby they may obtain public recognition of having attained these various levels of competence. Furthermore, having obtained this competence, it should open up opportunities for levels of archeological participation, contribution, and recognition beyond those available to them now. In this manner, both archeology and the individual will attain maximum benefit.

While the programs briefly outlined here will enable persons to work toward and achieve full professional levels of competence in one or more areas of activity, it is true also that many capable individuals who are seriously concerned with archeology and desirous of participating to some degree are not in a position for personal reasons (or, because of their own professional and business commitments, able) to devote the time necessary to participate in a formal program leading to certification. Such individuals will participate informally in various ways. Many will continue to report sites to the Survey, as they have in the past. These reports will not necessarily or always be in the detail expected of a certified surveyor, nor will any analysis necessarily accompany them, but they will make the Survey aware of sites not previously known and enable it to carry out whatever investigations or analysis seems warranted. They will make presentations about archeological needs to various public groups. They will volunteer to assist with the more routine aspects of archeological work, such as one group who backfilled a whole site for the museum, or another who over a period of years devoted one evening every other week to washing and numbering artifacts. They will investigate reports of site destruction when no archeologist is available, perhaps even making brief tests or standing by during destruction to keep the Survey as aware as possible of what is developing over the state and to recover as much data as the situation permits, not independent of or in competition with the Survey but as an auxiliary arm of the Survey, enabling it to extend its data-gathering base far beyond what it could otherwise accomplish. In Arkansas there are many such individuals who will assist the Survey in whatever way they can and are called upon to do.

In my experience, these individuals will do this because they recognize the need and want to and enjoy doing it, not for any public or even personal recognition that might thereby accrue to them. Nonetheless, it would seem desirable for the Society and the Survey to develop a mechanism whereby it would be possible to provide these individuals with the information and background necessary to enable them to be of maximum assistance and to recognize that assistance apart from the formal program of education and development toward a professional-type competence such as that which the certification program proposes. The best ways to make this background and information available or to provide this recognition remain to be worked out, but the facilities already available, such as Society publications, meetings, and digs, probably can be structured on occasion along these lines. Certainly, it is an important area for amateur contribution to archeology and therefore is of vital concern to all archeologists.

Whatever specific techniques are worked out in Arkansas or elsewhere, we all must recognize that public participation in archeology is inevitable and, in fact, eminently desirable, even essential. Only through public involvement will anything approaching the necessary funding become available, or can informed pressure to protect sites be applied to those who control the land, or can the always less than adequate professional staffs be supplemented with the capable experienced auxiliary aid so necessary if we are to recover and protect the maximum possible archeological data. Achievement of this maximum potential should be a primary goal of everyone interested in and concerned with archeology.

Designing a State Antiquities Act

General Considerations

Well-drawn regulatory legislation can be of considerable assistance to a state concerned with insuring that its archeological resources are best preserved for the benefit of all its citizens. But such legislation cannot do the job alone, and any state which assumes that it can is doomed to disappointment.

If enthusiasm for protecting antiquities should develop in a state legislature, then it is strongly recommended that the main legislative effort be directed first toward the establishment of an adequate state program of research and preservation. (See pages 63-80 for one example of such a program.) When the major force of legislative enthusiasm is allowed to expend itself on the establishment of regulatory legislation (an antiquities act), the state will soon learn that this essentially negative approach has created essentially negative results. Antiquities legislation can be an effective tool, but a tool is of value only to the extent that there are trained persons available to make proper use of it. In short, an adequate antiquities act presupposes an adequately financed and staffed state archeological program. Without such a program the most carefully drawn legislation will be of no real value and cannot even begin to accomplish its stated purpose of protecting the state's antiquities.

If antiquities legislation is to have any meaningful effect, the law must be so worded as to be constitutional, enforceable, and desirable. Weakness in any of these three areas can only result in an ineffective law that ultimately will fail in its essential purpose and may even cause irreparable damage to the very resources it seeks to protect.

Constitutionality. Court acceptance of the following two precepts is essential if any antiquities act is to be completely constitutional:

46

1. The public has a right to the historical and scientific information contained in archeological sites, and, therefore, no individual has the right to act in a manner such that this public information is needlessly destroyed.

2. The police powers of the state can be exercised to safeguard this aspect of the public welfare.

There have been decisions in the United States Supreme Court and in various state supreme courts accepting protection of the public welfare as a legitimate governmental concern. Nonetheless, most legal authorities still prefer to justify a law on the basis of protection of health and/or safety as well as on the basis of public welfare. If an effective antiquities act is to be legally acceptable, it must be on the basis of protection of the public welfare alone and, specifically, the public's right to the information contained in archeological sites.

Application of these precepts to state-owned or controlled land can be practical, but successful application to privately owned land is more difficult when the problems of enforceability and desirability are taken into consideration.

If these two precepts are not accepted by the courts, then protection of archeological information and materials can be effected only by indirect means, for example, laws prohibiting vandalism, forgery, and grave robbing, which can be defined as crimes or misdemeanors because of the nature of the activities themselves rather than because of the archeological nature of the media upon which the activities take place.

Legal discussions of antiquities acts that I have heard or read are nearly unanimous in the opinion that antiquities legislation cannot be applied to private land. It is probably true that the state may not claim ownership of the sites or of the artifacts themselves, though the principles of "treasure trove" or of escheat are possible legal avenues which might be explored in this regard, but full court acceptance of the two precepts just outlined would appear to provide a legal mechanism for exercising some measure of control over privately as well as publicly owned land. If it is legally established that the public has a right to the information contained in an archeological site, then, while the state cannot claim ownership or forbid excavation, it presumably can act to protect the public's interest by regulating the manner in which excavation takes place and by making certain that excavation does not needlessly destroy this information and thereby infringe upon the right of the public to that information.

Frankly, if this precept is not accepted, I fail to see how a state can act legitimately or effectively to protect sites and data even on state land. True, here the state owns the sites and the objects in the name of the public and can therefore make regulations concerning them, but only to the extent that these regulations are for the public good. A state law which merely protects the objects and ignores the related information does the public a grave injustice. If lawmakers adopt a myopic, materialistic view, then the data, which ultimately is of even greater value than the objects, will be lost. Adequate legislation—that is, legislation which protects information as well as objects and sites even on state land—must be based on the precept that the information has public value, and it must protect that information as well as, when possible, the sites and artifacts.

While it may be true that acceptance of these precepts offers a constitutional means for providing some measure of control over both public and private land, it also is true that the equally critical factors of enforceability and desirability argue, at least at present, against any wholesale application of this approach to private lands.

It is sometimes suggested that *any* antiquities act, even if it is unconstitutional, has value as a threatening weapon. Persons responsible for serious depredations of archeological sites are not likely to be discouraged by vacant threats, while others generally can be dissuaded without the dubious support of any such law. A law which the authorities fear to test in court is worse than useless and encourages disrespect for the law in general.

Enforceability.   Many state antiquities acts now on the books are unenforceable. In some instances this is because the law would not stand up under a court test and those in authority as well as others are fully aware of that fact. In other cases lack of enforcement has been the result of the absence of widespread public and official concern. No law, however constitutional, is likely to be effective if a majority of the people are not in favor of it. Prohibition should have taught us that. An antiquities act must be designed to facilitate, develop, and encourage public support and to avoid, insofar as possible, situations whereby the law is likely to be honored principally in the breach. No law should be worded so that it obviously is impossible to enforce under normal conditions. This weakens the law by encouraging disrespect.

With no obvious way to provide a special police force (similar to game wardens) to enforce an antiquities act, public support of any such law is absolutely essential if it is to achieve its aim. The best way to gain widespread public support is to encourage interested citizens and to publicize the problems and the needs through an active statewide archeological program.

Desirability.   In addition to being constitutional and enforceable, an antiquities act must be desirable. That is, it should serve to bring about the recovery of archeological information, not simply prevent its destruction. This is possible only if the act facilitates the cooperation of professional and amateur archeologists and encourages public support for the protection and preservation of archeological information and materials. An act which alienates the interested citizen, the amateur archeologist, or the landowner is worse than useless. Finally, a properly worded antiquities act must protect the rights of the landowner and other citizens as well as the integrity of the archeological information. At best, an antiquities act is only an aid, not an answer. Education, not legislation, is ultimately the most effective means of preserving our archeological heritage.

Drafting an Effective Law

Persons drafting an antiquities act must determine what lands are going to be affected by the act, who is to be permitted to do what, how these activities are to be controlled, what ultimate disposition is to be made of the objects and information recovered, and, finally, what penalties are to be set. [See also pages 92-101 for a discussion of the various provisions now actually in force in one or more of the states and for references to states having particular provisions in effect. The actual legal citation can then be obtained by looking up the state in question (see pages 125-192).]

Provisions Concerned Primarily with the Land. The first decision to be made is whether the law is to be applicable only to land owned or controlled by the state, to county and municipal land as well, or to all of these plus the extension of some or all provisions to private (or even federal) land.

Adequate protection of archeological material and data on state land is probably the minimal amount that should be attempted in any well-thought-out legislation. Some would say that it also is the maximum. Certainly, without the state having taken some steps toward protecting resources on its own land it would be difficult to initiate any program encouraging private landowners to protect similar resources on their land.

Normally, protection of antiquities on state land can be accomplished simply by declaring that the state asserts its interest and ownership of all such archeological materials and data. However, there should be a provision charging a particular state agency with responsibility for investigating and preserving this resource. Without provision for an agency with the personnel and funds necessary to carry out this responsibility, any pious statement of concern or ownership while having the force of law can have no practical effect.

In many states (Arkansas, for one) the state constitution assigns responsibility for certain lands to particular agencies. If this is the case, legislation may not reallocate responsibility for any aspect of that land without a constitutional amendment, which is likely to be impractical. Therefore it may be necessary, as it was in Arkansas, for the legislation to designate an agency to be responsible for the state's archeological resources and to request that the agencies actually controlling the land cooperate in every way possible in order to achieve this preservation. Since the legislature holds the purse strings for all agencies, if the archeological agency has statewide support and exercises normal tact, this type of provision should be adequate incentive to effect a good measure of cooperation from all concerned. Either by administrative direction or, preferably, by legislative direction, the agencies controlling the land should be required to notify contractors and others working on their land of the legislative intent and require that such contractors also cooperate with the agency responsible for archeological preservation.

With reference to state land, three additional approaches merit consideration. All involve state land made available for sale. This is not as insignificant an area of potential control as might at first appear, for actually a great deal of land passes through the hands of the state, however briefly, as a result of tax forfeiture, for obtaining highway rights-of-way, and for other reasons. One approach is a blanket reservation by the state of title to archeologically significant areas, objects, and information. While advantageous because it provides maximum protection, such a provision would entail considerable administrative effort and would, of course, serve to cloud the title of all land sold by the state. The latter factor could well be viewed as adequate reason for opposition to such a statute.

This principle already is being applied, however, in limited circumstances. Where urban property has been purchased initially by an authorized urban renewal agency with the cooperation and approval of the Department of Housing and Urban Development with federal funds, the redevelopment authority may include, and in at least one instance has included, in its purchase agreements for private buyers a covenant reserving to the state the right to enter the property to recover any significant archeological material or data encountered during development of the property.

Another similar approach is that of restricting sale of land containing valuable sites and/or retaining archeological rights to it, but only upon the request of the state agency responsible for archeological preservation. This approach is administratively much more acceptable but does presuppose a state agency with sufficient data and resources to provide adequate recommendations concerning such transactions. Mechanisms developed in connection with the National Register also could be employed in this regard. No state now possesses adequate state facilities for this, though some, such as Arkansas and Hawaii, are developing them. Where there is any reasonable potential for such development, legislative provisions for such protection would be very desirable. Not only does such a provision give a measure of protection to lands about to become less subject to protection but it does so without establishing a legal situation which is bound to be violated more often than it is honored as well. Its provisions would be initiated only following due consideration by the agency responsible to the state for archeological preservation.

A third mechanism, which in most instances probably does not require specific legislative authorization, would be to attach covenants to the sale of land on which were located significant archeological sites, requiring as a condition of purchase that the buyer provide and pay for the recovery of the data contained on the land. This too presupposes responsible state evaluation and supervisory agencies.

The extension of any measure of state control to sites on private land is, of course, the crux of many of the preservationist's problems. As discussed earlier, I believe that, contrary to most opinions I have read or heard expressed, there is a legal base for extending some control to private land. Knowledge concerning the past is of value to our understanding of the present and the future. The public has a right to this knowledge and a right to prevent its loss. It follows that no individual may knowingly and unnecessarily act to abrogate this right. Based upon this logic, it presumably would be possible to draft a bill which flatly prohibited willful, unnecessary destruction of archeological data on private land. But law is not solely a matter of logic or legislative enactment; in this case the factors of enforceability and desirability become paramount.

Even if this approach should be accepted as legal, I believe that at present the primary result of such a law in many instances would not be increased protection of data but a serious reduction of effective communication and cooperation between the archeologist and the landowner and consequent loss of data.

A number of factors lead to this conclusion. For example, in the phrase "a bill which flatly prohibited willful unnecessary destruction," it is necessary to set forth with clarity and precision the meaning of "willful" and "unnecessary." Willfulness implies knowledge. How is the public to be informed adequately of what constitutes damaging destruction? Similarly, destruction as a result of farming operations could not be totally prevented. What operations could be considered necessary and which would not? Even assuming that these key terms can be defined adequately, would there be enough archeologists available to make the law effective? In the long run, to be effective such a law must have solid public support. Each state must judge for itself.

I have rarely met a totally uncooperative landowner. I have never met one who thought *anybody* could tell him he could not dig a hole in his backyard if he wanted to, or if he wanted to let his neighbor do so. To expect an archeologist to convince a landowner that the landowner does not have this right at the same time he is trying to develop and retain the landowner's assistance and cooperation is to expect the impossible. For any type of blanket regulation prohibiting unnecessary destruction of archeological resources on private land to be an effective preservation tool will require far more and far stronger public support for the protection of our archeological resources than yet exists. As a matter of fact, if this level of public support is attained, the law will be largely unnecessary. Education is the answer. Ironically, unless states take prompt action, it seems just possible that before this level of public education and support is attained there might be precious little archeology left to preserve. This simple fact provides the strongest possible motivation for exploring alternate, less stringent but more practical approaches to the problem of preserving archeological resources on private land than a blanket application of the principle of the public's right to that archeological information. Two counties in California (see pages 230-234), however, actually have passed such legislation. Whether this legislation is too far in advance of public education remains to be seen. Let us hope not.

The federal approach of restricting the use of federal funds for projects that adversely affect archeological data contained in sites on the National Register is one that might also be explored by the states. Until practical guidelines are tested and, if necessary, various courts have spelled out in greater detail the lengths to which this principle can be applied, caution is advised. (See discussion on pages 112-117.)

It is always possible for legislation to include a section encouraging citizens to do nothing unnecessarily destructive of archeological resources, and a number of states have done this. Certainly, on the one hand, such legislative encouragement can do no harm and it does establish public concern. On the other hand, it alone is unlikely to be responsible for extensive positive action. A more positive approach is to provide the private landowner with a mechanism to protect sites on his property and to encourage its use. A number of possibilities present themselves in this regard.

While it is true that a landowner who wants to protect a site on his property can do so without benefit of legislation, it also is true that with proper legislative encouragement he is more likely to do so. In some states it may strengthen his hand if it is specifically spelled out that collecting archeological objects or excavation of sites on private land without the permission of the landowner is an act of trespass.

Easements provide another approach which, while yet largely untried, may prove to be of considerable utility in enabling the state to assist private landowners in protecting archeological sites. The principle of easement is one familiar to all who have worked with the United States Army Corps of Engineers on reservoir projects. It is also used to some extent by highway departments for scenic and other purposes, as well as by other governmental agencies, but the concept of providing a specific legal provision for obtaining an easement for the express purpose of preserving and protecting scientific data was first incorporated into law in the antiquities act of Arkansas. More recently, Texas and Mississippi have incorporated such a provision into their antiquities acts.

Under an easement a landowner surrenders certain of his rights concerning his property to another either by sale or donation. Depending upon the conditions of the agreement, the easement may apply to the land only while it is under the control of the present landowner, or it may be recorded on the deed and thus become more or less permanently attached to the land. (The duration of easements varies in different states, but easements are generally accepted as running for approximately seventy-five years.) In some instances easements might be purchased, in which case the purchase price itself could be a form of inducement to the landowner to protect sites on his property, but, given the limited financial resources available to most agencies concerned with archeological preservation, easements donated or given for a token fee are more likely to be feasible. Here the appeal must be to the landowner's concern for providing protection.

The Arkansas easement provision specifies that a landowner who desires to protect an archeological site on his property may voluntarily surrender sole control over that portion of his property containing the site by entering into a written agreement with the Arkansas Archeological Survey. Under the terms of this agreement the site is designated an archeological landmark and, more importantly, *both* the Survey and the landowner must then give permission before any activity which would be potentially destructive of the archeological data may take place on the site.

As noted previously, basically similar legislation has recently been passed in Texas and Mississippi, though in both of these states the wording is such that it appears that the landowner surrenders all control to the state when he enters into the agreement. Another variation appears in the recent Colorado legislation which authorizes the state to extend its permit controls to private land upon application of the landowner. One advantage to the landowner of such an easement is that by coassigning the right of permission to dig to a somewhat impersonal agency he is perhaps better able to ward off neighbors or others who might want to excavate or damage the site. He correctly can disclaim the right to grant such permission and can shift responsibility to the designated agency. This agency should have recognized standards as to who may dig and thus should be in a better position to protect the site from untrained excavators without causing undue antagonism toward either the landowner or itself.

The disadvantage of a permanent easement is that it clouds the title, and this may be enough to discourage its widespread use. Also an easement tied to a particular landowner can be readily rescinded by a new owner who may have purchased the property for the specific purpose of destroying the site. Nonetheless, scientific easements remain an avenue to be more thoroughly investigated.

Massachusetts has established a state committee of recognized competence to certify landmarks (historic and archeological) of significance to the state. This committee is empowered to establish the limits of such a site and, with the written permission of the landowner, may certify the site as a "landmark." This fact is then recorded on the deed. Once this has been accomplished, the committee must approve of any modification by the owner or other party which would affect the historic value of the landmark. In return, the landowner is protected in the sense that the property contained within the limits of the landmark cannot be taken by eminent domain without a special act of the legislature. The committee works closely with all state and federal agencies actively involved in modifying the landscape, but the committee's ability to define the limits of a landmark and thereby prevent its being taken by eminent domain gives them a strong voice in any negotiations with these agencies. Under the impetus of recent federal legislation (in particular, Public Law 89-665) more and more states are establishing similar committees. The experience of Massachusetts should be thoroughly investigated by any such state.

Federal legislation presently pending would authorize any federal agency whose programs adversely affect archeological resources to utilize program funds to recover or protect such resources. Hawaii, apparently following (though, in fact, legislatively preceding) this example, already has passed even more stringent legislation applicable at the state level (see pages 141-143), which requires that public construction funds be made available to recover archeological or historic resources endangered by such construction.

In some states it is possible to encourage private landowners to protect important sites by providing a certain tax exemption status to property which is set aside for historical or archeological preservation. This can be a very effective technique for inducing landowners to set aside property, but in other states such an approach would require amending the constitution, an impractical—indeed, in Arkansas, almost impossible—procedure.

In addition to statutes serving to encourage protection by the private landowner, there are a number of other approaches relating to the land itself and its control that have been employed or might be considered.

One approach is a statute spelling out the state's authority (or that of one of its agencies) to utilize its right of condemnation and eminent domain for the purpose of protecting the state's archeological resources. Such action again relates to legitimate extension of the state's police power to act solely with regard to the public welfare. Extension of the power in this area can and has raised serious public question, and a proposed antiquities act which contained such a provision might encounter opposition. I believe such a provision to be constitutional, but political desirability could become an overriding factor. Actually, I believe any fears of misuse of authority granted under such a statute are totally groundless. Any condemnation procedure requires just compensation, and adequate protection from arbitrary judgments of value is available through the courts. Before a state agency can condemn property for archeological preservation the legislature and the public must have provided that agency with adequate funds for this purpose, often by specific act. A state archeological agency with funds sufficient to permit abuse of eminent domain and condemnation is beyond my powers of conception.

The development and application of zoning laws, an approach widely used for purposes of historic house and similar preservation, would seem to have less general applicability to archeology, for often by the time an area is subject to zoning ordinances the land surface of that area already has been modified sufficiently to destroy any sites present. In specific instances, however, where there are known sites preserved within an area to be zoned, the zoning ordinance could well be brought into play to further protect the site.

Every state should review its legislation regarding the exhumation of human remains. In some instances the wording of the relevant statutes may cover excavation or disturbance of prehistoric graves or skeletons. In others it may be that the wording is such that it could be considered to include prehistoric graves but in a context or legal tradition which makes any such extension unlikely. It is my understanding that in most states court interpretation would be that the burial statutes cover graves or cemeteries for which there is legal record or for which there are present living relatives who are direct descendents of the individual(s) being disturbed. While it is true that by the nature of these limitations, prehistoric (and therefore the general but not directly identifiable ancestors of present-day Indians) are included, the statutes are not of themselves discriminatory (as some modern Indian groups have stated).

Burial statute limitations should apply to all burials and should recognize the need to treat all human remains with respect. While this is true, such legislation must have an element of practicality. It simply is not possible to extend the full protection of the law to every unmarked and previously unknown human skeleton or fragment thereof that comes to light during the course of agriculture, construction, or other activities that disturb the surface of the ground. To do so would slow such activity far beyond publicly necessary limits. Furthermore, burial legislation should and generally does recognize the legitimate public need for disturbance of human remains for causes of an overriding nature. Such overriding concerns range from removal and reburial in instances of public need caused by construction or other present-day forces, disinterment for legal, medical or legitimate scientific study, or the actual destruction of human remains where no other recourse is practical, including, for example, modern potters fields that often are periodically plowed and reused.

Legislation protecting human burials from unnecessary disturbance would be applicable to both public and private land. In fact, a recent New York law (see p. 168) specifically extends protection to Indian cemeteries recognized by the New York State Trust. Ideally such laws should permit excavation by qualified persons for scientific purposes (the Inyo County, California, ordinance—see pages 230-232—does do this), and exclude willful disturbance of the sort normally accomplished by pothunters. Properly drafted and enforced, such an ordinance could go a long way toward reducing the pothunting problem for graves often are disturbed or destroyed by such activity. A bill against grave robbing would be hard to vote against and could be more readily brought successfully before local courts than almost any other form of antiquities legislation. On the other hand, great care should be exercised for otherwise legitimate excavation could be disastrously curtailed. A corollary of this is that archeologists should not disturb human remains unless there is a scientific need to do so, and should exercise all care that any segment of the public which feels it has a legitimate concern is at least considered and, if possible, consulted. On the other hand, the principle of the greatest good for the greatest number must be taken to apply in this as in nearly every circumstance, so that important knowledge to which the public has a right is not lost because of the desire of a few that no burial or no burial of a particular sort be disturbed. Again, this is an important area of legislative concern, but is perhaps one of the touchiest areas. The greatest care, diplomacy, and expertise should be employed when dealing with it.

Another possible provision has been suggested but, to my knowledge, has not yet been tried. This has to do with requiring the private landowner to permit access to representatives of the state agency responsible for archeological preservation in order that they may search for sites, observe and record the results of ongoing excavations by others, or check other disturbance of archeological materials. This approach would not affect the right of the landowner to use the land as he saw fit or question his ownership of objects found therein; however, by extension of the principle of the public's right to the information contained in those sites or to be derived from that material, it would make some provision for protecting that public right. How effective, or even necessary, such a provision might be in actual practice is another question.

In the past a number of states have extended the provisions of their antiquities laws to federal lands within the borders of the state. The degree to which this is possible depends upon the conditions under which the state was admitted to the Union. In general the power of the federal government over its public lands may not be restricted by a state statute or regulation; however, states may prescribe reasonable police regulations applicable to public land areas of the United States as long as there is no conflict with congressional enactment (73 C.J.S. Public Lands Sec. 3). This could apply in the case of antiquities legislation if the goals of the state statutes were the same as those of the federal antiquities legislation, which also protects archeological materials on public lands.

Provisions Concerned Primarily with Personnel. In one sense at least the development of regulations concerned with the land is fairly simple. The situation relative to state land is fairly clear-cut, and it remains only to determine if and how archeological remains on private land are to be protected. In general, the situation is not so clear-cut when we face up to the interrelated problem of legislatively determining to whom permission to dig should be granted, under what circumstances, on what basis such controls are to be imposed, and how they are to be enforced.

Some states have attempted to extend blanket control over both public and private land in the state by providing that only the state archeological agency may excavate for archeological remains or, alternatively, that only educational or similar publicly oriented and competently staffed institutions may excavate. Although the intent of such legislation (to insure that only competent persons excavate and the results remain available to the public) is highly commendable, I am unaware that it has ever succeeded in achieving this end or even that any serious attempt ever has been made to enforce such a provision. If it is impossible to enforce, it is of little if any practical value.

Somewhat negative variations of this type of provision are to be found in one or two states, which prohibit a nonresident from excavating or which attempt to place greater restrictions on nonresidents than on residents. Actually, the fact that a state's archeological objects are going out of the state provides a popular base of support for antiquities legislation. Despite the possible local or even legislative popularity of what has been described as "that-carpetbagger-from-the-next-county-north" syndrome, however, it seems a poor basis for legislation and hardly an adequate means for determining who should excavate. A person's competence and the public availability of the results (both objects and data) should be the determining factors, not his residence. Arkansas artifacts properly cared for in New York might be considered by some to be less desirably placed (though wide distribution of study collections and exhibit material will always be desirable) than if they were properly cared for in Arkansas. But in the longer view Arkansas and the public obviously would be better served if the objects were safe and publicly available in New York than if they had been wantonly destroyed by a resident of Arkansas.

A number of other blanket regulatory approaches have been tried or suggested relative to controlling who may excavate on private land, but none would appear to have any notable chance of success irrespective of their possible legality, primarily because they assume a considerable staff to make them effective or else a majority of the citizenry dedicated to their enforcement. I am not aware that in any state such a situation yet prevails.

One such provision requires that all landowners notify a designated state agency of sites known or discovered on their land. As a suggestion, this has some merit, at least it could do no harm, but as a requirement, it would appear to be a mistake. Even in Arkansas, which has a coordinated and better staffed state agency than most, the thought of attempting to administer any such provision is staggering and I find it difficult to conceive of a local jury convicting a neighbor for failure to obey. In fact, effective wording of such a provision would be so difficult to achieve that I doubt if the law could be made to stand up in any court.

A related and more practical provision would require a landowner who had a state-recognized landmark on his property to notify the appropriate state agency a designated amount of time prior to taking any action which would have an adverse effect on the site. Hawaii has done this.

Another possible provision along these lines would be one requiring that any excavation of archeological sites on private land must be done in accordance with appropriate procedures to insure the preservation of the data—data in which the general public has a vested interest. As noted before, the principle is probably constitutional, but problems of wording (what is "proper procedure" and who is to judge "competence"?) and, even more important, the difficulties in enforcement, both in terms of the staff required and support by the public and in the courts, would seem to negate the practicality of this approach. That trench that Farmer Jones is putting right through an Indian mound is not an archeological excavation, it is simply an innocent trench silo! However desirable it might seem to the archeologist, it hardly seems practical to attempt to require that landowners owning sites conduct their agricultural or other pursuits according to accepted scientific methods of procedure for archeological excavations. This is one problem, however, that is going to have to be resolved with respect to sites placed on the National Register. If federal restrictions are interpreted to apply to land being farmed with any federal assistance, and most farmers utilize some form of federal assistance at one time or another, then either the landowner must cease farming any site on the Register or else he will have to farm in such a manner that the site is not adversely affected. Neither solution is apt to be accepted gracefully by some landowners, and court tests could readily develop which hopefully will serve to clarify the situation.

The most frequently adopted approach to controlling excavation has been via an extension of the state's permit-granting power. These permit regulations generally state that no one may excavate for archeological remains in the state or, even more frequently, on state-owned or controlled land without having obtained a permit from a designated state agency. A variety of other provisions generally are included establishing the qualifications of persons or organizations to whom permits will he granted, time limitations, inspections and control mechanisms, forfeiture of objects and data for failure to abide by the permit provisions, and, occasionally, spelling out a division of the artifacts between the excavator and the state.

For state property this is a practical method of procedure, where generally permits are restricted to properly staffed scientific organizations and by specification or implication are not available to individuals. The federal antiquities act is enforceable, even though it has not been strictly enforced with respect to theft or vandalism, and has been of inestimable psychological value. Any "division of artifacts" provision, however, can run afoul of other state regulations. In Arkansas, for example, the only approved method of disposing of state property is through public auction, and no state agency could be empowered to split state-owned artifacts with some nonstate agency except perhaps on a permanent loan basis.

For protection of sites on private property an extension of the state's permit authority to archeological sites is a less than satisfactory approach. If permits are restricted to scientific institutions, the responsible state agency is faced with an impossible enforcement problem. The law would be broken by individuals more often than it was honored, at least until such time as the landowners themselves were willing to enforce it. Without active support by landowners, a state, even one with a large archeological program, would be powerless to enforce such a provision adequately.

If, in contrast, particular individuals over the state are to be issued permits so long as they follow "approved procedures," serious diplomatic problems are going to be faced by the responsible agency. Someone has to determine to whom permits should be issued, must supervise the work, and must determine if "proper procedures" are being followed. Unless scientifically adequate and publicly accepted guidelines are established, not even a Solomon would be up to the task. There would be many instances when factors would come into play that cannot be spelled out in a permit law, many of which would be difficult or embarrassing to explain satisfactorily to the individuals concerned. A state archeologist placed in such a circumstance relative to amateurs and landowners would be in a difficult position at best. In short, a permit law applicable to private property and strictly enforced could result in a breakdown of cooperation and communication among professionals, amateurs, and land-owners, a situation fatal to any state program.

Implicit in much of this discussion is a second objection to provisions for permits. They simply are not enforceable under normal circumstances. True, such a provision does make someone responsible, which perhaps is better than having no one responsible, but in effect all the legislature has accomplished is to transfer its guilty conscience regarding loss of the state's archeological heritage to someone else—usually some archeologist with full-time duties and an overworked conscience already. In all probability he is already frustrated on the subject, and simple transference by the legislature of their feeling of guilt to his shoulders does little to alleviate or correct the situation. It should be noted that none of the many states having such a provision have provided adequate personnel or funds to supervise or enforce the permit provision. Prohibitive legislation which does not provide for supervision and enforcement is meaningless.

With respect to private land a slower, more frustrating, but ultimately more satisfactory solution is for the state to provide for a responsible state agency which has the personnel to work with the individual landowners. As just discussed, a variety of approaches can be utilized by such an agency ranging from simply receiving his assurance that sites on his property will be protected to working out a scientific easement whereby the state assumes control and responsibility for the archeological integrity of the sites. For this to succeed, however, the landowner must be contacted and convinced, and this requires a state agency adequately staffed and funded to carry out the work. Therein lies the crux of this potentially effective approach.

In sum, a permit provision for state land is (theoretically) enforceable and can be desirable but is largely unnecessary if a state declares its ownership of archeological resources on state lands and establishes an agency with adequate funds and authority to care for them. The agency itself normally can establish and exercise the necessary controls.

If a permit provision is used as a substitute for an adequate archeological program, it actually is, in the long run, a deleterious approach. With respect to private lands, permit provisions, though legal, normally are unenforceable and impractical. All states must recognize that there is no simple, easy, or inexpensive solution to protecting their archeological resources. Regulatory legislation alone can never succeed in preserving the archeological data required for the public good. A carefully thought out, well-funded state program is the only realistic solution.

For the reasons outlined here, I am less than optimistic concerning the efficacy of the usual permit laws; nonetheless, operation of the state program in Arkansas has made me increasingly aware that there is not only one additional drawback but that, despite all of these objections, there must be some recognition of the permit situation in any successful state program.

The additional problem is that such legislation in most states (but not all) prohibits issuance of permits to any but public scientific agencies. The qualified amateur who wishes to carry out competent work on state land is provided no avenue for doing so. As I have noted earlier, archeologists need all the help they can get, and if legislation is needlessly restrictive, it is thereby very shortsighted. If there is a qualified and adequately staffed state agency, it is better for the staff of that agency rather than the legislature to develop and set forth a set of guidelines which can be fluid and yet fair to all. Legislation alone is unlikely to achieve this.

Arkansas does not have permit legislation, but the Arkansas Archeological Survey, in cooperation with the Arkansas Archeological Society, is currently exploring possibilities whereby competent amateurs do not have the door slammed in their faces but instead are provided an opportunity to develop their archeological knowledge and skills to the maximum and then are provided a mechanism whereby they may utilize that knowledge and ability for the benefit of the public (see discussion, pages 40-45). A permit law which directly or indirectly paints all nonprofessionals with the same black brush of incompetence inevitably must contribute to a breakdown in communication between amateur and professional archeologists and will seriously reduce the potential effectiveness of the total state program. If a qualified amateur wishes to carry out a survey of an area on state or federal property, there should be a mechanism whereby the state agency can allow, indeed aid, him to do so by means of a permit or at least some similar mechanism. If he wishes to excavate, the situation is more difficult, for the state cannot give up title to the objects recovered; however, it seems at least possible that, when necessary and in return for the time and skills expended on the information gained, the responsible state agency, in some special instances, might be able to make some long-term loan agreement acceptable to that amateur. Of course, if the individual wishes to dig for his own profit, no such approach is possible. What we are concerned with here is designing a technique whereby the individual, if he wishes to, may contribute to the public good while at the same time achieving personal satisfaction, though not private gain.

Permit laws have a place, but they can be effective only if (1) a state agency or program adequate to supervise this approach also is provided for, and (2) the competent individual is not thereby prohibited from participating in and contributing to the total state program of archeological research and development.

Provisions Concerned Primarily with Ownership and Disposition. A few states have simply declared that all archeological objects wherever found are state property. This might work in Louisiana, which bases much of its law on the Napoleonic code, but it stands little chance of holding up in courts elsewhere in the country which are based on the principles of English common law. The only two possible approaches along this line would be a treasure trove provision or application of the escheat principle of state ownership of all private goods which belong to persons who died intestate—which presumably would include all precontact individuals! To my knowledge neither approach has been tried or tested in the courts.

Another approach, totally ineffective, forbids the exportation of archeological material from the state. This, obviously, can be traced to the "carpetbagger" syndrome. The legal basis for such action escapes me, but even if legal, it is impossible to enforce. The entire enforcement machinery of a state is by no means adequate to prevent private individuals from moving rather large quantities of alcoholic beverages across state lines. Expecting the state police to expend any appreciable amount of their time to prevent exportation of Indian pots, even with the possible assistance of a handful of archeologists, is completely unrealistic.

Provisions Concerned with Fraud and Vandalism. Provisions prohibiting fraudulent manufacture or sale of artifacts are of value and should be considered if this situation is not already covered adequately by the state's statutes.

Provisions prohibiting vandalism can be effective on state land but are of no assistance on private land. Agricultural practices, and authorized pothunting, not name scratching by individuals, are the cause of major destruction of sites on private property. Again it is the landowner, not the state, who must be looked to for adequate protection, and to obtain his understanding and assistance requires an adequate state program of archeological research and development.

Summary

Antiquities legislation cannot be the sole approach to preserving a state's archeological heritage. Given the fact that education rather than legislation is the real answer, is antiquities legislation of any value at all? I believe well-drawn legislation is of value. It publicly establishes the state's concern and interest in having archeological resources preserved and protected. Without such a public statement education would proceed more slowly and be much harder to effect. It also strengthens the hand (and moral fiber) of the concerned landowner or land user. These facts alone warrant its enactment.

Positive provisions, such as tax relief, and legal aids to the landowner (for example, trespass provisions and landmark provisions that enable the state to extend some measure of control to private land with the landowner's consent) are also valuable adjuncts to a well-rounded state program.

The negative provisions of antiquities legislation are likely to be of least value, for only occasionally will they, or should they, actually be brought into play. Unfortunately, it is these negative elements that have received the most attention from legislatures in the past, and this probably accounts, in large measure, for the disrepute of antiquities acts today, both within and without the archeological ranks.

An antiquities act which emphasizes the negative approach to the virtual exclusion of more positive actions, or which drains off the major force of legislative interest from support of a well-rounded state archeological program, can be a real threat rather than an aid to archeology. A carefully thought out antiquities act which supplements a total state program has a place, however, and can make a valuable contribution.

One Example — Arkansas

Brief Background

In May of 1957 State Representative John Bethell sponsored a proposal in the Arkansas Legislative Council to inaugurate a study of archeological programs and their cost in other states, and such a study was launched by the council. That fall, State Senator Charles F. Smith, without knowledge of the Bethell proposal, discussed with University of Arkansas President John T. Caldwell the problem of preserving Arkansas' past. As a result of this, President Caldwell requested that Mr. S. C. Dellinger and I explore the problem further with Senator Smith. I made a preliminary draft of the requirements for a state program, which was discussed with Senator Smith. At this point the two studies joined forces, and, after contacting key personnel in all (then) forty-eight states, I submitted to the Legislative Council in the fall of 1958 a summary of all state programs and antiquities laws, along with a draft of two bills, one to establish and the other to fund (at a cost of $50,000 a year) a state archeological program for Arkansas to be located at the University of Arkansas. Both bills were passed handily by the 1959 General Assembly, but, while the enabling legislation was signed into law as Act 82 of 1959, the appropriation bill was vetoed—primarily because neither the public nor any legislators had expressed to the governor any support for the bill. No public support means no money. The first hard lesson had forcefully been driven home.

Early in 1960 the Arkansas Archeological Society was founded, as had been the Northwest Arkansas Archaeological Society a little over a year earlier, moves which ultimately were to have far-reaching benefits for Arkansas archeology.

The 1959 enabling act had authorized and directed the State Highway Department to cooperate with the university in the establishment of a program of highway salvage archeology, but efforts to initiate such a program in 1960 came to naught.

63

During the 1961 legislative session, Representative Bethell and Senator Smith again considered introducing an appropriation bill. Dr. David W. Mullins, then and now president of the University of Arkansas, requested that the appropriation for this new program be considered as part of the regular university budget rather than having it funded separately. Despite assignment of a high priority to this new program by the university, funds were inadequate in the university's appropriated budget for implementation of the program during the 1961-1963 biennium. During this session, at the behest of the legislature, I drafted an antiquities act. This passed both the state house and senate but was vetoed by the governor on the grounds that it would "work undue hardships upon state, county, and municipal departments and employees" and that it would "interfere with and virtually prohibit the hobby of many people in the state." A few persons had protested vigorously while almost no one had spoken out for enactment.

In 1963, the university again made a strong plea to the legislature for funds to establish an archeological program as a part of the university budget, and again the effort was unsuccessful. Another antiquities act was drafted, but, as it became evident that no funds were to be available for a program, no serious move was made to introduce the antiquities legislation. It was felt that without personnel to work with it, no antiquities act could be effective.

Some progress, however, was made during this period. Toward the end of 1963 the State Highway Department was again approached concerning establishment of a highway salvage program. This time there was a more favorable reception, and a full program of survey and excavation on interstate rights-of-way was established in July of 1964. By July 1966, because all proposed interstate rights-of-way had been covered, the survey portion of the program lapsed, but the contract remains in effect and has been used for excavation of archeological material endangered by highway construction anywhere in the state on any type of state or federal road or highway.

The university adopted essentially the same legislative route in 1965 as it had during the previous two sessions. It asked for funds to implement Act 82 of 1959 as part of the regular university budget. The results also were the same as before. During this session, however, there was a new development. Representative Bethell again introduced legislation—this time a bill to establish a duplicate program to that established by Act 82, but under the Publicity and Parks Commission. This was later amended to be under a separate State Archeological Commission, and $11,000 was provided for the salary of an archeologist and a secretary. Both bills passed the state house and senate. The Arkansas Archeological Society had attempted to make this proposed program workable through amendments, but in the end the Society felt that the inadequate financing (there were no funds provided for operation of the program) and the almost complete duplication of responsibilities between the university and the

Commission would be fatal flaws in the development of an effective statewide program. The state Society was, therefore, instrumental in influencing the governor to veto this legislation. Thus, really for the first time, the Society effectively demonstrated that it could make its voice heard in the legislature. It could not, of course, directly affect the university appropriation and, as noted, university funds again proved to be inadequate to inaugurate any program under Act 82.

Shortly after the conclusion of the somewhat tumultuous (from an archeologist's point of view) 1965 legislative session, two significant moves were made relative to the future of Arkansas archeology. Representative Bethell and Senator Bob Douglas introduced a proposal in the Legislative Council for a second study of other state programs, and the Arkansas Archeological Society established a committee to work with the legislature and the university on archeological legislation.

At the request of the Legislative Council, I again compiled data on archeological legislation, the administrative structure of each state program if there was such a program, and the level of state support for archeological research in each of the fifty states, and I prepared an analysis of the requisites of an adequate state program. These reports were presented at a meeting of the Legislative Council attended by representatives of all state-supported institutions of higher education in April 1966. The council requested that a committee be formed of representatives from all state-supported institutions of higher learning, the History Commission, the two archeological societies, and any interested museums, and that this committee make recommendations concerning archeological legislation to the 1967 legislature. At about this same time representatives of the Arkansas Archeological Society met with President Mullins and received his agreement, if all other approaches failed, to a separate appropriation for the archeological program.

The special committee met a number of times during the spring of 1966 and after extended discussion, consultation with respective administrations, and more discussion, hammered out an enabling act, an appropriation bill, and an antiquities act which all the affected institutions and organizations felt they could support in the legislature.

The 1967 legislative session was a busy period for everyone interested in passage of this archeological legislation. A meeting was held with Governor Rockefeller, attended by the committee, sponsoring legislators, and interested citizens, at which time the program was reviewed and explained. Later, in a meeting between the sponsoring legislators, the chairman of the Legislative Joint Budget Committee, the state assistant comptroller, the governor, and me, the details of the budget request were ironed out, and the governor agreed to support the program on the level of $125,000 (a reduction of $100,000 from the committee's initial recommendation) for the first year of the biennium

(1967-1968) and $215,000 (the figure recommended by the committee) for the second year (1968-1969).

The Arkansas Archeological Society published a colored, illustrated brochure explaining the program, and this was distributed to all legislators, all newspaper editors, and many other interested individuals and groups over the state. Both archeological societies also saw to it that a member from the home district of almost every legislator contacted each legislator about the program, and all key legislators were throughly briefed by society members, usually constituents. As a result, the enabling act (which supplements Act 82 of 1959), the appropriation bill, and the antiquities act all passed both the state senate and house without a dissenting vote and were signed into law by Governor Rockefeller as Act 39, Act 270, and Act 58, respectively.

As a result of the intensive efforts of hundreds of people—members of the two archeological societies, one or more staff members and the administrations of all state-supported institutions, individual legislators, the governor, and various members of his legislative staff, plus the active interest of numerous other individuals—Arkansas now has a coordinated statewide program of archeological research second to none.

Pertinent Legislation

1. Act 82 of 1959, Acts of Arkansas. "An Act to Create an Arkansas Program of Archeological Research, and for Other Purposes." (See pages 199-201.)

2. Act 39 of 1967, Acts of Arkansas. "An Act to Designate the Program of Archeological Research and Discovery Provided for in Act 82 of 1959 as the Arkansas Archeological Survey; to Implement and Expand said Program by Providing for the Appointment of a Director of the Survey and a State Archeologist; to Prescribe a Procedure Whereby Any Public Institution of Higher Learning in Arkansas May Participate in the Program; to Authorize the Survey to Mutually Assist and Cooperate with the Arkansas Archeological Society in Furthering the Purposes of Public Archeological Education; and for Other Purposes." (See pages 201-204.)

3. Act 58 of 1967, Acts of Arkansas. "An Act for the Protection and Preservation of Arkansas' Archeological Heritage, Its Antiquities, Artifacts and Sites, and for Other Purposes." (See pages 204-207.)

4. Act 270 of 1967, Acts of Arkansas. "An Act to Make an Appropriation for Personal Services and Operating Expenses of the Arkansas Archeological Survey, for the Biennial Period Ending June 30, 1969; and for Other Purposes." (Act 550 of 1969 continued and increased somewhat that fiscal support of the program for the next biennium, as did Act 630 of 1971 for the 1971-1973 biennium.)

Purpose and Responsibilities

"The Arkansas Archeological Survey shall initiate, operate, and maintain a program in archeology which shall include, but not be limited to, the following areas of action:

(a) Excavation of historical sites, ruins, and mounds for the purpose of securing data and objects relating to early man in Arkansas;

(b) Fundamental research in Arkansas archeology and encouragement of public cooperation in the preservation of Arkansas antiquities;

(c) Research in and study of anthropology, geology, and related social and physical sciences, both prior to excavation and thereafter in order to plan and aid in discovery of sites and artifacts and their proper assessment once discovered;

(d) Publication of findings in terms of their scientific, popular, and cultural values;

(e) Display and custodianship of relics, artifacts, sites, and other tangible results of the program;

(f) Educational activities providing a stimulus to archeological efforts and the encouragement of archeological societies, parks, and museums." (Section 3, Act 39 of 1967, Acts of Arkansas.)

Administrative Structure

The funds for the Arkansas Archeological Survey are authorized by the state legislature in an appropriation bill separate from that of any other state agency. It is funded from the General Services Fund along with such other agencies as the Apiary Board and the Geological Commission, and not from the University of Arkansas Fund or any other fund directly available to the various institutions of higher learning. Thus, though it is avowedly a research and educational organization, which operates through and in cooperation with the institutions of higher learning, it is not directly in competition with them for funds.

A budget separate from that of the university is felt to be absolutely essential for an agency which has to cooperate with several state institutions. Only by means of a separate budget established by the legislature could questions or doubts be eliminated as to the true availability of Survey funds which might enable or prevent or limit participation by the various state institutions. The governor requested and the legislature approved of a budgetary level which made it possible for the program to be initiated at only three institutions during the first year. Thus five institutions (including the University of Arkansas) were unable to participate in the program during the first year of the Arkansas Archeological Survey's existence, for there simply were not adequate funds to hire and equip more than three archeologists plus the minimum essential coordinating staff. No problems were encountered in explaining this to the institutions which had to be left out during the first year. Had the Survey budget simply been included within the university budget and the source of the reduction not been so clear-cut, this might not have been the case.

Although the appropriation is entirely separate from that of any other agency, the Board of Trustees of the University of Arkansas is designated as the administrative agent for the Survey. This arrangement has a number of distinct advantages. It provides for maximum fiscal and administrative responsibility, while insuring minimum irresponsible or politically motivated interference with Survey operations. It also serves to make available to the Survey the accounting and purchasing facilities of the university as well as making readily available to the Survey other university facilities and services (for example, the computing center and legal counsel). One final advantage is that Survey personnel are members of the staff of the University of Arkansas and are thereby entitled to all university benefits, including retirement and insurance. (Tenure is with the Survey itself but otherwise follows normal university procedures.)

Coordinating Staff

The coordinating staff of the Survey is responsible for administering and coordinating the activities of all Survey archeologists, insuring the safety of the archeological data and materials recovered, and facilitating the production of the reports and other publications of the Survey. It consists of the following personnel:

Director. The director has overall responsibility for the operation of the Survey and for establishing its policies. He is responsible directly to and appointed by the University of Arkansas Board of Trustees from among the anthropologists on the university staff and, alone among the Survey staff, is paid by the university from its own budget and not from Survey funds. He may have university duties other than those of survey director. This arrangement could be disadvantageous if the director were expected to carry out this duty in addition to other full-time responsibilities. However, there are inherent advantages in this particular dual arrangement. At present, and probably for some time to come, the Survey director also will serve as director of the university museum. This greatly facilitates coordination of Survey research and registration with museum storage of the archeological materials and the establishment of joint study collections. The museum is officially designated as the repository responsible for maintaining Survey materials (if they do not remain at a cooperating institution), and it already possesses the largest single collection of Arkansas archeological material (for example, six thousand whole pottery vessels). A second advantage is that normally the administrative head of an agency with a separate legislative budget must appear before the legislature to defend his own salary (and salary increases) as well as those of the rest of the agency. The Survey director is relieved of this problem and can present the Survey budget without implications of direct personal involvement. The joint appointment of the director also serves to facilitate cooperation between the Survey and the rest of the university.

State Archeologist. The state archeologist is responsible for the daily operation of the coordinating staff and for the supervision and coordination of the activities of the Survey archeologists. In the absence of the director the state archeologist assumes full responsibility for the administration of the Survey. The state archeologist and all other Survey staff members are appointed by the University of Arkansas Board of Trustees upon the recommendation of the survey director. While the state archeologist may do occasional field archeology, this position, like that of the director, is largely administrative in nature. If there were *only* a state archeologist in a program of this size, such an individual could do *nothing* but administer. By sharing this responsibility both the director and the state archeologist are able not only to maintain occasional direct contact with field research, on the one hand, but also to have a reasonable opportunity to devote themselves to long-range planning and general theory, on the other.

Editor. The Editor is responsible for the detailed preparation for publication of manuscripts resulting from the work of the Survey and from directly related research on Arkansas archeology. Prompt publication of research results and of general guides and information is one principal goal of all Survey activity, and the Survey maintenance budget includes funds for such publication.

Photographer. The photographer is responsible for the photographic record, for making photographs in the field, and for preparation of illustrations for publication and of slides for use in educational and instructional talks by the Survey staff before interested groups and perhaps educational television. If possible, short training films about archeological techniques and their results will be prepared.

Photographic Technician. The photographic technician is responsible for laboratory processing of photographs and maintenance of the photographic record file.

Draftsman. The draftsman is responsible for the preparation of maps, sketches, and other scientific illustrations for publications and exhibits and for otherwise assisting in manuscript preparation.

Survey Registrar. The Survey registrar is responsible for maintaining a complete and consistent catalog and other records of all the material objects recovered by the Survey—their condition, location, and disposition, and for maintaining the master archeological site file. The registrar is also responsible for coordinating the daily operation of the coordinating office.

Clerk. The clerk oversees and maintains the purchasing and bookkeeping operations of the Survey and in general expedites this vital area of activity.

Typist-Technician. In addition to typing responsibilities the typist-technicians at the coordinating office are responsible for manuscript reproduction and production of copy for the printer.

Clerk-Typist. The clerk-typists are responsible for typing and filing correspondence, catalog cards, and other office records, and for carrying out normal office duties. The work load of the permanent clerk-typists can be eased, as occasion demands, through use of readily available part-time hourly student help—another advantage of the university affiliation of the Survey.

Graduate Assistant. One to two Survey graduate assistants inaugurate a two-year program toward an M.A. degree in anthropology each year. The summer immediately following their graduation with a B.A. degree they begin work (full time for two months) directly under a Survey or museum archeologist, and insofar as possible they are provided with diverse experience over the state. During their first school year they work half-time assisting with laboratory supervision or analysis of Survey material and assist with maintenance of certain Survey records, such as the archeological site file, which require some archeological background and experience. During their second summer they conduct full-time independent or supervised field research and then prepare this for publication (and as their M.A. thesis) during their second school year. They also are available for emergency research and salvage.

Cooperating Institutions

"All public institutions of higher learning in Arkansas desiring to participate in the program provided for in Act 82 of 1959 and this act [Act 39] may contract with the University of Arkansas for Survey Archeologists to be assigned to and in residence at the contracting institutions. Any such institution desiring to be assigned a Survey Archeologist in residence at the institution shall agree to provide the University under contract an amount not less than the equivalent of twenty-five percent (25%) of the salary of the Archeologist upon a nine (9) month basis, and when such contract is entered into by the University of Arkansas and a cooperating institution, the Survey Archeologist may be assigned to and based at the cooperating institution for the contract period which shall normally be twelve (12) months unless a shorter period is provided in the contract. During the portion of the Survey Archeologist's time contracted for by a cooperating institution, he may perform research, teaching, or other related functions as may be directed by the cooperating institution in accordance with the terms of the contract, provided such other functions shall not be such as to interfere with the effective performance of his duties as a Survey Archeologist.

"The University of Arkansas shall enter into contracts with cooperating institutions for the assignment of the Survey personnel to the extent that such assignments are consistent with the purposes and aims of the Survey, and insofar as funds and personnel permit such contracts to be made or renewed." (Section 4, Act 39 of 1967, Acts of Arkansas.)

Perhaps the key concept in the Arkansas program is that of full participation in the Survey by all state-supported institutions of higher learning which wish to participate. Such participation is not compulsory, but all six colleges and both universities have expressed a desire to do so. This results in a broad base of support for the program in the legislature and also serves effectively to eliminate problems of competition or inadequate communication among the institutions concerned with carrying out state-supported archeological research. The cost to the institution is minimal (from $1500 to $2500 annually plus office and laboratory space), and it receives full value for its investment in that the archeologist is authorized to teach up to six semester hours a year (all in a single semester) or to perform other archeologically related duties (for example, curatorial or research), though such activity must not interfere with the archeologist's Survey responsibilities. A cooperating institution also benefits, in the public eye, from having an archeologist-in-residence full time twelve months a year to carry out research in its region. In many cases, presence of a Survey archeologist enables the institution to offer, for the first time, one or two anthropology courses taught by an anthropologist.

The concept of requiring the institutions desiring to participate to contribute space and to reimburse the Survey for a portion of the salary of the archeologists was included for various reasons. In no case is the cash contribution from the institution's regular budget likely to be sizable, yet it must contribute some cash, indicating a positive desire to work with the Survey rather than simply to take part in a free program. Also, because of this reimbursement, the archeologist becomes in a psychological if not a legal sense one of the institution's own faculty. However, he is not someone foisted off on them willy-nilly. Since they are contracting for his services, the faculty and administration have a measure of control over whom they get, for if they do not like him, they can simply refuse to enter into a contract for the following year. Since it is to both the institution's and the Survey's advantage to have an archeologist present, it seems likely that something could be worked out, and, in fact, the Survey director gets approval of the participating institution prior to employing or renewing the contract of the archeologist to be based there. Finally, though the Survey maintains basic responsibility, any materials recovered by the Survey archeologist while he is in residence at a cooperating institution may remain there, if the institution requests it and provides adequate safeguards. Actually, the Survey will facilitate interchange of representative collections among all institutions in the state desiring to have them for study and/or display. The Survey also benefits from this approach, for it is provided with eight operational headquarters (including office and laboratory space) well distributed over the state, and thus is offered an unparalleled opportunity to coordinate fully the Survey program with any activities sponsored locally either by state or privately supported institutions and organizations or by individuals.

The Survey staff at each cooperating institution consists of the following personnel:

Archeologist. The archeologist has a research title approximately equivalent to similar teaching titles, and, in fact, each archeologist carries both titles: research and academic. A research associate has experience or training equivalent to an instructor, while an assistant archeologist or an associate archeologist has experience equivalent to an assistant professor or associate professor, respectively.

During the major portion of his time each archeologist is responsible for conducting archeological research. He is expected to familiarize himself thoroughly with the archeological situation in his general area of the state, including the archeological sites, agricultural and construction activities which are endangering or could endanger these sites, the landowners, the amateur archeologists, and the private collections. Although by the very nature of the areal distribution of the colleges the archeologists have geographic areas of primary concern, these are not strictly delimited nor are they adhered to at all times. The coordinating staff is in a position to arrange for the archeologists to work wherever they are most needed in the state (several could be, and have been, involved simultaneously at a single site) or where the archeologists' particular research interests require. Similarly, it is not planned that all investigations be of an emergency or salvage nature, and the archeologists are encouraged to develop problem-oriented research interests.

Each archeologist is provided an office and laboratory space by the local institution, while the Survey provides a typist-technician, in some cases an archeological technician, a vehicle, necessary office and field equipment, travel funds, and some funds for field and laboratory crews.

Coordination of the activities of these archeologists and the resultant records and materials is, of course, a major concern in itself, and one or more persons either on the coordinating staff or at the cooperating institutions devote a portion of their time to research on these aspects of the program, including research on descriptive techniques, utilization of computers, and data retrieval.

Typist-Technician. The typist-technician is responsible for maintaining the office records and catalog of the material recovered by or in the custody of each archeologist. This person also supervises the laboratory processing of the archeological specimens. In some instances, it might be desirable for this to be two persons, each working half-time, one to handle the office routine and the catalog, the other (perhaps a student or someone with archeological background) to assist with the laboratory processing and to some extent with the field work.

Archeological Technician. There has been apparent an increasing need for persons interested in and trained to perform field and laboratory duties in archeology who are intermediate in experience between the office staff and the professional with an advanced degree in anthropology. The position of archeological technician was created to fill this need. These individuals (the Survey has only one full-time and several part-time technicians to date) contact landowners and agencies affecting land use, investigate sites reported to the Survey, carry out regional surveys, briefly test sites, and assist with analysis. With these areas of responsibility covered the archeologist can devote his major attention to analysis, writing, and development.

Extra Help. These part-time employees are hired on an hourly basis by the archeologists for specific research projects, to carry out actual excavations of archeological sites, and to wash and number specimens in the laboratory. Insofar as is possible, students from the cooperating institutions are hired for this work. The amount of hourly help required by an archeologist in a given year varies depending upon the nature and scope of the specific projects he undertakes.

Coordination of the Survey with Other Agencies

Federal Agencies. Prior to establishment of the Survey, the University of Arkansas Museum served as prime contractor with the National Park Service for archeological research in Arkansas. The Survey has gradually assumed this function.

State Highway Commission. "The State Highway Commission is hereby authorized and directed to enter into appropriate contracts and cooperative agreements with the University of Arkansas and U.S. Bureau of Public Roads and to expend funds, both State and Federal, in aid of archeological salvage and archeological preservation on all or any part of the lands and rights-of-way now or hereafter coming into its control in order that the beneficial purposes of this Act shall be achieved." (Section 7, Act 82 of 1959, Acts of Arkansas.)

As discussed earlier, this has resulted in the survey and excavation of all sites threatened by the interstate rights-of-way. The contract to recover data from threatened sites on any rights-of-way in the state remains in effect and has been activated in several instances, including one where no federal funds were involved.

Commissioner of State Lands. "Upon a written notice to the Commissioner of State Lands given by the Arkansas Archeological Survey, the Commissioner of State Lands shall reserve from sale any State lands, including lands forfeited to the State for non-payment of taxes, on which sites or artifacts are located or may be found, as designated by the Arkansas Archeological Survey; provided, however, that the reservation of such lands from sale may be confined to the actual location of the site or artifacts. When such sites or artifacts have been explored, excavated, or otherwise examined to the extent desired by the Arkansas Archeological Survey, said Survey shall then file with the Commissioner a statement releasing such lands and permitting the sale of same." (Section 5, Act 58 of 1967, Acts of Arkansas.)

Arkansas does not have as much state-owned land as some of the western states, but a surprising amount of land passes through the state's hands, however briefly, as a result of tax forfeitures and for other reasons.

Other Agencies Controlling State Land. "The State of Arkansas reserves to itself the exclusive right and privilege of field archeology in sites owned or controlled by the State, its agencies, departments, and institutions, in order to protect and preserve archeological and scientific information, matter, and objects. All such information and objects deriving from State lands shall be utilized solely for scientific or public educational purposes and shall remain the property of the State." (Section 2, Act 58 of 1967, Acts of Arkansas.)

"All State agencies, departments, institutions, and commissions, as well as all counties and municipalities, shall cooperate fully with the Arkansas archeological Survey in the preservation, protection, excavation, and evaluation of artifacts and sites; and to that end, where any site or artifacts may be found or discovered on property owned or controlled by the State or by any county or municipality, the agency, bureau, commission, governmental subdivision, or county or municipality having control over or owning such property or preparing to excavate or perform work upon such property or currently performing work of any type upon such property is urged to notify the Arkansas Archeological Survey of the discovery and location of such sites or artifacts and shall cooperate to the fullest extent practicable with the Arkansas Archeological Survey to preserve and prevent the destruction of such site or artifacts and to allow the Arkansas Archeological Survey to assist in and effect the removal of such artifacts by means designed to preserve and permit the study and evaluation of such artifacts; and the provisions of this Act shall be made known to contractors by the State agencies doing the contracting." (Section 3, Act 58 of 1967, Acts of Arkansas.)

"In order that sites and artifacts on State-owned or controlled land shall be protected for the benefit of the public, it is hereby made a misdemeanor for any person, natural or corporate, to write upon, carve upon, paint, deface, mutilate, destroy, or otherwise injure any objects of antiquity, artifacts, Indian painting, or sites, and all such acts of vandalism shall be punished as misdemeanors according to the provisions of this Act." (Section 7, Act 58 of 1967, Acts of Arkansas.)

"The Arkansas Archeological Survey shall serve as the repository for copies of all archeological field notes, photographs, publications, or other records obtained through the use of State funds by whatever agency. All archeological objects found through the efforts of the Survey shall be deposited at the University of Arkansas Museum, provided archeological objects obtained by Survey Archeologists while under contract to and assigned to a cooperating institution may, upon request of the cooperating institution, be assigned to the custody of such institution if appropriate and adequate safeguards are provided." (Section 5, Act 39 of 1967, Acts of Arkansas.)

The Survey is not designated the sole agent responsible for archeological materials on state lands. Such usurpation of authority over property presently under the complete control of another state agency would require a constitutional amendment.

A legal basis is provided for full cooperation with the Survey by state agencies, governmental subdivision, and contractors working with the state. But, as in all such instances, personal contact must be established, and a certain amount of rational give-and-take and experimentation is essential to the development of procedures and techniques that protect the maximum amount of data without so burdening the other agencies that local or agency-wide antagonism develops. The Survey and the other agencies also will have to work out procedures for curbing vandalism on state-owned or controlled land.

The Survey and the University of Arkansas Museum are, at present, the only state agencies involved extensively in archeological research and development. As the Survey's work proceeds and other agencies and the public become more aware of the archeological situation, it is quite possible that other agencies may begin to expend some of their own funds in this field. Some of this might be jointly financed by the Survey and the second agency, whereas in some instances work might be undertaken independently of the Survey (though presumably with the knowledge and cooperation of the Survey). The Survey should encourage work by others. In any event, Section 5 of Act 58 insures that the Survey has the authority to obtain copies of all records pertinent to Arkansas archeology which are obtained through use of state funds, and thus the state is assured of being able to obtain all relevant archeological data from a single source. This centralization of records also will facilitate the coordination of the total state effort by the Survey and its personnel.

Private Landowners. "An archeological site of significance to the scientific study or public representation of Arkansas' aboriginal past may be publicly designated by the Arkansas Archeological Survey as a 'State Archeological Landmark' provided that no sites shall be so designated without the express written consent of the State agency having jurisdiction over the land in question or, if it is on privately owned land, of the owner thereof. Once so designated, excavation for the purpose of recovery or the recovery of artifacts from such sites by persons other than the Arkansas Archeological Survey or their duly designated agents shall be a misdemeanor." (Section 4, Act 58 of 1967, Acts of Arkansas.)

"It shall be deemed an act of trespass and a misdemeanor for any person, natural or corporate, to remove artifacts and antiquities of the kind described herein from the private land of any owner thereof without his permission being first obtained." (Section 6, Act 58 of 1967, Acts of Arkansas.)

No attempt was made in the antiquities act to regulate strictly archeological activity on private land. While there might be constitutional means to effect this end, it was felt that public awareness of the present perilous position of the state's archeological resources was not yet sufficiently developed to make any such regulatory act of value. In fact, it was felt that public antipathy toward a sternly drawn antiquities act pertaining to private land might well endanger the Survey itself. Instead, every effort was made to encourage the landowner concerned with protecting archeological material on his property to do so and to assist him in this effort. Essentially, the two provisions just quoted give the private landowner the same opportunities to protect sites on his property as has the state.

The effectiveness of these provisions depends upon the initiative of the individual landowner and this, in turn, will depend in large measure on the initiative of the Survey. A punitive or restrictive approach also would have depended almost entirely on Survey initiative. It was felt that the positive approach of obtaining the understanding and cooperation of landowners adopted here would, in the long run, have more far-reaching and longer-lasting beneficial effects.

The Arkansas Archeological Society. "The Arkansas Archeological Survey is hereby authorized to assist and support the programs of the Arkansas Archeological Society to the extent that the purposes and aims of the two coincide." (Section 8, Act 39 of 1967, Acts of Arkansas.)

"The Arkansas Archeological Society is hereby requested to annually review and evaluate the programs and activities of the Arkansas Archeological Survey and to provide written reports of such evaluation to the director of the Survey, each state-supported institution of higher learning and such other interested institutions and agencies that may request the same." (Section 9, Act 39 of 1967, Acts of Arkansas.)

Section 8 of Act 39 explicitly recognizes the fact that the Survey alone cannot possibly achieve the goals set for it. Only through the cooperation and concern of an increasing number of people over the state will this goal even be approached. The principal statewide avenue for expressing both interest in and concern over Arkansas' archeological resources is and has been for a number of years the Arkansas Archeological Society. (The Northwest Arkansas Archaeological Society also has been very active, particularly in the northwestern quarter of the state.) The Arkansas Archeological Society and the University of Arkansas Museum have worked closely together since the inception of the Society, and Section 8 authorizes the Survey to continue this close working relationship.

The Survey, of course, is a public agency, and as such, its operation is subject to review. However, because of the close interrelationships of the various institutions of higher learning in the operation of the Survey and the diplomatic difficulties inherent in one such institution specifically reviewing even a small portion of the operation of any of the others, it was felt that the establishment of a mechanism for review by another group closely concerned but not administratively involved would be highly desirable. Section 9 of Act 39 established the Society as this reviewing agency. (This was not a duty the Society sought, and, indeed, its officers accepted it with considerable reluctance.) Opinions expressed by the Society in its annual review are backed by no power of enforcement, but a carefully considered critique of the Survey's operation can and should have a salubrious effect. Perhaps there is danger as well—particularly if the Society should move away from its present close identification with the same basic goals as have been set for the Survey. Should that happen, the possibility of adverse publicity, and the creation of divisive elements within the Survey and the state, would be great; however, this, in itself, would be an eloquent, if damning, critique of the job the Survey had been doing!

Summary

The goals of the Survey can be summarized as follows:

a. To recover and preserve archeological material and data from all parts of Arkansas and related areas

b. To analyze these materials and data and make public their interpretation as rapidly as possible

c. To increase general public respect for and ability to work with archeological materials and data

d. To develop and improve theories and techniques for recovery, recording, processing, analyzing, retrieving, and publishing these materials and data.

The effective operating budget of the Survey for its first year (1967-1968) was $125,000. (Ten percent of this was held in reserve pending determination of total state income for the year and did not become available to the Survey.) This sum made it possible to employ about half of the coordinating staff and to place Survey archeologists and their assistants at three cooperating institutions. In procuring the archeologists for this first year, every effort was made to place the right individual at the right institution with the various institutional and personal factors and variations taken into consideration. In addition, an effort was made to obtain good geographic distribution of the three archeologists during the first year. The appropriation for the second year ($215,000, again with ten percent held in reserve), the third year (the full $215,000), and the current biennium (which approaches $250,000 for each year) has enabled the Survey to become more fully operative by placing archeologists at seven of the state colleges and universities and by filling out the coordinating staff. In briefly reviewing the first four years of the Survey's existence, I believe it is possible to say that it has made noticeable progress toward each of its goals.

In the forty years prior to the Survey, the museum had recorded less than one thousand archeological sites in the state. The Survey files now contain records—and generally they are far better records—on over five thousand sites, and they are accumulating at a rate of almost a thousand a year. The Survey has managed to acquire copies of the basic field records known to exist from almost all field research carried out in Arkansas, including those of such earlier work as that of C. B. Moore and M. R. Harrington. It is gradually building up its photographic files as well, with the ultimate goal of having a record of all known significant artifacts from Arkansas. To this end it already has photographed the more than five hundred whole vessels from Arkansas in the Gilcrease Museum and has borrowed from Peabody Museum at Harvard the extensive negative files (more than two thousand) accumulated by P. Phillips of Arkansas collections in many other museums in the East and Midwest. This is in addition to the approximately six thousand whole vessels (many of which are already photographed) in the University of Arkansas Museum's collections. Gradually, too, private collections are being studied, photographed, and added to the record.

Probably a quarter to a third of all the original field research ever undertaken in Arkansas has been done in the past four years. This material is being actively studied, as is the data already available from earlier work. The results of some of this work have appeared heretofore in the publications of the Arkansas Archeological Society, but the Survey has begun a Research Series in which most of the results directed to other archeologists will be published. Two publications in this series have appeared to date, and two more are nearly ready; research papers probably will appear at a rate of two to four a year. There is also a Popular Series directed toward a more general audience. For most issues of the

Research Series it is planned to have a summary, directed at this nontechnical audience, which will appear in the Popular Series, though the Popular Series will not be restricted to such summaries.

Having seven archeologists scattered over the state actively carrying out research in itself creates public awareness of archeology. But each archeologist also works directly toward achievement of this goal through talks to local civic groups and schools, by affiliation with other groups having similar goals, and in many instances through establishment of a chapter of the Arkansas Archeological Society. When it has been possible to provide the archeologist with a research assistant or an archeological technician, even greater strides are taken, for this assistant devotes a major portion of his time to contacting those who own and control the land and its use—not just the occupants of the land itself but also state and federal agencies, such as the Soil Conservation Service. In this connection the Survey currently is conducting a series of studies, in cooperation with the National Park Service, to determine which agricultural programs and land use practices are causing significant destruction to archeological resources and how best to meet each situation.

The Survey's first number in the Popular Series, entitled "Indians of Arkansas," was a review written for the layman of what we presently know concerning Arkansas' prehistory. It also contains a statement about the importance of archeology, about the Survey, and about the Arkansas Archeological Society. Over three thousand copies were distributed without charge, one to each public school library in the state and to each classroom teaching the required unit in Arkansas history, and it is made available to the rest of the public at cost. In several instances Survey archeologists have been instrumental in starting, or have worked with, high school archeology clubs, and, as noted earlier (see page 40ff), the Survey is working actively with the Society in developing and promoting increased knowledge about archeology. Newspaper articles are frequently employed, but personal contact is the most effective approach. On a more general level Survey personnel conceived and were largely responsible for writing (in conjunction with Carl Chapman in Missouri and the University of Missouri Extension Service publication facilities) the booklet "Stewards of the Past." This booklet explains to the general public that there is a national crisis relative to our archeological resources and, of equal importance, that there is something which everyone can do about it. To date almost forty thousand copies of this booklet have been distributed, with nearly every state having purchased copies for (usually free) distribution.

The Survey also has endeavored to be innovative in its approach to all aspects of archeological research. It currently has taken the lead in experimenting with and developing a computerized data bank and retrieval system for archeological information, including both artifacts and sites. Survey personnel were instrumental in establishing and coordinating the Mississippi Alluvial Valley Archeological Program. This loose affiliation of all archeologists actively working in that geographical area has not only increased communications and knowledgeable planning among them but also led indirectly to the production of "Stewards of the Past" and more recently the introduction of legislation [the Moss-Bennett bill now being considered by Congress (see pages 249-251)] to facilitate federal participation in the effort to recover and protect our archeological resources on a national level. Survey personnel helped author this legislation and have led the effort to develop support for it and to carry out the legislative leg work, which is as essential on the federal level as on the state level.

The Arkansas Archeological Survey was created by the people of Arkansas to benefit Arkansas. This, I believe, it has done and is doing in full measure. I also believe, however, that by their action Arkansans have benefited the nation as a whole, not only directly in ways such as those which have been suggested here but also indirectly by having provided a model of what a state can do to preserve its past.

There seems little question but that the Survey has been able to launch one of the most effective programs to be found anywhere in the country on the problem of the preservation of a state's archeological resources. This is true both because of the nature of the administrative organization and because of the total effective finances. Nonetheless, even in Arkansas, both the public and the archeologists are going to continue to be frustrated and, at least on occasion, dissatisfied. There will always be more farmers than archeologists, more destruction than conservation, more valuable sites lost than can possibly be even superficially investigated. The Arkansas Survey is not able to claim, as did the University of Arkansas Museum staff for years, that it has neither time nor funds to get out over the state, or that there are no funds for publication. But neither is it able to meet all of the demands made upon it, no matter how urgent they may be. Patience and a degree of cheerful resignation, counterbalanced by hope and determination, are still key elements in the personality of the successful archeologist—amateur or professional.

Establishment of the Arkansas Archeological Survey effectively demonstrates what an interested, concerned citizenry and legislature can do. They can present archeology and archeologists, of all types, with a tremendous opportunity and an even greater challenge. The Survey is attempting to meet that challenge with a continuing, effective, coordinated, and imaginative program.

A SUMMARY OF CURRENT STATE AND FEDERAL SUPPORT

State Support of Archeological
Research and Development

Basically, there are three general types of legislation which affect archeological resources and archeological research. The first of these is funding legislation which provides the wherewithal for state-supported archeological research. The second might be termed "enabling legislation" in that it is concerned with the establishment or designation of an agency responsible for developing the state's archeological resources. The third is regulatory legislation designed to control investigation and disposition of a state's archeological resources. All three forms of legislation could be found in a single state but often are not. (Only twenty states have all three forms.) Some forty-three states have regulatory legislation of one form or another, whereas only twenty have any realistic enabling legislation, though another ten states at least mention archeology in connection with some state agency. Probably in no more than twenty states is archeological research an identifiable budgetary item, and in no more than half of these is it subject to specific funding by the legislature. Of the fifty states, five have no archeological legislation at all (Indiana, New Hampshire, New Jersey, Rhode Island, and Vermont), and in Louisiana archeology receives only passing mention in one recent bill.

Associated with all three types of legislation there are occasionally, but not inevitably, one or more sections which establish legislative intent regarding and concern for the preservation and development of the state's archeological resources. More pointedly, there generally are other sections in these laws which endeavor to establish the nature or extent of state ownership and control over archeological materials. These ownership statutes take three basic forms: (1) The state is declared to be the owner of all archeological material found within the state, whether on public or private land (the constitutionality of claiming ownership on private land is in serious question); (2) state ownership of or

83

concern for all archeological materials on land owned or controlled by the state is proclaimed (this provision is sometimes extended to include lands controlled by municipal or county governments); (3) state ownership is asserted over archeological materials on all public land, state and federal, within the state. The constitutionality of extending state ownership to objects on federal land reverts to the provisions of initial statehood, and this differs from state to state.

FINANCIAL SUPPORT

A detailed review of state financial support of archeological research at the beginning of 1971 reveals a rather varied picture. Financial support ranges from none whatsoever in some states to annual amounts well in excess of $100,000 in others. For purposes of a summary discussion the fifty states can be divided into four groups on the basis of the total amount of financial support provided.

No Program

Four states expend no funds for archeological research. (In 1958 this figure was nine.) These include Vermont, New Hampshire, Massachusetts, and Rhode Island, all in New England. Another six states really fall more properly into this category, but as some state money is or has been spent on occasion, they are included in the next category.

Less Than a Minimal Program

Unfortunately, this is the largest category, for the situation in twenty-three states (twenty-three in 1958 also) can best be described in this manner. Six of these states (Connecticut, Maine, Montana, Nevada, North Dakota, and South Dakota) cannot be considered to have any real state-financed program at this time. Though a small amount of state funds is spend on archeological research, it is available spasmodically and generally amounts to much less than a $1000 a year of operating funds spend on archeological research. The others (Alabama, Alaska, Colorado, Georgia, Idaho, Indiana, Kentucky, Louisiana, Michigan, New Jersey, Oklahoma, Oregon, Tennessee, Utah, Virginia, Washington, and Wyoming) are generally only a little better off. In only a few instances (for example, Louisiana and Oklahoma) is there a full-time state-supported research position. In the other states, although there is sometimes the equivalent of one to two state-supported research positions, this generally consists of several people, often at different institutions, doing a little research now and then as the opportunity presents itself or as salvage becomes essential. In no case do any of these persons have any significant research funds available to them; the range is from approximately $1000 to $5000 each year with a marked tendency toward the lower end of the scale. No one could be expected to mount any type of realistic statewide archeological research program with no more time or resources available than this.

Oklahoma and Louisiana appear to be making a start toward a real program, but even should the full-time research position created in each state be provided with completely adequate operating funds, it is unrealistic for any state to expect one individual to be able to do anything more than the most urgent tasks. In fact, he will be so busy with emergencies that he might never have time to sit down and evaluate the state needs, much less design, develop, and execute a full-scale program to meet those needs. Nonetheless, creation of a full-time research position certainly is a step in the right direction. The next step should be development of a staff and budget (and this, normally, means one separately recognized by the legislature, or by the agency of which the program is a part) which will permit making a realistic attempt to meet the state's needs.

Of course, it should be noted that sometimes a considerable amount of archeological work is being done in these states. The pertinent point here, however, is that this research is largely unsupported by the state.

Minimal Basic Program

Fifteen states support programs which to some degree provide the basis for an adequate program (Arizona, Iowa, Kansas, Maryland, Minnesota, Mississippi, Nebraska, New Mexico, New York, North Carolina, Ohio, Pennsylvania, South Carolina, West Virginia, and Wisconsin). In each of these states there is the equivalent of at least two persons paid by the state to do research, and in almost every instance one or more of these are employed basically for research. Furthermore, specific budgeting and/or legislative recognition is taken of the program, and state funds are channeled primarily through one source. In other words, most of the basic requirements for developing a coordinated statewide archeological research program are present. For several of these states the level of operating funds available is still inadequate, but in the others (for example, Arizona) it approaches a realistic level.

In general, it would appear that from at least $10,000 to $15,000 of operating money (including salaries for supporting part-time field and laboratory staff) should be provided annually for each full-time research position if the research person is to be able to perform efficiently. This figure should be much higher, of course, if the program is not affiliated with a university, a museum, or other organization which provides the program with space, maintenance, utilities, security, and similar facilities at no cost to the program. Actually, only one or two of the states included here attain this level of support with state funds, the gap being made up in some instances by nonstate and contract funds. Dependence upon nonstate funds for basic operation is unfortunate. A state archeological research program should have the flexibility to work where a statewide problem-oriented plan indicates work is most needed. Rarely is this essential flexibility possible when nonstate funds must be depended upon for operation.

In none of these states is the level of staffing or operating support adequate for a fully developed state program, but a sound base has been established from which such a program could be developed.

Developed Program

Six states appear to have what can be described as developed programs (Arkansas, Delaware, Florida, Hawaii, Missouri, and Texas). Two others (California and Illinois) are expending as much or more than these five but without the statewide coordination which is essential to any developed program. Illinois has attempted to achieve this coordination with some measure of success through an informal but incorporated organization made up of all archeologists active in the state. California has initiated similar steps with the organization of the Society for California Archeologists. Though California has a long way to go, its legislature currently is considering enabling legislation patterned after that of Arkansas.

In each of the six states with developed programs two or more persons are employed more or less full time specifically for research; in each the program has a separate budget and, except in Missouri, is legislatively recognized. Only in Arkansas, Delaware, and Hawaii can it be said that the state's program is totally coordinated through a single agency, but in Florida and Texas there is a legislatively established and funded program with a state archeologist to provide a central depository and data bank in addition to the activity at other state institutions. Theoretically, there is no reason why the total programs in Florida and Texas cannot be coordinated by means of personal contacts among the archeologists concerned. The near-total Missouri effort is centered at the University of Missouri, where it operates separately but in close affiliation with the Department of Anthropology and the Museum of Anthropology. It doubtless is significant that Arkansas, Delaware, Florida, Missouri, and Texas have active, well-led amateur archeological societies, while in Hawaii, much more than in most states, a close personal identification is felt by the present voters with their precursors who inhabited the historic and prehistoric sites.

Summary

While at first glance it might be comforting to find that in round numbers just over two-and-one-quarter million dollars a year is being provided by the states for archeological research, it becomes considerably less reassuring when one realizes that less than ten states are providing more than half of that amount and that fewer than half of the states (twenty-three) account for nearly ninety percent of the total.

It is particularly discouraging when the 1970 situation is compared with that of my survey in 1958. Only at the bottom and at the top is there any marked change. Now only four states expend absolutely no money on archeological research, whereas nine were in that category twelve years earlier. The brightest (and almost only) ray of hope, however, is the really marked development which has occurred in a few states (Arkansas, Delaware, Florida, Hawaii, and, to a lesser degree, Texas). With these exceptions, progress over the past twelve years has been less than spectacular, and, in the majority of cases, nonexistent. Time is growing short. Archeology cannot afford another twelve years of similar somnolence.

At the present time over half of the states are making no realistic effort to preserve or protect their archeological resources. This ominous fact is of vital concern to everyone. Those states with reasonably adequate programs cannot sit back and relax, for to interpret the prehistory of their states, they need the data being lost in the others. Until *every* state has an adequate program, everyone concerned with this nation's vast archeological resources must be willing to turn to and work overtime, for the best and often the only capital available to invest in this development is the time and energy of the professional and amateur archeologists.

ADMINISTRATIVE ORGANIZATION

The details of the administrative organization of the various programs are unique to the individual states, but, in grosser terms, the administrative location or affiliation of the archeological research program in those states which have to any degree officially recognized the program can be considered under six headings.

Separate State Agency

Arkansas and Delaware are the only states which have established essentially separate agencies funded directly by the legislature to handle the state program. In Delaware this took the form of an Office of Archaeology as a separate office of the Department of State receiving funds directly from the legislature. The Office of Archaeology is the single responsible state agency with, evidently, no other state agencies likely to become active in the near future; thus they could be in a position of leadership and find it possible to coordinate all available data within their own organization. In Arkansas the funds are legislatively separated from any other organization, but the Board of Trustees of the University of Arkansas is designated the responsible body, while coordination of the program with all state institutions of higher learning is precisely spelled out. Thus the program has the advantages both of independent recognition and support and of legislatively directed coordination of all interested state agencies. (See pages 67-68 and 128 and 129 for more complete information.)

Operating a state archeological research program as a separate administrative and budgetary organization (and this would include not only Arkansas and Delaware but also Florida, South Carolina, and others of the states discussed later) is totally different from operating a research program through a teaching department, or as a staff member attached to some agency with other basic responsibilities, or even from a museum curatorial position. For one thing the total energies of the director and everyone on the staff are directed toward the program. This affects the director's attitude as well as the manner of operation and the capacity to conduct research. He is available to do what needs to be done when it needs to be done. It is not necessary for him to wait until summer or to interrupt his analysis while he teaches two, three, or four courses for a semester. The increase in efficiency and resultant output is impressive. If a state wishes to achieve a maximum return on its investment in archeological research, it should give very serious consideration toward establishing such an administratively and budgetarily separate agency. This does not mean that it has to be divorced entirely from any other administrative unit. It can be placed within the framework of a university, a museum, or some other state agency. Nor does it mean that provision should not be made for utilization of part-time personnel. The archeological budget should, however, be a separate entity and not simply an unspecified part of a larger operating budget. The senior archeologist and his staff should be reasonably free of other responsibilities and must be in an administrative position such that their determination of where and how they are to operate is not subject to any more specific control or overview than is appropriate for a legislature to apply toward any state program or agency.

Program within a University

Arizona, Connecticut, Iowa, Louisiana, Missouri, Nevada, Oklahoma, South Carolina, and Utah all have programs recognized within the organizational framework of a university. In Louisiana, Missouri, and Utah the program is recognized as a separate budgetary unit within the College of Arts and Sciences; in the case of Arizona as a separate unit within the museum (which in this case is also the state museum); in Iowa it functions through the University Division of Research and Administration; while in South Carolina and Oklahoma it operates directly under a university vice-president and is funded separately by the legislature. In an operational sense the programs in all of these states may well be as independent as in Arkansas and Delaware. Connecticut has legislative recognition but not legislative funding. Perhaps not coincidentally, it does not have university funding either.

Illinois, Michigan, and Wisconsin have separate programs only in a somewhat unusual sense. In all three states a number of organizations (mostly university affiliated) are active, and, though in every instance the archeological research budget of each individual organization tends to be at or below the minimal range and generally is not specifically recognized, the total for the state can be fairly considerable. In these three states the archeologists from the interested institutions have banded together in an informal (but legally constituted) organization to coordinate the state program. This is perhaps the best practical arrangement for states which have several institutions already active but which lack direct legislative recognition or funding of a program. Nonetheless, its voluntary nature, the multiple and therefore potentially unstable sources of funds, and the lack of legislatively recognized structure, while all having certain advantages, would seem to argue against establishing this as an ideal model to emulate.

Programs such as those found in Arizona and Missouri conclusively demonstrate that active leadership can result in the establishment of effective programs within the university structure, but the situation at some thirty or forty other universities suggests that such development is not readily accomplished. There are good reasons for this. Separate "pure" research programs are not readily undertaken by most universities (except, perhaps, in the field of agriculture), even when the identification with teaching is a close one. The association between archeological research and teaching is close, of course, which doubtless accounts for the large number of minimal or less than minimal programs, but teaching needs alone are not likely to provide adequate justification from the point of view of the university for providing for a fully developed statewide research program. On the more practical level it is difficult, and in situations of close budgetary decisions almost impossible, for a research program, even one closely allied to the teaching program, to compete for funds successfully against departments that can cite the teaching of core courses, expanding course coverage, and ever-increasing enrollment as arguments in their favor. The approach taken by Wisconsin, Michigan, and Illinois, that of carrying out the necessary research as a part-time activity from within the teaching department, is a practical alternative open only to states having a number of institutions actively interested in pursuing archeological research, and there are serious disadvantages to this approach, as noted previously. Certainly, no single teaching department is likely ever to be in a position to support enough research time on the part of its faculty to provide for an adequate state program.

Nonetheless, an administratively separate and legislatively recognized program at a university is potentially one of the most effective organizational structures for a state program. This is, of course, particularly true if full responsibility for carrying out the program has been designated by the legislature *and* has been accepted by the university, and, further, if it is associated with a strong active university museum. The latter association frees the program as much as is possible within a university community from budgetary competition with enrollment and places it within a research-oriented organization. As a part of the university, the program has statewide contacts, is assured of high standards for its personnel, and is reasonably free from nonacademic pressures. It has ready access to supplementary support by trained personnel in other fields (for example, geology, botany, physics), to essential auxiliary facilities such as the library, specialized laboratory equipment, and a vehicle pool, and to the other resources of a university. If there is a university museum, the program can avail itself of the museum's facilities for storing comparative study collections and for housing in an adequately scientific manner its own collections. Finally, a state program under a university umbrella has a high degree of stability. But here, as elsewhere, separate administrative and budgetary recognition of the archeological research program is crucial to success.

Program within a State Museum

This administrative organization is to be found in New Mexico, in essence in Pennsylvania, and at least potentially in New Jersey. Such an organizational arrangement could have even greater advantages than the situation within a university, for, being associated with an organization which is, or should be, research oriented, the program is not in the position of competing against enrollment, while most of the other advantages present in a university could also be found in association with a fully funded state museum. The difficulty in most states is simply that no such well-staffed and fully equipped state museum exists, and one adequately equipped and financed to provide proper support for a state archeological program is unlikely to appear overnight. The three states utilizing this approach have physical plants (new ones in Pennsylvania and New Jersey) totaling several million dollars in value, while the archeological program budget forms only a small portion of the total museum budget.

Program within a State Historical Society

Again three states have chosen this administrative route as their principal one (Kansas, Nebraska, and Ohio). In these circumstances an archeological program generally has been undertaken by the state historical society as a part of its total field of responsibility but, for some reason, without establishing it as a separate budgetary entity. If the program is carried out by staff members as a part-time activity, it can be said frequently to suffer problems similar to those experienced by programs carried out on a part-time basis by archeologists attached to teaching departments within a university. However, as was the case with the state museum, in a setting where the historical society is a large organization with an active statewide program and a museum organization, there are many positive factors working for the development of a program. In Colorado the State Historical Society is responsible for issuance of permits, but the Society itself does not carry out any active archeological research program.

Program within Other State Agencies

In the states where this has developed (Florida, Georgia, Hawaii, Maryland, Mississippi, New Jersey, New York, Texas, Virginia, and West Virginia) it generally has worked well up to a point. It would appear, however, that state programs attached to such organizations potentially could suffer from being peripheral to the main purpose of the organization (the Florida archeological program, though under the Florida Department of State, was legislatively established as a specific division so may be less subject to the problem than some of the others), and in most instances the auxiliary facilities and personnel present in a university are unlikely to be as readily available. Growth and development beyond the level of initial funding, while certainly possible, may prove to be more difficult than within a university, museum, or society organization which has a basic research orientation to start.

In Georgia (Historical Commission) no real development has yet occurred. In New York (Department of Education), though it has a minimal basic program with a research orientation and museum organization attached, the program has not grown noticeably over the years. In Florida (Department of State), Hawaii (Department of Land and Natural Resources), Maryland (Geological Survey), Mississippi (Department of Archives and History), Texas (Historical Survey), and West Virginia (Geological Survey) the programs are too new to judge growth. Hopefully, growth will prove possible, particularly in those states where the initial funding was not as adequate as could be desired.

Separate Programs within a Number of State Agencies

In this instance "separate program" implies both that the program is normally treated as a separate budgetary entity within each agency and that, furthermore, essentially separate (though occasionally coordinated) programs exist in more than one type of state administrative unit. This situation holds for California, Minnesota, and North Carolina. In North Carolina and Minnesota the programs appear to be well coordinated with essentially the university-based program accepting responsibility for prehistoric archeological sites and material while the Historical Society (Minnesota) or the Department of Archives and History (North Carolina) undertakes preservation of historic sites and materials. In California there is little evidence of coordination, though informal (nonlegislative) and formal (legislative) efforts are being made to correct this situation. In other states where there are separate agencies charged with or accepting some measure of responsibility in the archeological area no effective programs have developed.

Multiple support can indicate a broad base of state interest and concern, which is, of course, a healthy sign and conceivably could bode well for the development of greater financial resources than any one agency might be able to provide. Furthermore, if the various advantages unique to one or another agency affiliation can be utilized by archeologists at all of the other agencies, this approach could obviously be quite successful. Two serious dangers exist. A "let George do it" approach could arise both with respect to funding and to areas of responsibility. Also, lack of coordination and the danger of competition between agencies working in the same general area with the same financial base (the state government) is a very real one. This evidently has become a serious problem in California. Both of these potential problem areas might be avoided in part by legislative recognition and direction, as has been done in Minnesota and North Carolina. Unless there is effective coordination by some means, the disadvantages of this approach far outweigh the advantages.

REGULATORY LEGISLATION

Of the forty-five states which have some form of archeological legislation, forty-three have regulatory legislation of some nature (Connecticut and Louisiana are the exceptions) with the majority taking the approach of regulation via permit. In addition, a considerable variety of other provisions (over fifty) have been brought into play. In a few instances one particular prohibition is all that a state has attempted. In general these acts are patterned after the federal law of 1906 (see pages 235-238) and have been referred to collectively as "antiquities acts."

State Ownership

Twenty-two states (Alaska, Arizona, Arkansas, Colorado, Delaware, Florida, Georgia, Hawaii, Idaho, Illinois, Kansas, Missouri, Maryland, Michigan, Minnesota, Mississippi, New Mexico, North Dakota, South Dakota, Tennessee,

Texas, and Wisconsin) reserve to themselves exclusive ownership of archeological resources on state land (Florida restricting it to "abandoned" archeological material). Florida, Georgia, Maine, Michigan, Mississippi, South Carolina, and Texas extend coverage to underwater areas under state control. Nevada and Oklahoma specifically forbid excavation on both state and federal land, while Alabama goes the total distance and proclaims itself the owner of all archeological material within the state (probably unconstitutionally and certainly to no avail).

Arkansas (indirectly), North Carolina, and Ohio provide for the use of the state's right of eminent domain to acquire archeological resources, and Illinois and Iowa specifically state that archeological resources can be considered when adding lands to the park system. Some states, such as Arkansas and Minnesota, make provisions for state agencies to loan or exchange archeological objects in possession of the state in the furtherance of the state's interests.

Permits

Issuing Authority for Permits

Alaska	Commissioner of Natural Resources
Arizona	Director of the Arizona State Museum, University of Arizona
California	Director of the Division of Beaches and Parks (for park land)
Colorado	State Historical Society
Delaware	Governor or agent (Office of Archaeology)
Georgia	Georgia Historical Commission
Hawaii	Department of Land and Natural Resources
Idaho	Board of Trustees of the State Historical Society
Illinois	State department controlling property with review and counsel by the Illinois State Museum
Kansas	Secretary of the Kansas Antiquities Commission
Kentucky	Department of Anthropology, University of Kentucky
Maine	Director of the Maine State Museum and senior archeologist at the University of Maine
Maryland	Maryland Geological Survey
Michigan	Director of the Department of Natural Resources
Minnesota	Director of the State Historical Society
Mississippi	Board of Trustees of the Department of Archives and History
Montana	Commissioner of Public Lands on the recommendation of the State Historical Society
Nebraska	University of Nebraska, Conservation and Survey Division
Nevada	Board of Directors of the Nevada State Museum
New Mexico	Cultural Properties Review Committee with concurrence of the state archeologist

New York	Heads of the state departments or agencies with approval of the commissioner of education
North Carolina	Director of the State Museum or the director of the Department of Archives and History
North Dakota	Superintendent of the State Historical Society
Oklahoma	Chairman, Department of Anthropology, University of Oklahoma
Oregon	State Land Board and president of the University of Oregon
South Carolina	Institute of Archaeology and Anthropology, University of South Carolina (underwater only)
South Dakota	Secretary of the State Historical Society
Tennessee	State Archaeologist, Division of Archaeology, Department of Conservation
Texas	Antiquities Committee
Utah	State Park and Recreation Commission
West Virginia	Antiquities Commission
Wisconsin	Director of the State Historical Society with approval of the state archeologist
Wyoming	State Board of Land Commissioners

Even cursory perusal of this list suggests that there is little consistency among the states in who should bear responsibility for granting permits to carry out archeological work. It is even more disconcerting to discover, after a little study, that the permit-granting authority occasionally is only distantly related administratively, if at all, to whatever archeological expertise is available in the state. I can only suggest that if a state determines that it wishes to require permits, it make a determined effort to coordinate this authority with the state archeological program and avail itself of the resident expertise in that program. Only by so doing is there any hope or assurance that the permit provision will be of maximum benefit and assistance to the state in protecting its archeological resources.

Permit Coverage. Thirty-three of the forty-three states with regulatory provisions require permits to excavate on state land, and three of these specifically require state permits for work on both state and federal land. Alabama, Montana, and Oklahoma require a permit for anyone to excavate or explore for archeological material anywhere within the state. Taking the opposite tack, in Missouri and California the legislation refers only to state park lands, in Iowa only to Conservation Commission lands, and in South Carolina only to state-owned underwater property. The Florida, Georgia, Maine, Mississippi, and Texas permit laws specifically include state-owned underwater property as well as other state land, and the law has recently been so applied in Michigan. In Nevada surface collections of material are specifically exempted, while Alabama, Michigan, and Wisconsin stipulate that the landowner's consent must likewise be obtained. In Maine, Arkansas, and a few other states permission of the state agency controlling the land also is required. North Dakota authorizes landowners to issue permits for archeological work on their own land. Hawaii forbids issuance of a permit to excavate if an ancient monument or structure can be interpreted *in situ*.

Permit Eligibility. Most of the states restrict permits to qualified educational or scientific institutions where, by implication or explicit provision, the material must remain available to the public and result in gainful knowledge. A few others stipulate that only "persons with training" or "qualified persons" are eligible. The Wisconsin act allows issuance of permits only to qualified individuals. Institutions cannot be issued permits in Wisconsin. Other states, implicitly or explicitly, leave the establishment of qualifications to the permit-granting authority. Oregon has a special provision exempting other active public organizations within the state if they deposit copies of records in the Oregon State Museum. South Dakota and Oklahoma require that the responsible state agency carry out an investigation of the site and of the requesting agency before issuing a permit. Alabama flatly states that no nonresident may excavate in Alabama, while Tennessee *requires* the state archeologist to grant a permit to *any citizen* or group of state citizens! Arkansas, while not requiring a formal permit, does require in addition to permission from the appropriate state agency, that a full set of records on archeological research carried out by anyone with state funds be deposited with the Arkansas Archeological Survey.

Permit Fees. Oklahoma, North Dakota, and South Dakota establish permit fees, presumably to facilitate the investigation of each permit, but in the case of North Dakota and South Dakota the fees are so low ($5.00 and $2.50) as to be of no real assistance. The $50.00 fee of Oklahoma is slightly more realistic but still would not cover the cost to the state agency of the investigation required. South Carolina may charge a fee for underwater work.

Revocation and Forfeiture. Eleven states (Colorado, Maine, Minnesota, Mississippi, New York, North Dakota, Oklahoma, South Dakota, Texas, Utah, and Wisconsin) specifically provide in their legislation for revocation of the permit if the work is not done scientifically, and forfeiture of any materials generally is implied or specified should this happen. Nevada provides for revocation if the work is not begun within six months, while Nevada, Hawaii, Oregon, and Tennessee provide for forfeiture of objects obtained without a permit. Colorado requires annual reports and a final report within three years (plus an inventory and a sample collection if the state desires one) and provides for revocation of permit if these conditions are not met. Hawaii has similar provisions. Others accomplish much of this by the specific regulations promulgated by the issuing agent. Minnesota goes a step further—it retains state title in all materials gained under permit with the stipulation that if the agency to which the permit was granted should ever cease to exist or for some other reason can no longer protect them, the objects shall revert to Minnesota. Kansas and Maine have similar provisions, and this approach would seem worthy of consideration by other states as well.

Disposition of Archeological Items Recovered.   Seven states (Georgia, Kansas, Maine, Maryland, Minnesota, New Mexico, and Wisconsin) explicitly state that all artifacts obtained under permit remain state property, four others (Delaware, Idaho, South Carolina, and Wyoming) provide for exceptions to this rule, and another eight (Colorado, Mississippi, Montana, Nevada, Oklahoma, Oregon, Texas, and Utah) specifically state that a portion may be required by the state. Four of these last (Montana, Nevada, Oklahoma, and Oregon) specify fifty percent. Alabama states that no archeological materials may be exported from the state, and Idaho prohibits exportation of materials from state property. Tennessee stipulates that they cannot be removed for periods longer than three hundred sixty-four days. (How these exportation provisions are to be enforced is not stated.) Arkansas (as a part of its enabling legislation), New Mexico, and to some extent South Dakota have provisions authorizing the official depository to redistribute items to properly safeguarded places around the state in order that they may be of greater benefit to the public. Arkansas (again in its enabling act) and Minnesota also are permitted to exchange objects with other states in order to further their research.

Other Permit Provisions. Most such legislation or the accompanying regulations also stipulate a variety of other conditions such as duration of the permit (generally one to three years) and the possibility of renewal. Wisconsin and Minnesota make provision for waiving normal permit stipulations in an emergency. Under Tennessee law all scientific records made under permit remain state property, and North Dakota requires that copies of all such records shall remain in the state. North and South Carolina, Texas, and a few other states authorize or direct law enforcement officers to assist in enforcing the permit provisions. In Colorado any municipality, county, governmental agency, corporation, or private individual may request the state to assume permit-granting authority over lands under their control.

Fraud and Vandalism

Seven states (Arizona, Hawaii, Mississippi, Oklahoma, Pennsylvania, Texas, and Wisconsin) have specific provisions to the general effect that it is a misdemeanor to rework or falsely label archeological objects or to manufacture, offer for sale, or exchange such objects with intent to defraud. Arizona also includes the sale or exchange of objects known to have been collected illegally.

Seventeen states (Alabama, Arizona, Arkansas, California, Hawaii, Idaho, Iowa, Maine, Mississippi, Missouri, Montana, Nevada, New Mexico, Tennessee, Texas, Washington, and Wisconsin) have statutes specifically prohibiting defacement, disturbance, or other vandalism of archeological sites of one or another type over which they exercise control. Idaho's law extends only to landmarks (except insofar as the permit provision provides broader protection), Missouri's only to state park land, and Washington's only to cairns, graves, or glyptic or pictured records. Alabama perhaps goes farthest in this regard by requiring that all excavated sites shall be restored to the same or like conditions as before excavation.

Acquisition and Disposition of Land and Easements

The enabling acts of a number of the state archeological agencies (including Arkansas) empower them to acquire and administer archeological sites, and two (North Carolina and Ohio) are specifically empowered to employ condemnation proceedings if necessary to save important sites.

Eight states (Arkansas, Colorado, Idaho, Massachusetts, Mississippi, New Mexico, Tennessee, and Texas) make provisions for establishing what might be termed "state archeological landmarks" and for the placement of markers. Texas has established an Antiquities Committee to do this and to be the legal custodian of items recovered under the Texas antiquities act (it also issues the permits). Generally, such state landmarks cannot be excavated or destroyed without permission from the state. At least in the case of Arkansas, Mississippi, and Texas these amount to scientific easements obtained by the state over private lands which thus give the state a measure of control over that property.

Iowa authorizes the county conservation boards to give consideration to archeological features when acquiring land for recreational purposes. A similar law is on the books in Illinois. In Illinois, Michigan, North Dakota, and South Dakota the state is directed to retain rights to any archeological sites or materials on any land subsequently disposed of by the state. In Arkansas, Hawaii, and Tennessee the state may withhold from sale or disposition land containing sites until these have been investigated, perhaps a somewhat more realistic approach.

In Hawaii sites recorded are to be placed on the tax map and state agencies are required to expend up to one percent of construction funds to recover archeological and historical remains affected. This certainly is a revolutionary provision. Private agencies and individuals are required to give three months notice if recorded sites are to be affected.

Trespass

Trespass laws and practices evidently vary considerably in the different states, and their relevance to activities affecting archeological resources should be determined. In some states (Alabama, Arkansas, Michigan, North Dakota, and Tennessee) it has been felt necessary to stipulate that it is an act of trespass to enter on private land for the purpose of collecting or excavating archeological materials. Making this a misdemeanor greatly strengthens the landowner's hand and better enables him to protect sites on his own property. All that remains is for the state archeological agency to encourage him to do so.

Tax Reduction

Providing landowners tax relief for sites being well protected is one of the few positive rewards a state can provide as a means of encouraging such protective activities. Used with discretion, this could be a powerful inducement and should be encouraged, though in some states it is not possible under present constitutional requirements. At present only New Mexico, Virginia, and Wisconsin specifically provide for this.

Provisions Requesting Cooperation

A number of states have included in their antiquities acts sections requesting the assistance and cooperation of citizens and landowners, or of other state agencies. Arkansas, Delaware, Georgia, Maryland, Minnesota, North Carolina, and Wisconsin include statements requesting that private landowners endeavor to insure that sites on their property be protected and that any excavation therein should employ the same safeguards for preserving the archeological information for the general public welfare as is incorporated into the statutes regarding state land. North Carolina even requests that persons with private collections insure that these are properly safeguarded and preserved by donating them to public institutions.

Arizona, Arkansas, Delaware, Kansas, New York, North Carolina, North Dakota, and Wisconsin urge citizens to report sites on state land to the proper state authorities, while Arkansas, Minnesota, North Dakota, Tennessee, and Wisconsin ask the other state agencies to cooperate with the specific state agencies responsible for the state's archeological resources. In Arkansas and Tennessee the agencies also are requested to notify contractors of the provisions of the act and to cooperate with the archeological agency.

In two states (Arkansas and Tennessee) the state archeological agency is authorized to cooperate with and assist amateur groups in the state.

In Mississippi, Montana, Nevada, South Carolina, and Texas law enforcement agencies are specifically charged with helping enforce the act, and in North Carolina employees of the state Department of Archives and History are deputized by the act for this purpose.

Arkansas and Tennessee provisions specifically authorize and direct the state highway departments to assist and to expend state and federal funds for this purpose. Colorado, Iowa, Kansas, Maine, Montana, Nebraska, New Mexico, New York, Wisconsin, and other states have provided, by legislative act or administrative practice, for establishment of a highway salvage program. Similar legislation in other states where it is required to enable the state highway department to expend funds for archeology would make possible more highway salvage work.

Other Provisions

Georgia and Florida specifically mention "treasure trove" as belonging to the state. However, the intricacies of treasure trove law relative to archeological findings, Internal Revenue Service interests, the state, the legal rights of the finder, and those of the landowner are less than clear at the moment and are likely to remain unclear for some time. This would be a likely area of investigation for a legally trained person interested in archeology, for it might well hold some promise as a legal test providing a measure of protection for archeological materials. The same might be said with regard to the possible application of the principle of escheat to archeological materials.

The Massachusetts Historical Commission, with its powers to protect sites on public and private lands by making them relatively immune to eminent domain procedures, has an approach which warrants serious consideration by other states, particularly those with many historic and archeological sites being encroached upon by construction and urban renewal activities.

Among innovative procedures Georgia's provision of a "finders' fee" or reward payable by the state to those reporting sites is unique and presently of untested value. Attention is called particularly to several innovative and important provisions contained in Hawaii's antiquities legislation, including the requirement that state construction agencies expend up to one percent of construction funds on the recovery of archeological finds, the placement of sites on the tax roles, the three-month notice provision before there can be any modification of a designated landmark, and others (See pages 207-215 for the complete text.)

Although not written with the protection of archeological remains in mind, archeologists in Iowa feel that the Iowa law prohibiting the disturbance of human remains can be applied to the protection of aboriginal remains; legal authorities in Arkansas feel that similar Arkansas statutes would not be so applied by the courts. Hawaii's law spells out the conditions under which human remains may be disturbed.

Texas's involvement with offshore wrecks and related problems has caused that state to institute a number of specialized provisions, including authority to enter into contracts with salvagers, the right to buy back material from salvagers, and the authority to do restoration and conservation work (for a fee) for nonstate individuals or agencies (and much of this has been copied in recent Mississippi legislation). Other states, such as Florida, Georgia, Maine, and South Carolina have also become concerned in this area.

In a number of states (for example, Connecticut, Arkansas, Georgia, Iowa, Kansas, New Mexico, Tennessee, West Virginia, and Wisconsin) legislation specifically establishes the post of state archeologist. There is no one-to-one correlation between such acts and the establishment of an adequate state program.

In Arkansas, the Arkansas Archeological Society—a group made up of amateurs and professional archeologists—is asked to provide the legislature, concerned institutions, and others with an annual evaluation of the state archeological program. This responsibility, urged on them by the institutions, was accepted with reluctance by the Society and with some concern by the professionals attached to the state program. Actually, it has been of great benefit, for it provides the Survey with a report on its public image and the legislature and participating institutions with an unbiased view of the progress or problems of the program, as well as valuable data on the Survey's needs.

As a result of the Historic Preservation Act (P.L. 89-665), most states have made some provision, legislative or administrative, for grants-in-aid for archeological work, but care should be exercised that such grants do not become the only source of state (and federal) aid. The Historic Preservation Act provides valuable assistance but is not so structured that it can assume the entire or even a major portion of the burden of recovering the nation's archeological resources.

Summary

A majority of states have some form of regulatory legislation. Most regulation takes the form of controlling exploration and excavation on state-owned or controlled land by the issuance of permits. A number of states have extended this control to all land in the state and in some instances have actually declared state ownership of archeological material on private land. Though this last provision has never been tested in the courts, it is unlikely to stand up.

It should be noted that despite considerable inquiry I am acquainted with only rare instances where one of these state regulatory laws has been actually applied or a case brought to court, in spite of the fact that over forty states have regulatory legislation, some of which has been on the books for over thirty years. A number of correspondents noted that, while well-designed laws have value, education rather than legislation is the best means of achieving effective conservation and development of archeological resources. Despite this fact, well-designed regulatory legislation has a definite place. What must be emphasized is that for effective education and effective enforcement of any regulatory legislation an adequate, active state-supported program of archeological research and development is essential.

Federal Support of Archeologial Research and Development

INTRODUCTION

Legislatively expressed concern for archeological resources by the federal government (the Antiquities Act of 1906) antedates that of any state of which I am aware, though in several states earlier legislative action had served to preserve individual sites. Subsequent legislation has further strengthened the federal role in historical and archeological protection, recovery, and preservation. This legislation and resultant federal activity has been not only of a regulatory nature but also has affected the establishment and funding of federal programs for this purpose, and has provided a source of funds through contracts and grants—often matching grants—by means of which the states have been able to initiate or increase their own efforts. This support on the federal level has been extremely important, not only for the support itself but for the example it has placed before the states and for the very significant contribution it has made to the development of many of the present state programs as well.

PRINCIPAL FEDERAL AGENCIES INVOLVED

Smithsonian Institution

The Smithsonian Institution has actively supported archeological research within the United States by its own staff longer than any other federal agency. The actual amount and direction of this research has varied considerably, depending upon both budgetary restrictions and the personal interests of the staff members. Unlike the National Park Service, the other principal federal agency involved in actually carrying out research, the Smithsonian research orientation for over thirty years has been worldwide and is not specifically directed toward research on and recovery of archeological resources within the territorial limits of the United States. It is, of course, highly desirable that at least one federal agency have this worldwide breadth and scope to its operation. Archeological information does not readily conform to current political boundaries, and if archeologists working within the United States are to be able properly to interpret their findings, they must possess comparative information from elsewhere. Thus not only is it self-serving for the federal government to help provide this worldwide data but any more narrowly defined parochial approach to scientific knowledge would be inexcusable for a nation with the resources and responsibilities possessed by the United States.

Actually, Smithsonian personnel often have been in the forefront of archeological development on the American scene through individual research by archeologists attached to the National Museum of Natural History, United States National Museum, Bureau of American Ethnology, and through operation of the River Basin Survey, which was so active in the Missouri basin after World War II. The Bureau of American Ethnology has now been abolished, and responsibility for the River Basin Survey has been transferred entirely to the National Park Service.

At present, archeological research activities at the Smithsonian have been pulled together into the Department of Anthropology within the National Museum of Natural History, and a new publication series "Smithsonian Contributions to Anthropology" was initiated in 1965. There is, however, no major program of activity at the present time directed specifically toward archeological research within the United States.

Department of the Interior—National Park Service

The National Park Service was created in 1916 as a bureau within the Department of the Interior and was at that time charged with responsibility for administration of national parks and monuments. In 1933 the Government Reorganization Act authorized transference of historical and military parks to the National Park Service. During this period and since, the National Park Service has carried out such archeological research as was necessary for the development of these park areas. In so doing, they have doubtless contributed more than any other single group or agency to the absolutely vital task of creating in the minds of the average citizen an appreciation of our past heritage and a desire to know more concerning it.

The Antiquities Act of 1906 had long been available, though often of little avail, to protect archeological resources on federal lands in a prohibitive or passive way, but it was not really until the Historic Sites Act of 1935 further enlarged the Park Service's responsibilities that there was any legislative basis for the development by an agency of the federal government (other than the Smithsonian) of any positive program of archeological and historical research not restricted in scope entirely to federal lands. The Historic Sites Act authorized the National Park Service to make surveys, secure data, and investigate archeological and historical sites anywhere in the country in order to determine which might have national value, and to seek and utilize the aid of other federal, state, or private agencies in so doing. This led to the formalization (it actually had been begun as an emergency measure in 1933) of the extremely valuable Historical American Buildings Survey (carried out in cooperation with the Library of Congress and the Architectural Institute of America) and initiation of the Historic Sites Survey (later designated as the National Survey of Historic Sites and Buildings), but not, at least immediately, to any equivalent activity on the archeological front. This was in some measure due to the intervention of World War II. Of course, prior to World War II, and also curtailed by it, there was the extremely important archeological program undertaken by the federal government as a part of the Tennessee Valley Authority development with the archeological effort being directed by William S. Webb. Subsequent to World War II, the National Park Service undertook a series of thematic studies particularly in connection with its Mission '66 program. These surveys and thematic studies included archeological as well as historical sites. The Mission '66 studies appeared (the archeological ones in extremely limited editions) in the late 1950's and early 1960's and resulted in the designation of a considerable number of sites as National Historic Landmarks and thus automatic placement on the National Register. In recent years an Historic American Engineering Register has been established.

Thus, while the Historic Sites Act did not serve as an instant clarion call for vastly increased federal activity, this landmark legislation—and it was that—has served as the foundation upon which most subsequent federal activity has been based. Certainly, without this act there is little reason to believe the Inter-Agency Archaeological Salvage Program would ever have gotten off (or into) the ground.

It was this latter program which got the National Park Service actively committed to archeological research outside of the actual park areas themselves. With inauguration of this program the National Park Service, for the first time, was thoroughly involved in (as it—sometimes fondly—is known to express it) out-house as well as in-house archeology. This was in 1945. To those of us who entered and grew up in archeology subsequent to World War II, it is difficult to realize the metamorphosis this development caused, albeit gradually, in the National Park Service. To us, their involvement in nonpark areas was ever there. What needs to be recognized is that this adjustment is still going on, not only to this but to the equally drastic changes, to be discussed later, being brought about by the national Historic Preservation Act of 1966. (Perhaps even further adjustments will be necessary as a consequence of legislation now pending in Congress. See pages 249-251.)

In 1945 nonfederal archeologists, concerned with the greatly expanded United States Army Corps of Engineers program of dam building, formed the Committee for the Recovery of Archaeological Remains. This four-man committee was sponsored by the American Council of Learned Societies, the Society for American Archaeology, and the American Anthropological Association. (It consisted at that time of Dr. J. O. Brew, Dr. Fred Johnson, Dr. A. V. Kidder, and Mr. William S. Webb. The present members include Dr. Brew, Dr. Emil Haury, Mr. Henry Hamilton, and Dr. Richard Daugherty.) This group served as the coordinating link between the National Park Service, the United States Army Corps of Engineers, and the Bureau of Reclamation (which also was involved in dam building). Later, other federal agencies entered the picture as it became clear that their programs too affected archeological resources. The ensuing dialog resulted in the development of the Inter-Agency Archeological Salvage Program with two subprograms.

The Inter-Agency Archaeological Salvage Program is the high-sounding name of an informally organized but certainly vitally important and highly successful operation. It is important not only for the archeological research which has taken place under the program but also because it served as the initial fulcrum upon which it has proven possible to raise the interest not only of the National Park Service but also of other government agencies in the need for archeological salvage. Of almost equal importance, in the sometimes bureaucratically fragmented world which is the federal (or any) government, the members of the Committee for the Recovery of Archaeological Remains (CRAR) were able to serve as a communications link among these agencies, allowing them to reinforce each other in their evolving interest in the development of archeological resources, and to become informed of each others' activities.

The Smithsonian Institution, with funds requested from Congress by the National Park Service, established within its Bureau of American Ethnology the River Basin Surveys. The River Basin Surveys, a federal agency operating with federal funds, established an office in Lincoln, Nebraska, and undertook to carry out archeological explorations and excavations in sites threatened with inundation behind the numerous large dams the United States Army Corps of Engineers and the Bureau of Reclamation were constructing within the Missouri River basin. In 1960 this program of archeological research in reservoirs was backed up by specific legislation (see pages 247-249).

A second subprogram, operating from 1947 through 1956 with National Park Service funds transferred to the River Basin Surveys, was set up to take care of similar problems caused by dam construction elsewhere in the country than the

Missouri River basin and, to a lesser extent, to carry out additional work in the Missouri River basin itself. Under this subprogram three additional offices were established (in Eugene, Oregon, in conjunction with the University of Oregon, at Austin, Texas, in conjunction with the University of Texas, and at Athens, Georgia, in conjunction with the University of Georgia) which were responsible for contracting with museums, universities, and other institutions which were equipped to carry out archeological research. Contracts in the form of cooperative agreements were then let to these institutions to carry out the necessary work. In 1956 federal funding for this portion of the program was almost totally eliminated and the three centers largely ceased operation. Subsequent to 1957 the National Park Service assumed full responsibility for the program within and without the Missouri River basin. This innovative subprogram had a number of beneficial results. It kept general coordination of the program (and now total operation) within the hands of the National Park Service but did not require of it the impossible task of hiring the necessary full-time staff or acquiring the facilities necessary to undertake this expanded program. Since these normally were cooperative agreements between the local institutions and the National Park Service rather than simply contracts to do research, it generally was true that the local institution made available funds or services equal or almost equal in value to the funds being provided by the National Park Service, thus nearly doubling the amount of research it was possible to accomplish. Viewed from the point of view of the local institution, this approach had (and has) much to recommend it. In addition to providing a source of research funds for both faculty and students, the impetus provided by this federal program, in more instances than a few, has been directly responsible for the growth and development of local and state programs. It certainly was a contributing factor in Arkansas. On occasion too, during this period the National Park Service utilized its own archeologists to do research outside of the Missouri River basin when, for various reasons, a local agency was not able to undertake the research.

This, then, was the picture up to 1966. In that year Congress passed the national Historic Preservation Act (discussed in greater detail later). As a consequence of this act, National Park Service activities and responsibilities in the area of archeological and historical research have been further expanded. An administrative reorganization which established an Office of Archeology and Historic Preservation within the National Park Service has taken cognizance of these expanded activities.

Within this office there are three divisions: history, historical architecture, and archeology. Also in the Office of Archeology and Historic Preservation, serving directly under the chief of the office, is the keeper of the National Register (see pages 241-242). The Division of Archeology has assumed responsibility from the Smithsonian for the operation of the presently somewhat reduced Missouri River Basin Surveys program and continues as the responsible coordinating and letting agent for the cooperative agreements with nonfederal institutions, as well as for establishing standards of archeological research within and without national parks boundaries by its own personnel.

Under an even more recent reorganization (fall 1971), a service center has been established in Denver responsible for coordinating all research, development, and construction within the national parks themselves. This center is not administratively under the Office of Archeology and Historic Preservation; rather the director of the center and the chief of the Office of Archeology and Historic Preservation report to the same associate director. Archeologists, as well as naturalists, historians, engineers, and architects, are attached to this center. The Division of Archeology, as noted, is responsible for establishing the standard of work by these archeologists but is not administratively responsible for their work except insofar as division archeologists are called upon for support by the center.

One major difficulty is that the vastly expanded horizons of activity which have now been provided the National Park Service have not been accompanied by any significant expansion of its operating budget in this area. This must be the next and essential step, for the National Park Service now possesses the legislative authorization and direction to continue to expand and develop its archeological programs along several lines. First, of course, there is an ever-expanding need for development (and stabilization) of the archeological areas under the control of the Department of the Interior, as well as provision for continuation of a carefully directed program of additions to the park system. It is to be hoped, too, that under the Division of Archeology the program of cooperative agreements with local institutions for archeological research outside the park areas can be continued and enlarged. This should be true, too, of the research activities carried out by the division's own archeologists.

The Division of Archeology has established archeological centers in the Southeast, Southwest, and Midwest. These centers (plus one for the Northeast and one for the West) could, and I believe should, become regional archeological resource centers, which would also serve as the nucleus for the development of the national problem-oriented archeological overview which is essential to the successful preservation of our archeological resources.

Through the National Register it is possible to provide at least a certain measure of legal protection to the more important known sites and through the grant-in-aid program provided for by Public Law 89-665 it is possible to assist states in recovering, protecting, and preserving specific sites that have been placed on the National Register.

It cannot be emphasized too strongly, however, that if the National Park Service archeological program is to be of maximum effectiveness, its efforts must not be restricted to sites on the National Register. Such a restriction conceivably could be relatively logical with respect to houses or similar structures of known historic or architectural value, but it is not a feasible approach in the realm of archeology. For one thing, the very existence of sites requiring investigation by federal funds (either directly by National Park Service personnel or by means of cooperative agreements with the states) might be unknown until far too late to go through the process of getting them on the Register. Second, with these, and indeed with many (though not all) archeological sites, placement on the Register more logically follows rather than precedes excavation, for only then is the site's importance known. This statement is not meant to preclude or even discourage the practice of placing unexcavated sites on the Register if there is reason to believe they are significant, or if doing so may serve in whatever measure to protect them, but it would be patently ridiculous to put every site known to archeologists on the Register. In short, while the work carried out under the grants-in-aid program of the National Register should be coordinated with that of the Division of Archeology and vice versa, neither one can serve as a substitute for the other. Both are vitally necessary to the continued healthy development of public support and to the success of archeological research on the federal level.

National Science Foundation

In the years since its establishment the National Science Foundation has been of considerable importance to the development of archeological knowledge in the United States and, indeed, over the world. It has been from the first a problem-oriented rather than a situation-oriented organization. As such it is a unique and essential portion of the total federal program to develop and support archeological research by this country.

The significance of the National Science Foundation's contribution can best be appreciated in relation to the current need and practice of expending much of both Park Service and state funds for emergency salvage. National Science Foundation funds also are occasionally so utilized, but, more importantly, they can be and are utilized for specific problem-oriented research, nearly the only federal funds so available to nonfederally employed investigators.

Department of Transportation—Federal Highway Administration

In 1954 an archeologist, Dr. Fred Wendorf, and state and federal highway personnel in New Mexico recognized that many of the programs of the state and federal highway departments were causing the destruction of archeological resources. From this realization grew an effort largely initiated and coordinated by Dr. Wendorf which resulted in the promulgation of several directives from the (then) Bureau of Public Roads.

These directives were concerned specifically with the salvage of archeological resources. This precedent resulted first in provision for archeological salvage in the Federal-Aid Highway Act of 1956 and currently in mechanisms being included in the National Transportation Act of 1966 and the Federal-Aid Highway Act of 1966 for the development of highway salvage programs in each state wishing to participate in such a program. The Department of Transportation thus became one of the few federal agencies authorized by federal law to take into consideration expending its own funds for the purpose of salvaging or protecting archeological resources.

Despite this federal leadership, acceptance or even cooperation on the state level has been less than universal. In the period 1956-1969 there have been one hundred sixty highway salvage projects in twenty-six states. Nearly half of these (sixty-nine) have been in two states (Illinois and New Mexico), while another thirty-seven were in Arizona, California, and Idaho. The remaining fifty-four projects were scattered among twenty-one other states. In twenty-four states no highway salvage projects at all were initiated despite the availability of federal funds.

There are several explanations for this. State highway departments tend to look upon incoming federal monies as a part of their appropriation, so any diversion of these funds must be carefully reviewed. Also, however favorably inclined the state highway department may be, there still must be a legal provision by the state for the required matching state money to be utilized for recovery and protection of archeological resources and, of at least equal importance, the availability of those funds. A further factor in the establishment of a state highway program is the incidence of Indian sites on the proposed right-of-way. In some instances, despite the interest of all parties concerned, the Indians just did not "cooperate" by placing their villages on present highway rights-of-way! Sometimes, however, the problem can be relegated to a basic lack of initiative or enthusiasm by either the archeologists or the state highway personnel or both. In contrast to this situation, my experience and that of others has been that the Federal Highway Administration will do everything within their power to assist in the development of such a program in every state. All they ask in return, and they have a right to ask it, is the submission of reliable readable reports which adequately communicate the results of the work to the layman as well as to the scientist, reports which will further the program itself by demonstrating that such research is important.

Department of Housing and Urban Development

The Department of Housing and Urban Development is the third federal agency to be authorized to expend its funds for archeological and historic preservation. Acts pertaining to this agency as well as those affecting the

Department of Transportation and some of the more sweeping acts affecting the Department of the Interior have been passed within the last four years. I believe they represent and express a growing trend in federal legislation toward the acceptance of federal responsibility in this critical area of concern.

The nature and area of the concern of the Department of Housing and Urban Development can best be shown by quoting from two departmental directives:

"A principal concern of the Department of Housing and Urban Development is improving the quality of urban life. Over the past few years, conviction has grown that one vital aspect of a dynamic urban program is the recognition, care and use of those parts of the physical environment embodying our heritage and culture. Homes and commercial buildings from an earlier time have much to teach us about ourselves, add grace to a community, refresh the eye, and emphasize the beauty of newer lines and forms. Open spaces of historic significance add to the pleasure of a community while reminding us of events of an earlier era. A section of homes, stores and structures preserved or restored in an adaptive way may become the focus of a neighborhood, or spark the redevelopment of a decaying area. For these reasons, HUD is deeply committed to utilizing historic resources of the city in a way which adds to the lives of the citizens and to the beauty of the environment; historic preservation for the sake of people holds an important place in HUD programs.

"In recognition of the vital aspect of the recognition, care, and preservation of those parts of our physical environment which embody our heritage and culture, urban renewal projects financed with Federal assistance may include the acquisition, relocation and/or restoration of land areas as well as individual structures which have special historic or architectural value."

It should be pointed out that these programs are almost invariably oriented toward urban areas and are matching grants. They have been utilized in some instances for archeological surveys of a specialized nature within urban areas as well as for reconstruction or the removal of historical houses to new locations.

National Trust for Historic Preservation

The National Trust for Historic Preservation is, technically, a nonfederal agency, but it receives federal funding through the grants-in-aid provisions of the National Historic Preservation Act. Its orientation to date has been exclusively historical and architectural, but as a source of information on preservation legislation and related activities of all types it is unequaled.

Other Federal Agencies

A number of other federal agencies have become increasingly concerned with archeological resources and salvage. At the 1970 meeting of the CRAR some two-dozen federal agencies were represented. A few, such as the Bureau of Land Management and the United States Forest Service, have recently hired one or more archeologists to advise them on needs in this area. The Bureau of Land Management recently has tightened somewhat its regulations by requiring, in some instances, a review of permit applications by a qualified archeologist and by requiring the permittee to assume the cost of necessary archeological salvage.

PRINCIPAL FEDERAL LEGISLATION

The Antiquities Act of 1906
(Public Law 34-209; 34 Stat. 225) (See pages 235-238 for text.)

This is the first as well as the most basic piece of federal legislation affecting archeology. It clearly established the principle that the government, acting for all the people, should not only protect archeological and historic objects and sites but should also actively work toward their preservation and public availability. The act and the accompanying rules and regulations have served as guidelines for the development of most state regulatory legislation.

The act provides for a fine and imprisonment for the excavation, removal, or vandalism of archeological and historical (and by administrative practice, paleontological) sites on government property. It provides for the establishment, by presidential proclamation, of national monuments for structures or objects of historic, prehistoric, or scientific interest which are located on government property and sets up a mechanism for permits to conduct investigations to be issued scientific organizations, provided the results are permanently preserved in a public museum.

The permits required under this act are obtained from the departmental consulting archeologist, who is also the chief archeologist of the National Park Service, for all federal lands except those under the jurisdiction of the Department of Agriculture (principally land controlled by the Forest Service) and the commissioner of Indian affairs. For permission to excavate on these properties application is made directly to the Department of Agriculture or to the commissioner of Indian affairs. It would seem far better if *all* such federal permits were handled by the Division of Archeology of the National Park Service, for they alone of the federal agencies are equipped with the personnel and the experience to evaluate and oversee the work done under such permits.

Perhaps the principal value of this act has been the solid base it has provided for subsequent federal legislation and for the operating control it has permitted and fostered over federally owned archeological resources, as well as for its psychological effect. It cannot be said as yet to have been used widely as a legal basis for prosecuting offenders. The basis for such prosecution is there, however, and may well see wider use in the future as public concern for the preservation of the nation's fast-disappearing archeological and historical resources increases.

The Historic Sites Act of 1935
(Public Law 74-292; 49 Stat. 666) (See pages 238-241 for text.)

This is the second of three basic pieces of federal legislation affecting archeological and historical resources.

This act declares it to be national policy to preserve for (in contrast to protecting from) the public, historic (including archeological) sites, buildings, and objects of national significance. Furthermore, the National Park Service is directed to "make necessary investigations and researches in the United States relating to particular sites . . . or objects to obtain true and accurate historical and archeological facts and information concerning the same."

This act in large part has formed the legal basis for the growth and development of the National Park Service program of archeology culminating for the present, in conjunction with the Historic Preservation Act of 1966, in the recently established Office of Archeology and Historic Preservation and the development of the current programs discussed previously (pages 106-108). It is important to note that under the wording of this act the National Park Service is charged with a nationwide responsibility in the area of archeological and historical resources—a responsibility which is in no way restricted to areas in federal ownership or to sites being destroyed in whole or in part by federal funds. In short, this act provides both authorization and a directive for the National Park Service to assume a position of truly national leadership in the area of protecting, recovering, and interpreting this nation's archeological and historic resources. If it does not assume such a position of leadership over the next few years, the National Park Service, the public, and even more, archeologists everywhere must share in the blame, just as they must all share the tragic loss of the resources which surely will accompany such a failure.

The Historic Preservation Act of 1966
(Public Law 89-665; 80 Stat. 915) (See pages 241-247 for text.)

This act is easily the third most important piece of federal legislation affecting historic and archeological research and preservation. In essence it provides for a vastly expanded National Register of important sites and objects—expanded principally in the sense that now sites of local, state, and regional as well as national significance are eligible for inclusion. It establishes a program of matching grants to the states for projects having as their purpose surveys of state resources and establishment of a state preservation plan, as well as matching grants for specific projects to protect or preserve sites or properties significant in American history, architecture, archeology, and culture which have been placed on the National Register. It sets up a program of grants-in-aid to the National Trust for Historic Preservation. Finally, it establishes an Advisory Council on

Historic Preservation. Everyone concerned with archeological research and preservation should become thoroughly familiar with the details of this law and the guidelines worked out for its implementation for, inevitably, it is going to have an effect on every state program and is likely to affect not only the funding but also the administrative and the regulatory aspects of the state programs.

The act requires that each state make a survey of its significant sites, designate a state liaison officer to be responsible for the program, and set up a state review committee composed of professionally competent persons to recommend sites to be placed on the National Register. Procedures also are established for the states to apply each year for matching grants to obtain and preserve sites on the National Register. The state preservation plan drawn up by the review committee and the state liaison office must be the official plan of the state and must meet with the approval of the Office of Archeology and Historic Preservation after review by the division chiefs and the National Register with respect to the competence of the personnel and adequacy of the administrative machinery for recommending sites and projects. A state's archeological program obviously should be involved with the state's total preservation plan.

Section 106 of the Historic Preservation Act is best quoted in its entirety:

"The head of any Federal agency having direct or indirect jurisdiction over a proposed Federal or federally assisted undertaking in any State and the head of any Federal department or independent agency having authority to license any undertaking shall prior to the approval of the expenditure of any Federal funds on the undertaking or prior to the issuance of any license, as the case may be, take into account the effect of the undertaking on any district, site, building structure, or object that is included in the National Register. The head of any such Federal agency shall afford the Advisory Council on Historic Preservation established under title II of this Act a reasonable opportunity to comment with regard to such undertaking."

Guidelines have been established and the advisory council has taken a number of difficult situations under consideration with considerable success. Nonetheless, the total implications of this section are broad and it may be some time before all details are worked out. In essence this section of the act implies that federal funds or authority may not be utilized to affect adversely sites on the National Register if any alternative is feasible. This key regulatory provision of the act also is going to affect directly archeological efforts within the states.

It should be emphasized that placing a site on the National Register may contribute to its protection and preservation but by no means assures this. Legally, a site can be placed on the Register without the consent or even the knowledge of the landowner. Diplomatically, this generally is not to be recommended. At least two factors are operative here. In a positive sense, an appeal to the pride and sense of responsibility of the private landowner who possesses a site to be placed on the National Register often will form the strongest base for preservation of that site—far stronger a base than the prohibition of the use of federal funds for its destruction. Agencies and individuals other than the federal government possess most of the bulldozers and related equipment in this country, and the landowner himself is the only possible protection against these. On the negative side, failure to inform the landowner would easily arouse his ire, particularly if he finds that presence of the site on the National Register prevents him from receiving federal assistance to do work in the area. This could readily lead him to destroy the site deliberately (with nonfederal resources), thus, incidentally, making it once again possible for him to get federal assistance to work in the area, where now the site would no longer exist. In short, failure to work closely with the owner of a site could lead directly to the destruction of the very site one is striving to protect. In Arkansas it is the practice of the State Review Committee to be aware of the reaction of the landowner when it is considering a nomination. It thus is in a better position to determine whether nomination will be truly beneficial or, in fact, potentially deleterious to the preservation of the site. Of course, in some circumstances, nomination, even over the intense objection of the landowner, could be the wisest course with respect to the preservation of a site, though this perhaps is more likely to be true of historic houses than archeological sites. Certainly, when nominating an historic district, total agreement by every landowner is not likely to be possible.

The situation just outlined suggests one of the factors which must be considered when recommending placement of a site on the National Register. Another potential area of concern is the policy of publishing the precise location of sites on the Register. Though the Register currently is willing to be somewhat vague with regard to these locations, it is unlikely to be sufficiently so to provide any realistic protection against the increased vandalism which could arise from this increased public awareness of the location and "value" of the site or object.

The National Register certainly is a valuable weapon in our arsenal and should be an important aid in convincing landowners that sites on their property are worthy of an effort on their part to protect them. But like any weapon it must be used with care and discretion, and the federal program envisioned under this act does not provide adequately for the archeological needs of this country. In fact, current policy restricts the use of funds under this program to the protection of only those archeological sites which are going to be permanently exhibited to the public. Excavation or investigation to preserve information only, the primary archeological need, is not covered and therefore is not eligible for funding.

There also is, at least potentially, a very real danger that federal agencies and others will conclude that unless an archeological site is on the National Register it need not be taken into consideration. Assuming a completely adequate state survey, such a conclusion might be valid for historic, architectural, and cultural resources, except insofar as new ones are created, but it can never be true for archeological resources.

This situation pertains with regard to archeological sites for a number of reasons. The quantity of archeological sites (in Arkansas, for example, we currently know of five hundred sites in one small mountainous county, and an intensive survey of the county has not even been attempted) and the shortage of archeologists makes it impossible to carry out anything even approaching a really adequate survey in the few years presently envisioned by the National Register for completing the surveys which will form the basis for the official state plans. True, other sites can always be added, but the fact remains that the approximation of completeness possible for historic, architectural, and cultural sites can never even be approached in the archeological area.

An archeological survey, no matter how thorough or expertly done, can never succeed in recording all of the existing archeological sites. Some will be missed because of vegetation or other surface cover, others will be revealed only through erosion or construction activity which exposes previously buried sites. When a site is revealed under circumstances of clearing prior to construction or during construction, rarely if ever is there time to go through the process of getting the site on the Register. Other mechanisms must be established, such as making funds available to the Division of Archeology specifically to meet such needs.

Like historic sites, each archeological site is unique and therefore valuable, and like architectural sites it often is possible to save only samples of types. Unlike historic sites the only possible documentation of the significance of an archeological site lies in the ground. With an historic site the documentation of its significance generally lies outside of the structure itself, though additional information (or even proof of authenticity) may lie in the ground. If the structure or site is destroyed, however, it still is possible to say why it was important and (generally) where the site was even though the location is now drastically altered. Unless an archeological site is adequately excavated prior to its disturbance, we never will know why or even if it was significant. Thus despite their similarity of uniqueness, the devices and programs for the investigation and protection of archeological sites must differ not just in degree but in kind from those established for historic sites. Similarly, though a trained historical architect can examine a structure and evaluate whether or to what degree the structure is representative of a type or style of architecture and thus is worthy of preservation, no archeologist can perform a like feat for an archeological site. Archeologists are thoroughly aware they cannot excavate or preserve *every* site, so they can and do make "best judgments" as to which of several (or hundreds of) sites, which appear on the surface to be similar, are most worthy of investigating. Unlike the situation in architecture, there never can be any assurance that this judgment is correct. The best that can be done is a program of surface evaluation of all known sites, accompanied by testing of many and detailed excavation of as many as possible. All of which again requires a program different in kind from that of an architectural and historical survey, even one complete with measured drawings and recommendations for unique or typical examples to be preserved.

It is true that each archeological site is unique and that its full importance can never be known short of complete excavation. Nonetheless, this does not provide a valid case for placing every archeological site on the National Register in an effort to "protect" it. For one thing, archeology alone could more than occupy the full time of the present National Register staff should it adopt this approach. Even were it administratively possible to do so, it would not be desirable, for if every known and newly discovered site were placed on the Register (and every one is unique and does have national, state, or local significance and thus would qualify), the resultant slowdown in construction, farming, and other activities brought about by the mass of sites which would need to be checked would present an impossible situation. Obviously, in this sense alone, discretion is called for. This, of course, is true with respect to the other categories of sites as well, but in archeology the uniqueness of each site combined with its unknown degree of significance prior to excavation and the sheer number of sites (most of which are yet undiscovered), along with the rapidity of their current destruction, combine in such a way as to require more approaches to the problem of protecting and preserving archeological resources than can be provided by the mechanism of the National Register.

One critical difference between archeological sites, on the one hand, and historical or architectural structures and sites, on the other, is brought out by the present discussion. The process of history already has established, has provided the data to establish, or will establish because of future events which sites or structure are significant and worthy of attention. The archeologists are faced *first* with the task of determining history and the cultural processes which went on at a site. Only after this has been done can significance for preservation be determined. Thus the first goal of the federal as well as all other archeological programs over the next few decades must be the determination of history and of cultural processes. Only if this is successfully achieved will archeology be in a position to make intelligent recommendations as to which unique or typical examples should be protected, preserved, and interpreted for the public's edification by being placed on the National Register.

For the present it must be emphasized that the fact that an archeological site is not on the Register does not mean that it is not important or that it does not warrant consideration and investigation by any agency or individual which threatens its disturbance. Every threatened site warrants evaluation in the light of the immediate circumstances (apparent importance of the site relative to current knowledge, time available before its destruction, availability of funds and personnel for investigation, practicality of altering plans in order to preserve it). Factors such as these, not simply presence on the National Register, must be the principal considerations in every case.

The decisions made concerning the actual interpretation and operation of the act could have a very marked effect on archeological preservation on the state level, but it will be some time before all of the details have been ironed out. For example, the National Register is of the opinion that the provisions of the act apply to the operations of individual farmers who utilize in part federal funds to carry out agricultural practices over the area of an archeological site on the National Register. That is, he can no longer obtain federal aid to landlevel the area if this practice adversely affects a site on the Register (or at least not until the Advisory Council has been afforded the opportunity to comment). This also applies to other Soil Conservation Service programs. But who is to determine what agricultural or other practices "adversely affect" the archeological sites? How are these rapidly developing programs to be administered relative to the provisions of this act? In the end it seems likely that both the strategy and tactics of state programs of archeological research and development will be strongly affected.

The Reservoir Salvage Act of 1960
(Public Law 86-523; 74 Stat. 220) (See pages 247-249 for text.)

This law really is simply an extension or specific application of the more general authorization and direction provided by the Historic Sites Act. Here it is specified that an attempt shall be made to recover historical or archeological data affected by the construction of a dam (greater than 5000 acre feet or 40 surface acres of detention capacity) by any federal agency or federally licensed agency. The provisions apply regardless of size if the constructing agency finds or is provided with evidence that archeological resources are affected. The extension of the provisions of the law to agencies operating under a federal license was a valuable innovation. This law now serves as the principal legal basis for the National Park Service's extensive salvage efforts behind the United States Army Corps of Engineers and Bureau of Reclamation reservoirs, though, as indicated earlier, this program originated well before passage of the law.

At the present time (Spring 1971) both houses of Congress are considering an amendment to this law which, if passed, will authorize any federal agency whose programs adversely affect archeological or historical resources to expend program funds to protect or recover those resources. (For full text see pages 249-251.) The agencies may accomplish this either through direct expenditure of their own funds, through contracting with state or private agencies to accomplish the desired result, or through transfer of the necessary funds to the National Park Service so that agency may evaluate the need and carry out or contract for the necessary research. This amendment has been introduced by Senator Frank E. Moss of Utah in the Senate (S.1245) and by Congressman Charles E. Bennett of Florida in the House (H.R. 6257). Should this legislation become law, all archeologists and all state and federal agencies will need to rethink their programs in order that maximum scientific benefit may be gained.

Pertinent Department of Transportation Legislation
(See pages 256-258 for text of appropriate sections of the United States Code.)

The Highway Archeological Salvage Program, which began in New Mexico and spread across the country, was initially an administratively established program taking its legislative authority from the Antiquities Act of 1906. In most states it has been used largely with respect to the interstate highway system. Subsequent legislation (49 U.S.C. 1651; 23 U.S.C. 138; and 23 U.S.C. 305) establishes a firm legislative base for highway salvage and this plus administrative policy does everything possible to assure that adequate policies will apply to all highway work in which federal funds are involved.

Now, for the first time, state highway departments must get views of all related agencies (for example, a state agency responsible for archeology) before submitting a program to the Bureau of Public Roads. These programs will be available for public inspection and a hearing procedure will be established. If an objection is voiced but the state highway department does not feel it can alter its plan, it must demonstrate as a part of its proposal submitted to the Bureau of Public Roads that there is no feasible and prudent alternative and that the program includes all possible planning to minimize the harm. In short, state highway department programs are now subject to a form of review before they are approved for federal aid—a drastic change over previous procedures. If there is a state archeological agency available to do survey and excavation on proposed rights-of-way, it will be very much to the advantage of the state highway department to avail themselves of that agency's services. Nonetheless, the initiative for developing appropriate procedures will (and should) rest with the state archeological agencies.

Pertinent Department of Housing and Urban Development Legislation
(See pages 258-265 for text of appropriate sections of the United States Code.)

Involvement of the Department of Housing and Urban Development in the preservation field is more likely to affect historic house preservation than archeological sites; however, this legislation does make funds available on a matching basis for acquiring, restoring, and improving significant sites. Provision also is made for conducting surveys, and, in a few instances, these have had an archeological orientation. Persons involved in archeological preservation on the state level should be aware of the assistance available in the perhaps rather special circumstances provided for under this act.

The National Environmental Policy Act of 1969
(Public Law 91-190; 83 Stat. 852) (See pages 251-256 for text.)

Though directed at a much broader horizon, this act has and will continue to have considerable impact upon the archeological scene. The act states that it is the "continuing responsibility of the Federal Government to use all practicable means, consistent with other essential considerations of national policy, to improve and coordinate Federal plans, functions, programs, and resources to the end that the Nation may ... preserve important historic, cultural, and natural aspects of our national heritage." It also directs that "to the fullest extent possible" all federal policies, regulations, and laws shall be interpreted in a manner consistent with the aim and purpose of the National Environmental Policy Act. It charges all federal agencies with responsibility for reviewing all of their present and future programs to determine their total environmental impact and to prepare statements and recommendations which set forth in detail the nature of the impact, any adverse effect, alterations, total short- and long-term effects, and any irreversible and irretrievable commitments of resources resulting from their programs. Finally, responsible federal officials must consult with and obtain the comments of any federal agency which has jurisdiction by law or special expertise with respect to any environmental impact involved. Federal expertise with respect to the nation's archeological resources clearly rests with the National Park Service, and this act would seem to require that federal agencies consult with the National Park Service with respect to archeological impact. Copies of these statements are to be made available to the public.

As a direct consequence of this act, all federal agencies are formulating impact statements about each of their projects and programs. The initial push for data is far greater than either our knowledge or available human and financial resources will permit for the requirements of the bill to be totally satisfied. Both federal agencies and concerned environmentalists, including archeologists, are going to have to work hard to achieve a viable compromise consistent with the intent of the act. Not all construction nor every program can be brought to a complete halt pending development of fully adequate data. At the other extreme, inadequate use of available data or statements that there is no impact in instances where obviously critical changes or losses will occur (even if the extent of these losses is not yet fully documented) cannot be permitted. This act provides a powerful means for seeing that the impact on archeological resources by federal programs is not ignored, but the demands on everyone, particularly the National Park Service, to provide archeological data are going to be heavy. In complying with this act, archeologists and others are going to have to steer a narrow line between idealism and pragmatism.

SUMMARY

The Eighty-ninth Congress in particular, and federal agencies in general, have been taking an increasingly positive view of the value of historic and archeological preservation and have assumed much of the initiative and burden of developing new approaches for supporting efforts to accomplish this preservation. It is an example the states would do well to study and emulate.

In the specific area of archeological research and development I believe that there has been an unnecessary restriction of the federal effort to federal lands alone or to salvage efforts in areas where federal funds were directly responsible at least in part for the destruction of the sites. I believe the legislative authorization is already present in the Historic Sites Act and the Historic Preservation Act for a much more comprehensive view of federal support for archeological research. We can no longer afford to condone the practice of digging only where we absolutely have to do so because the site is about to be destroyed within a week or a month or a year. The vast majority of archeological sites in the United States are going to be lost long before we ever have a chance to excavate them properly. We need, therefore, to determine where we are going to expend our limited resources (funds and personnel) on the basis of *what we need to know* and where (and how) we can best derive the necessary data. These decisions must be made on a problem-oriented basis, nationwide, not on one restricted to the geographic limits of individual states, or of United States Army Corps of Engineer reservoirs, or Soil Conservation Service landleveling projects.

In short, legislative authorization already is available for federal support of broadly based, problem-oriented research—if the necessary funds can be made available. This brings the problem back to the states and to you and me. If we want this type of broadly based, problem-oriented support—and in my view it is absolutely essential if we are to protect or recover any meaningful portion of the past—then it is our responsibility to develop the necessary regional overviews and to convince our state and national legislatures of the need. To a large degree on the federal level, but as yet in only a few of the states, the necessary legislative machinery already has been provided or has been introduced. The responsibility for initiation, passage, and effective utilization of this and additional legislative opportunities rests almost entirely with us.

THE STATUS OF STATE SUPPORT
FOR ARCHEOLOGY IN EACH STATE

Introduction

The following state summaries are designed to provide a brief review of the level of *public* support for archeological research being provided by each state at the beginning of 1970 (and, in most instances, early 1971). It further presents a brief summation of the administrative organization utilized by each, accompanied by the legal citation and a summary of any legislation that directly affects or controls archeological research in the state.

Information summarizing each state program was initially gathered between September 1965 and March 1966. (There had been an earlier summary done in 1958.) The resulting compilation was returned to each informant for correction or revision during late 1966 and early 1967, and the results were submitted to the Arkansas Legislative Council along with the recommendations for the establishment of a state program for Arkansas. It was planned to publish this compilation at that time, but local developments relative to the legislative establishment and formation of the Arkansas Archeological Survey became so demanding that publication had to be postponed. During the summer of 1967 Paul Schumacher of the National Park Service in San Francisco conducted a poll of the states and upon learning of my efforts generously turned over his information for inclusion in this report. An even later National Park Service compilation also was placed at my disposal.

Every effort was exerted to make the summaries accurate as of the first part of 1970 by again referring them to each state, and an attempt (doubtless incomplete) has been made by the author to update them to early 1971. In every case, the author must bear full responsibility for both the sum and the substance of each state summary. Each state is unique, with its own personalities, potentialities, and problems. Any attempt to summarize these from a distance must inevitably present a somewhat skewed picture of the actual situation. I acknowledge this and must absolve my local sources of information from any responsibility for my particular interpretations and presentations. I can only hope that a reasonably accurate picture has been presented and that good rather than harm will result.

The files of the Arkansas Archeological Survey now contain probably the most complete information available on state legislation and state support of archeological research programs. If the following summaries are of value, and corrected up-to-date revisions would be of continued value, then it is requested that those responsible for or concerned with these programs keep the Survey informed of any significant errors in the present summaries and of later changes.

Remember, *these summaries are of state-supported research only*. They rarely provide a summarization of *all* of the archeological research being undertaken in a state, for the work of nonstate-supported agencies in each state was not considered and is not included herein. Also, *the number of archeologists indicated is my estimate of the equivalent of full-time personnel being paid out of state funds to do research*. Archeologists carried on the staffs of state agencies or institutions to teach or carry out other nonresearch functions are not included.

ALABAMA

State-Supported Archeological Research Programs

Principal State Agencies Involved. University of Alabama, Department of Sociology and Anthropology, and the Museum of Natural History, University, Alabama 35436.

State Funds Allocated Annually for Research. A portion of the salary of one archeologist plus approximately $3000.

Discussion. Archeologists in the Department of Sociology and Anthropology carry out research on their own time and with funds provided by the federal government and by private organizations, most notably in recent years by the Alabama Archaeological Society through its affiliate, the Archaeological Research Association of Alabama, Inc., which through public subscription has received thousands of dollars in each of the last several years to enable archeologists employed by the state to carry out important research.

The University of Alabama Museum of Natural History owns and operates Mound State Monument. It and the museum serve as de facto central depositories for state-owned archeological artifacts and records.

No annual program of research is budgeted by either organization with state funds; however, limited state funds are used for maintenance of the present collections and those collections incoming as a result of privately sponsored research.

Archeological Legislation

Citation. Ala. Code, Title 55, Sections 272 through 277 (1966); Ala. Act 168 of 1966.

Principal Provisions. The 1966 law establishes a Historical Commission with authority to receive and manage archeological or historical sites and buildings. By the remaining legislation (passed in 1915) the state reserves to itself the exclusive right to explore, excavate, and survey all aboriginal works and antiquities within the state, and state ownership of all such antiquities is expressly declared, subject only to the landowner's rights for agricultural, domestic, and industrial purposes. No nonresident may excavate. No one may remove any antiquities from the state, explore without the landowner's consent, or deface any aboriginal remains. It also requires that after excavation such remains "shall be restored to the same or like conditions as before" excavation.

Comments. If nothing else, strict enforcement of the last provision outlined should result in some of the best field notes around, though it might be presumed that this provision was intended to have sole reference to restoration of the external features of sites rather than requiring replacement of everything just as it was found. The state peremptorily assumes ownership of all antiquities. The difficulties inherent in such provisions have been mentioned (see pages 92 and 93). In 1958 the comment was made that "the law is not strictly adhered to," which probably is an understatement.

The Alabama law shares with certain other states a greater concern with whether nonresidents obtain antiquities and/or whether they are shipped out of state than with whether the antiquities are accorded proper scientific treatment. This attitude of antipathy to the "carpetbagger from the next county north" is not uncommon but, as in this case, is often overemphasized to the detriment of a law's true value and effectiveness.

ALASKA

State-Supported Archeological Research Programs

Principal State Agencies Involved. Alaska Division of Parks, Historic Preservation and Archaeology Unit, 323 East Fourth Avenue, Anchorage, Alaska, 99501.

State Funds Allocated Annually for Research. Salaries equivalent to less than one archeologist full time plus approximately $5000.

Discussion. The Department of Natural Resources is constitutionally charged wtih responsibility for conservation and planning for use for maximum public benefit of historic and archeological resources. The department's responsibilities in these areas are administered by the Historic Preservation and Archaeology Unit, Alaska Division of Parks. Research to date is being done on a contract basis for the Division of Parks by archeologists on university faculties in the state.

Archeological Legislation

Citation. Alaska Comp. Laws Ann., Sections 38.12.010 through 38.12.050 (Supp. 1970).

Principal Provisions. It is unlawful to excavate, remove, or injure archeological materials on state land without a permit from the commissioner of natural resources. Permits are restricted to those qualified to make scientific investigations and then only if the results will become and remain public.

Comments. This essentially is a permit law affecting state-controlled land only. Of course, in Alaska, as in some other western states, effective control over state and federal land serves to protect a major portion of the state. Extensive additions to the state's historic preservation legislation currently (early 1971) are under consideration.

ARIZONA

State-Supported Archeological Research Programs

Principal State Agencies Involved. (1) University of Arizona, Department of Anthropology, and Arizona State Museum, Tucson, Arizona 85721. (2) Arizona State University, Department of Anthropology, Tempe, Arizona 85281.

State Funds Allocated Annually for Research. Salaries approximately equivalent to that of six archeologists full time plus perhaps $75,000 of which approximately ten percent is allocated to student field training.

Discussion. The Arizona State Museum is the principal agency responsible for state-supported archeological research and most of the personnel and funds are there or at least are channeled through the museum. It is currently establishing a central clearing house for all site survey files being kept in the state and hopes ultimately to include data compiled by non-Arizona institutions. The director of the museum, an archeologist, has principal direct "control" over the size and nature of the budget, subject, of course, to university and legislative overviews. Archeologists on the staff of the Departments of Anthropology at the University of Arizona and Arizona State University carry out research, but, since they are primarily teaching rather than research oriented, their work naturally is directed toward training of students and individual research interests.

Archeological Legislation

Citation. Ariz. Rev. Stat. Ann., Sections 41-771 through 41-776 (Supp. 1969. (See pages 195-199 for complete text.)

Principal Provisions. No one may excavate archeological material from state-owned or controlled lands except under permit from the director of the Arizona State Museum. Such permits shall be issued to public or nonprofit scientific and educational institutions. Persons working on state land shall report archeological sites to the museum. Archeological materials shall not be defaced or reproduced or sold with intent to defraud nor shall any objects collected in violation of this act be sold or exchanged.

Comments. This is one of the better laws that restrict efforts solely to the protection of archeological materials on state-owned or controlled land. It has proved useful as a tool for convincing other state agencies of the appropriateness of setting aside land on which important sites occur, and it encourages communication among all concerned.

ARKANSAS

State-Supported Archeological Research Programs

Principal State Agencies Involved. (1) Arkansas Archeological Survey, University of Arkansas Museum, Fayetteville, Arkansas 72701. (2) University of Arkansas Museum, Fayetteville, Arkansas 72701.

State Funds Allocated Annually for Research. Salaries equivalent to nine archeologists full-time plus approximately $95,000.

Discussion. (See also pages 63-80.) Arkansas appears to be the only state to have a fully coordinated statewide program of archeological research and development involving all state-supported institutions of higher education and other concerned state agencies. The enabling act creating the Arkansas Archeological Survey (and a related bill which protects archeological resources on state land and establishes a procedure for designating archeological landmarks which also are protected) was passed by the 1967 session of the Arkansas General Assembly. An appropriation, entirely separate from the university appropriation, is made to the University of Arkansas Board of Trustees to provide for operation of the Survey. The board appoints a director of the Survey from among the anthropologists on the university staff and, on the director's recommendation, it appoints all other Survey staff members.

The key concept of the Survey is that all state-supported institutions of higher education in Arkansas, including the University of Arkansas, may participate in the program (if they desire to do so) on an equal basis. To participate, each of the six state-supported colleges and the two universities may contract with the Survey by agreeing to reimburse the Survey an amount equivalent to three-sixteenths of an archeologist's salary (quarter-time for nine months) and to provide the Survey with necessary office and laboratory space. In return the Survey places a Survey archeologist at the participating institution on a full-time year-round basis. The Survey archeologist may teach anthropology or perform archeologically related museum work or other research for the institution, as mutually agreed upon in the contract, for an amount of time not to exceed the equivalent of quarter-time for nine months. If teaching is involved, it must all take place in a single semester, leaving the archeologist completely unhindered for research at least eight months of the year. Each archeologist assumes primary responsibility for the archeological resources within his particular region, but his own research need not be restricted by such areal bounds. Similarly, should the need arise, several archeologists could work at a single site.

A coordinating staff consisting of a director and a state archeologist, who administer the program, a registrar to maintain the records, and an editor, photographer, and draftsman to process popular and scientific reports for publication are housed at the University of Arkansas Museum. Funds for secretarial, laboratory, and field assistants are available to both the coordinating staff and the Survey archeologists. The Survey has ultimate responsibility for the safety and distribution of the artifacts recovered by Survey personnel (and is the repository for copies of *all* archeological records obtained by state funds through whatever agency), but artifacts recovered by a Survey archeologist remain at the participating institution to which he is attached if that institution so desires and can provide proper security. Otherwise they are deposited with the University of Arkansas Museum, and all are made a part of the university museum records, which are in the process of being computerized.

In essence, each institution obtains, for minimal financial outlay, a full-time staff member to teach some anthropology and do archeological research in the area in which that institution is located. In turn, the Survey obtains eight regional operational bases well distributed over the state at no cost, and problems of personal or institutional competition over funds or areas are eliminated by having a single coordinating agency.

The stated purpose of the Survey is to provide the general and scientific public, both present and future, with meaningful information concerning Arkansas' past. To accomplish this, it encourages preservation of the state's archeological resources; effects both salvage and problem-oriented recovery of data and artifacts; develops and refines concepts and techniques; describes and interprets the total available data; and, finally, informs the public by means of popular and scientific publications, formal and informal instruction and lectures, and individual contacts. By providing for centralization of all records, complete coordination of the state's effort, and maximum flexibility of approach and operation, Arkansas has assured itself that it will receive maximum return on the funds invested.

The University of Arkansas Museum conducts an annual archeological training session. The museum also houses the coordinating staff of the Survey and is the official repository for all Survey records and materials. It is responsible for display and custodianship of all artifacts except those retained in Survey collections at other state institutions.

Archeological Legislation

Citation. Ark. Stat. Ann., Sections 8-801 through 8-808 (1967), Ark. Stat. Ann., Sections 9-1001 through 9-1017 (1967). (See pages 199-207 for complete text.)

Principal Provisions. Sections 9-1001 through 9-1017 (Act 82 of 1959 and Act 39 of 1967) encompass the enabling legislation establishing the Arkansas Archeological Survey as just outlined. Sections 8-801 through 8-808 (Act 58 of 1967) is an antiquities law which reserves to the state the exclusive privilege of field archeology on state-owned land and establishes legislative intent that similar work on private land be discouraged except in accordance with the spirit of the law. Persons are encouraged to report sites to the Archeological Survey. All state agencies, as well as counties and municipalities and contractors working with such bodies, are required to cooperate with the Survey. An archeological site on state or private land with the written consent of the landowner or the state agency responsible for the land may be declared a "state archeological landmark," subsequent to which the consent of both the owner and the Survey must be obtained before excavation can take place at that site. Upon written notice from the Survey the land commissioner shall reserve from sale land containing sites until such time as they have been released by the Survey. Removal of archeological materials from land without the owner's permission is specifically declared to be an act of trespass. Vandalism of sites on state-owned or controlled land is declared to be a misdemeanor.

Comments. Basically, the antiquities legislation takes a positive rather than a negative approach and endeavors to encourage communication among all affected. On the one hand, the landmark and the trespass sections, as well as those requiring or requesting cooperation with the Survey, should make it possible and relatively easy for both private landowners and public agencies desiring to protect sites on land under their control to do so. On the other hand, the legislation places most of the burden of initiative in this regard on members of the Survey, the most logical ones to exercise it, while not denying others the opportunity to display such initiative. So far as is known, the landmark statute is the first to set forth a specific legal basis for a state agency to obtain what is in essence an easement on private property for the purpose of protecting scientific data and materials. Recently, Texas and Mississippi have enacted similar laws. In order to permit flexibility in this regard, depending upon the needs or practical possibilities at individual sites, the duration of the easement was not spelled out. State constitutional prohibitions ruled out inclusion of several otherwise desirable provisions, including ones providing for transferring direct responsibility for archeological sites on state land to the Survey, and the possibility of offering tax relief to owners for property declared to be a landmark.

CALIFORNIA

State-Supported Archeological Research Programs

Principal State Agencies Involved. (1) Department of Parks and Recreation, Post Office Box 2390, Sacramento, California 95811. (2) University of California, Berkeley, Archeological Research Facility, Berkeley, California 94720. (3) University of California, Los Angeles Archeological Survey, Los Angeles, California 90023. (4) Various of the other divisions of the University of California. (5) Several California State Colleges, notably Sacramento, San Francisco, Chico, San Diego, and Long Beach.

State Funds Allocated Annually for Research. While it is difficult to arrive at a precise figure because of the number of institutions involved, yearly fluctuation, and other factors, the amount may total as much as the equivalent of eight archeologists full time and $100,000 or more with the major portion of the directly appropriated research funds being channeled initially through the State Department of Parks and Recreation.

Discussion. The State Department of Parks and Recreation is the agency with primary legislated responsibility for salvage archeological work, and until 1970 it administered the Highway Salvage Program with funds derived from the State Division of Highways. Since that time, the Division of Highways, in cooperation with the Department of Parks and Recreation, has assumed active administration of the program, which is being carried out through the Society for California Archaeology (on an interim basis pending new legislation) via direct salvage contracts with individual institutions. The department currently concerns itself with in-house work and contracts with the State Department of Water Resources, which provides funds for salvage when its construction program necessitates it. The Department of Parks and Recreation accomplishes the work with its own permanent personnel or with temporary employees, usually students from the branches of the university, the state colleges, or other organizations. Both the Berkeley and Los Angeles campuses of the University of California have administratively separate archeological research organizations, and, though the Berkeley facility is currently not very active, the UCLA Survey has the equivalent of at least one full-time research worker as well as some maintenance funds specifically allocated to archeological research. The latter organization carries out survey work (not provided for in the parks and recreation organization) and contracts with federal, local, and private agencies for specific projects. The various other state-supported institutions also do some archeological research with state funds, largely as an adjunct to their teaching programs. California is only one of any number of examples, though perhaps on a larger scale than most, illuminating the fact that today the major portion of the funds available for archeological research is for salvage operations.

There is no state organization equipped to assume the responsibilities of a truly central coordinating or record-keeping agency. This has caused, and is causing, severe administrative and other problems, the most obvious of which is the lack of any master file of sites, with resulting overlap of site numeration and effort, and the impossibility of anywhere obtaining an overview of present data concerning the California archeological situation. While thoroughly aware of and disturbed by the situation, the California archeologists are inhibited in taking effective corrective action by lack of legislative direction and support, as well as, in part, by some growing pains of the sort which are inevitable when a number of agencies working in similar fields with similar sources of revenue exist side by side without clear-cut areas of responsibility. Some efforts toward an informal but perhaps ultimately legislatively recognized central records agency is currently underway, and the still young but vigorous Society for California Archaeology can do much to resolve these operating problems. It is the principal initiating and coordinating agent in the current (1971) attempt to introduce and pass legislation establishing an effective statewide program not unlike that in Arkansas. Until some such legislative direction is provided, California will continue to have serious problems.

California currently is one of the most active states with reference to involvement by archeologists in local situations. In addition to the two county archeological ordinances discussed later there have been several instances of local governmental units taking action to save or protect archeological sites because the archeologists (professional and amateur) made their views known.

Other states whose programs have not yet reached the proportion and scope of California's should study this situation in order that they may attain the enviable total size of this state's program while avoiding some of its problems. Often an effective organizational arrangement which readily can be put into effect when an operation is small in scope, and which serves advantageously to direct growth and development, becomes increasingly difficult if not impossible to institute after the program has increased in size and complexity. When this happens, there is resultant waste and loss to all. Growth without direction and organization is inevitably wasteful.

Archeological Legislation

Citation. Cal. Department of Parks and Recreation, Administrative Code Title 14, Chapter 5, Sections 1307 through 1309; Cal. Penal Code, Section 622½ (West 1939); Cal. Water Code, Section 234 (West Supp. 1970); Cal. Pub. Res. Code, Sections 5097 through 5097.6 (West Supp. 1970).

Principal Provisions. The Director of the Division of Beaches and Parks may grant a permit to remove archeological materials with the sole restriction that it must be "for the best interest of the state park system and for state park purposes." Otherwise, removal or defacement of archeological materials on park land is prohibited. The penal code provides that there shall be no willful destruction or defacement of archeological materials, whether on private or state lands, except by the owner thereof. Any state agency, and the State Department of Water Resources specifically, may provide the Department of Parks and Recreation with construction plans and may authorize archeological survey and investigation by the Department of Parks and Recreation of sites to be damaged during construction (or the agency itself may act after receiving the recommendations of the Department of Parks and Recreation) so long as such investigation does not impede said construction. In this section willful removal, injury, or destruction of archeological or paleontological resources on public land without express permission from the public agency having jurisdiction is forbidden.

Comments. None of these acts appear to be worded in a manner adequate to provide consistent or adequate protection to the state's archeological resources.

In addition to the state laws, at least two California counties—Marin and Inyo—have passed archeological ordinances (Marin County Ordinance No. 1589, and Inyo County Ordinance No. 146). (See pages 230-234 for complete texts.)

The Marin County ordinance essentially declares that the information contained within archeological shell middens is of public concern, and uncontrolled disturbance or excavation of those middens, whether on public or private lands, by untrained persons is forbidden. Contractors or others who wish to excavate or who discover such middens must obtain a permit from the county. Prior to granting a permit, the county notifies an archeological agency, which has five days to evaluate the site, and if it warrants investigation, the owner or contractor must provide at least ten days for such investigation to be carried out. Each day of nonconformance is considered a new violation and is a misdemeanor.

The Inyo County ordinance prohibits excavation in any active or recent cemetery and restricts excavation in older Indian burial grounds to professional archeologists or those working under their direction who have first obtained a permit. This permit must be approved by the county coroner, the board of trustees of the Owens Valley Piute-Shoshone Indians, and the county superintendent of schools and then be submitted to the board of supervisors of the county, who shall affirm or deny permission. Violation is a misdemeanor.

Although I have heard some say they believe any such an ordinance is unconstitutional, it is my contention that it is constitutional (see the discussion on page 50). The only thing prohibiting use of such legal protective measures is the absence of public acceptance of the principle of the public's right to archeological information, wherever it is located, and a public willingness to uphold statutes protecting that right. Bringing the public to this state of awareness while there are still some archeological resources left to protect is archeology's greatest challenge today. Wherever this awareness is achieved, it should be backed up by carefully thought-out, well-worded legislation.

COLORADO

State-Supported Archeological Research Programs

Principal State Agencies Involved. (1) University of Colorado, University of Colorado Museum, and Department of Anthropology, Boulder, Colorado 80302. (2) The State Historical Society of Colorado, Colorado State Museum, East 14th Avenue and Sherman, Denver, Colorado 80203.

State Funds Allocated Annually for Research. The salary equivalent to one archeologist plus $8000.

Discussion. There is no separately constituted program of archeological research in Colorado. Some research time and limited funds are made available to archeologists through the State Historical Society or to archeologists who are employed primarily in teaching, curatorial, or administrative capacities at various other state-supported institutions. The University of Colorado Museum serves to some extent as a central clearing house and repository for data.

Archeological Legislation

Citation. Colo. Rev. Stat. Ann., Sections 131-12-1 through 131-12-6 (1963).

Principal Provisions. All historical, prehistorical, and archeological resources, fossils, and objects of natural history within the boundaries of land owned by the state are reserved to the state. It is also noted that access to the site of such objects shall be provided. The State Historical Society is directed to enter into agreements with the State Highway Department and other agencies relative to such sites and is authorized to issue or deny permits for their investigation. These permits shall be issued only to qualified institutions, and annual reports shall be required, as well as a final report within three years of the completion of any work. The Historical Society shall also receive a complete inventory and may request a representative sample of the materials. A permit may be revoked at any time if the work is being done unlawfully or improperly. By request of any municipality, county, governmental agency, corporation, or private individual the Society may also assume permit-granting authority. Violation of any portion of the act is declared a misdemeanor. The governor also is authorized, on recommendation of the Society and with approval of the state agencies having jurisdiction and the county or municipality within which a site is located, to declare by public proclamation that any historic or prehistoric site is to be a state monument.

Comments. This is a relatively standard act establishing the state's right to archeological resources on state property, with the added provision enabling the governor to establish state monuments. The provision authorizing the Society to assume permit-granting authority over properties not owned by the state upon request of the owner is not unlike the easement provision in the Arkansas law.

CONNECTICUT

State-Supported Archeological Research Programs

Principal State Agencies Involved. University of Connecticut, State Archaeologist, Storrs, Connecticut 06268.

State Funds Allocated Annually for Research. A portion of the salary of one archeologist plus well under $1000.

Discussion. The state archeologist, legally appointed by the Board of Trustees of the University of Connecticut serves "without compensation" and presently is an anthropologist employed for full-time teaching-curatorial duties. Some departmental funds are made available for limited travel.

Archeological Legislation

Citation. Conn. Gen. Stat. Ann., Section 10-132a (1964); Conn. Gen. Stat. Ann., Sections 10-321a and b (1967).

Principal Provisions. The state archeologist is charged with conducting research on Indians and archeology and with cooperating with others to preserve archeological remains threatened with loss. The Historical Commission can administer grants-in-aid for "historic structures," which the legislation defines as including archeological sites.

Comments. The office of state archeologist has been established, but the occupant has been given precious little with which to work. The extension of the Historical Commission's grants-in-aid program to archeological sites obviously is a response to the Historic Preservation Act (P.L. 89-665). It permits but still does not provide for state funding of archeology.

DELAWARE

State-Supported Archeological Research Programs

Principal State Agencies Involved. Office of State Archaeologist, Hall of Records, Dover, Delaware 19901.

State Funds Allocated Annually for Research. The salary of two archeologists plus approximately $35,000.

Discussion. The Office of Archaeology is a separate office of the Department of State operating under the Division of Archives and Cultural Affairs and receiving funds directly from the state legislature. One full-time archeologist is charged with implementing the state program. The office is charged to sponsor research and to cooperate with other public institutions and encourage work by any archeological societies, to protect archeological sites and materials, to enforce the regulations concerning same, and to disseminate information to the public and schools via publications and museum exhibits.

Archeological Legislation

Citation. Del. Code. Ann., Title 7, Sections 5301 through 5306 (1953); Del. Code Ann., Title 7, Sections 5403 through 5405; Del. Code Ann., Title 29, Section 8705 (Supp. 1970).

Principal Provisions. Excavation or injury of any archeological site or material on land owned or controlled by the state is prohibited except by permit from the governor (or his designated agent). Such permits shall be issued only to recognized scientific institutions with a view to increasing knowledge of such objects. All objects recovered shall be deposited in the Archaeological Museum of the University of Delaware or the Delaware State Museum unless the permit makes specific exception. Excavation on private land is discouraged except when pursuant to the spirit and policy pertaining to state lands, and persons are encouraged to report sites. Sections 5403 through 5404 establish the responsibility of the Delaware Department of State to engage in site excavation, protecting and encouraging preservation of sites on private land, assisting other responsible agencies, disseminating information, and enforcing relevant laws. Section 8705 transfers the operation of the archeological program, initially established under a commission of the Division of Archives and Cultural Affairs of the Department of State.

Comments. This is a relatively standard set of regulations with regard to state lands, with a passing mention of private property.

FLORIDA

State-Supported Archeological Research Programs

Principal State Agencies Involved. (1) Florida Department of State, Division of Archives, History, and Records Management, Bureau of Historic Sites and Properties, Archaeological Research Section, Underwater Archaeological Research Section, Historic Preservation Section, and Research Laboratory Section, Tallahassee, Florida 32300. (2) University of Florida, Florida State Museum, and Department of Anthropology, Gainesville, Florida 32601. (3) Florida Atlantic University, Department of Anthropology, Boca Raton, Florida 33432. (4)

Florida State University, Department of Anthropology and Archaeology, Tallahassee, Florida 32300.

State Funds Allocated Annually for Research. Salaries equivalent to eight archeologists full time plus approximately $150,000.

Discussion. Florida has one of the larger, more active state programs. Legislative developments over the past four years have led to the establishment of the Bureau of Historic Sites and Properties with an archeologist as chief. This is a full-time research agency with four sections: Archaeological Research, Underwater Archaeological Research, Historic Preservation, and a Research Laboratory Section. The underwater section is occasioned by the large number of underwater wrecks currently being salvaged. The bureau is staffed with archeologists, field assistants, graduate and undergraduate assistants, a preservationist, and secretarial and laboratory help. It also has a newly constructed archeological preservation laboratory. The bureau is oriented largely toward salvage archeology, concerning itself primarily with underwater and highway salvage or the salvage of other sites or materials about to be destroyed, and is probably better staffed and equipped to do this than any other state with the possible exception of Arkansas.

The Florida State Museum has a Division of Social Science which devotes a major portion of its efforts to archeological research both within Florida and out of state. In contrast to the bureau, the archeologists at the Florida State Museum are in a position to devote their attention more to problem-oriented research. Archeologists attached to the various anthropology departments do some research of both types, but, as is usually the case, the state funds available to them are provided primarily with student training in mind. All of these state agencies contract with federal agencies for archeological research projects.

Archeological Legislation

Citation. Fla. Stat. Ann., Section 267 (Supp. 1969).

Principal Provisions. This act (as slightly amended subsequent to the citation given above) creates a Division of Archives and History under the secretary of state, thus placing responsibility for all Florida-owned historical sites and properties under a single state department. It also creates an Advisory Commission which is to assist the Division of Archives and History. This commission consists of the director of the Florida State Museum, the state geologist, the department heads of the respective established departments of anthropology and archeology and history in each accredited institution of higher learning in Florida maintaining such departments which offer graduate degrees in such subjects, the president of the Florida Historical Society, the president of the Florida Anthropological Society, the director of the Florida Board of Parks and Historic Memorials, the director of the Internal Improvement Fund, the state librarian, the president of the Florida Library Association, and the director of the university presses of any state university in Florida.

Administratively, the act creates a Division of Archives, History, and Records Management under the secretary of state with the following bureaus: Archives and Records, Historical Museum, Publication, and Historic Sites and Properties. The Bureau of Archives and Records does not affect archeology nor does the Historical Museum, except insofar as it is directed to display archeological materials. The Bureau of Publication, however, does provide an outlet for research accomplished by the Bureau of Historic Sites and Properties. The Bureau of Historic Sites and Properties is empowered to employ a state archeologist. At present, the state archeologist is also the chief of the bureau, though this need not be the case. A Research Laboratory Section is supportive to the operation of the Archaeological, Historic Preservation, and Underwater Archaeological Research sections of the Bureau of Historic Sites and Properties. The Historical Preservation Section is designed to coordinate the development of Florida's preservation plan and facilitate the placing of sites on the National Register and other historic and prehistoric inventories.

The act declares that it is state policy to protect and preserve historic sites and properties, buildings, artifacts, treasure trove, and objects of antiquity which have scientific or historical value or are of interest to the public, including, but not limited to, monuments or memorials, fossil deposits, Indian habitations, ceremonial sites, abandoned settlements, caves, sunken or abandoned ships, historical sites and properties, and buildings or objects or any part thereof related to the history, government, and culture of the state. It also declares it to be public policy "that all treasure trove, artifacts and such objects having intrinsic or historical and archaeological value which have been abandoned on state-owned lands or state-owned sovereignty submerged lands shall belong to the State of Florida."

The Bureau of Historic Sites and Properties is charged with the following responsibilities: to locate, protect, and preserve historic, archeological, and related artifacts, including everything just discussed; to develop a comprehensive statewide historic preservation plan; to encourage and promote the acquisition, preservation, restoration, and operation of historic sites with the provision that before any state funds may be expended for this purpose the Advisory Commission must have so recommended and the bureau must have determined that there exists historical authenticity and a feasible means for acquiring, preserving, and operating the property, and that the property shall have been approved by the bureau for such purpose; and to cooperate with the Florida Board of Historic Memorials in operating and managing historic sites subject to the Division of Archives, History, and Records Management.

Comments. This act sets up a reasonably independent archeological research agency which has its own budget within the state government. The state archeologist is charged with emphasizing salvage archeology, but the wording is not such that he is limited solely to this. All in all, it appears to be an eminently workable and well-organized arrangement, particularly with respect to the preservation laboratory and potential for coordinated publication and museum facilities. The work of this agency, plus the work being done by the Florida State Museum and archeologists associated with the various anthropology departments, should provide Florida with one of the better statewide archeological programs in the country. The total state effort is not coordinated through a single agency, as is the case in Arkansas, but, since the activities of the various state agencies seem to be reasonably complementary, coordination of the effort is possible.

The St. Augustine Restoration Commission and the Pensacola Restoration Commission are also under the Department of State and each has an archeologist on its staff.

GEORGIA

State-Supported Archeological Research Programs

Principal State Agencies Involved. (1) University of Georgia, Laboratory of Archaeology, Athens, Georgia 30601. (2) Georgia State College, Department of Anthropology, Atlanta, Georgia 30303. (3) Georgia Historical Commission, 116 Mitchell Street S.W., Atlanta, Georgia 30303.

State Funds Allocated Annually for Research. Salaries equivalent to one or two archeologists full time plus $5000-$10,000.

Discussion. The Georgia Historical Commission is charged by legislative act with overall responsibility for archeological sites and materials and is authorized to employ a state archeologist. Funding to date has been minimal, however, and an attempt by the commission to set up a highway program foundered, as did an attempt by the university to establish such a program. Both the University of Georgia and Georgia State College carry out occasional projects with some state money, but there is no regularly funded program or extensive coordination of effort among the three institutions involved. An effort currently is being made to develop a program, and the commission has established a laboratory for archeological work.

Archeological Legislation

Citation. Ga. Code Ann., Sections 40-802a through 40-814a (Supp. 1969).

Principal Provisions. The 1969 act, which amends slightly a law initially passed in 1951 (Sections 40-802a through 41-809a), established the Georgia Historical Commission, nine individuals appointed by the secretary of state with the duty, among others, to promote and increase understanding of the state's archeology by preserving archeological sites, erecting markers, creating museums, and issuing publications. Five members of the commission constitutes a quorum.

Sections 40-813a and 40-814a declare state ownership of all archeological materials on state lands or tidelands (except for property under the jurisdiction of the board of regents). The Historical Commission is authorized to grant properly staffed institutions permits to do research on state lands if the results are used for scientific purpose and provided that the state retains ownership of the objects. It also urges private landowners to allow excavation only by qualified institutions or individuals. The Historical Commission is authorized to pay a "finders' fee" set by them to persons who report finding sites, treasure, treasure trove, or ancient or abandoned ships. A state archeologist may be appointed by the commission to carry out research, cooperate with other agencies, establish training programs, and otherwise disseminate archeological information. The commission also is empowered to work on private property with the written consent of the landowner if the results of such work are to remain available to the commission.

Comments. The Historical Commission has the enabling legislation for initiating an active program, hopefully in coordination with the University of Georgia Laboratory of Archaeology and the Georgia State College, but adequate funds still are unavailable to any of these institutions. The "finders' fee" is a unique aspect of this legislation.

HAWAII

State-Supported Archeological Research Programs

Principal State Agencies Involved. (1) Department of Land and Natural Resources, Division of State Parks, Post Office Box 621, Honolulu, Hawaii 96809.

State Funds Allocated Annually for Research. Salaries equivalent to seven archeologists full time plus approximately $100,000.

Discussion. The Division of State Parks in the Department of Land and Natural Resources has been established as the state agency primarily responsible for carrying out an archeological program of research and preservation, and it employs both full-time and part-time archeologists for this purpose.

A Hawaii Foundation for History and the Humanities has been legislatively established as a nonprofit corporate foundation to accept gifts of objects, sites, and buildings significant to Hawaii's history and culture and to manage such properties. It is also charged with responsibility for reviewing the work of the Department of Land and Natural Resources, presumably including the archeological research, and is to approve properties for nomination to the National Register. Unfortunately, the foundation is not yet funded or organized to carry out these functions.

The designation of a single state agency responsible for archeological research, the scope of the state funding, and the related antiquities legislation are such that Hawaii could have an excellent program leading to the recovery, preservation, protection, and operation of its archeological resources.

Archeological Legislation

Citation. Hawaii Rev. Laws, Section 734-1 (1968); Hawaii Rev. Laws, Sections 6-1 through 6-15 (1968); Hawaii Act 216 of 1969; Hawaii Act 236 of 1969. (See pages 207-215 for complete text.)

Principal Provisions. Section 276 sets forth specific conditions under which human remains may be disinterred. Act 254 and Chapter 6 are basically enabling legislation for the archeological program established under the Division of State Parks. Permits for archeological excavation may be issued by the Department of Land and Natural Resources with the stipulation that these are restricted to educational and scientific institutions or organizations and that no permit will be granted for the removal of any ancient monument or structure which can be permanently preserved and remains an object of interest. The conditions of the permit are quite stringent, but reasonable and feasible. The provisions, in addition to the more standard ones, include the requirement that all vehicles in camp sites be identified with a sign saying archeological field work and a permit number. Discrimination is specifically prohibited, as is the committing of any waste or nuisance. There is a requirement for both preliminary and final reports, the latter to be submitted within one year of the expiration date of the permit.

Act 216 is unusually strict and comprehensive antiquities legislation. It provides that any public construction or improvement of any nature undertaken by a government agency on lands owned or controlled by the state shall expend one percent of the appropriation for such public construction or improvement or so much thereof as may be necessary for the archeological investigation, recording, and salvage of such sites known or encountered which are affected by such construction. All sites recorded by the Division of State Parks are to be communicated to the director of taxation, who will locate them on all tax maps, and those persons planning any public construction or improvement must consult these maps to determine if any archeological site will be affected. If so, such public construction shall not be commenced until the Department of Land and Natural Resources has been advised. The department must take action concerning the resource or, within ninety days, file a notice of objection with the agency doing the construction. If no notice has been received from the department or if the department objects, the construction agency may appeal to the governor, who may take appropriate action to resolve the problem.

Before any alteration, construction, or improvement of any nature is undertaken or commenced on a designated private historic or prehistoric site by any person, he shall give the Department of Land and Natural Resources three-months' notice of his intent. After the expiration of the three-months notification period, the department shall either commence condemnation proceedings for the purchase of the site remains, permit the owner to proceed with his construction, alteration, or improvement, or undertake to permit the recording and salvaging of any historical information deemed necessary to preserve Hawaiian history, by any agency qualified for this purpose. The Department of Land and Natural Resources must obtain written permission from the owner before it can do any work or remove any archeological objects from such private land.

Act 216 also declares that the Department of Land and Natural Resources may issue permits for investigation on lands owned or controlled by the state or county to qualified individuals or institutions. Objects taken without permit may be seized. Forgery also is prohibited. It is declared unlawful for any person to remove, injure, or destroy any prehistoric remains found on lands owned or controlled by the state. In leases of public lands rights shall be retained to all prehistoric and historic remains found thereon.

Act 236 established the nonprofit Hawaii Foundation for History and Humanities, which is charged with responsibility for cooperating with agencies concerned with these subjects, for receiving and managing gifts of objects and sites, and for reviewing the archeological programs, including the archeological programs of the Department of Land and Natural Resources, for designating sites to go on the National Register, and other activities, such as providing matching grants-in-aid to governmental or private agencies and assisting in the training of competent museum personnel.

Comments. This is perhaps the most comprehensive and strict set of antiquities legislation in the country. The legislation requiring (not just authorizing) state agencies to expend construction funds to recover archeological and historical remains affected by such work is perhaps the most revolutionary and far-reaching of the Hawaii regulations. It parallels what is being considered by the federal government (see pages 249-251), though in the latter instance the agencies are only authorized to expend such funds rather than being required to do so.

A requirement that all sites be properly located on all tax maps, though again paralleling the federal situation of the National Register, has certain benefits in connection with the requirement that public and private actions which could affect such designated sites must either take them into account, in the case of public agencies, or provide for a three-month notification, in the case of sites on private land. Nonetheless, there would seem to be certain potential problems in that this means that all site locations must be made public. Unless the level of public concern, and the ability of law enforcement agencies or that of archeologists to prevent looting or disturbance of such sites greatly exceeds that of any other state of my acquaintance, problems relative to the safety of those sites may ensue from this legislative requirement. The requirement for private landowners who have designated sites on their property to provide the Department of Land and Natural Resources with a three-month notification is also innovative, one of the few reasonably effective attempts which has not been tried elsewhere to provide some measure of control of archeological sites on private land. The requirement that rights to prehistoric and historic remains shall be retained on all public land leased is also helpful. No mention is made of retention of such rights for any public lands which are sold. The only other legislation along these lines is that of Arkansas and Tennessee which authorizes the archeological agency to prohibit sale of state lands which contain archeological resources until adequate investigation has been made.

However, all of this legislation, to be effective, must be backed by a well-funded professionally staffed state program. The administrative details alone, while necessary, are rather staggering to contemplate. For example, the Tax Department will not place a site on a tax map without a proper survey and, at present, neither the archeologists nor the state surveyor's office has the staff or funds to accomplish this. If the professional archeologists have to spend all of their time administering, then precious little archeology will get done and the legislation will be self-defeating. Further coordination and improvement of this legislation is currently under consideration.

IDAHO

State-Supported Archeological Research Programs

Principal State Agencies Involved. (1) Idaho State University, Idaho State University Museum, Pocatello, Idaho 83201. (2) Idaho Historical Society, 610 Julia Davis Drive, Boise, Idaho 83706. (3) University of Idaho, Department of Anthropology, Moscow, Idaho 83843.

State Funds Allocated Annually for Research.   A portion of the salary of one archeologist plus approximately $3000.

Discussion.   The Idaho Historical Society is involved primarily because it is the state agency charged with the preservation and interpretation of Idaho's historic resources and is the agency to which application is made to conduct archeological excavations under the antiquities act. Most of the state-sponsored archeological research is conducted by the Idaho State University Museum, which also serves as the principal contracting agency for federally supported research. State support is provided through the museum and the state's portion of the highway salvage program. Some work is carried out with special funds by the University of Idaho on emergency salvage projects.

Archeological Legislation

Citation.   Idaho Code Ann., Sections 67-4114 through 67-4118 (1957). Idaho Code Ann., Sections 67-4119 through 67-4122 (1963).

Principal Provisions.   The Historical Society is authorized to designate and preserve historical and archeological sites, and the law requires that a permit be obtained from the society before archeological investigation can be made on state lands. It restricts permits to applicants qualified by experience or professional training to conduct such excavations in a proper scientific manner. The society is authorized to promulgate and enforce necessary regulations. No person shall remove archeological material from state lands without permission of the society, which may require that a portion of the archeological materials recovered under permit shall remain in the state.

There is also a provision (Sections 67-4116 and 67-4117) which authorizes the governor to designate specified locations as archeological sites, and markers may be placed thereon with the permission of the state agency responsible for the land or of the owner if on private land. All persons are forbidden to willfully damage or destroy such sites or markers.

Comments.   With the owner's permission, this second provision could be used as a means for establishing some protection for important sites on private land. Whether or not it is spelled out in sufficient detail to be workable is questionable.

ILLINOIS

State-Supported Archeological Research Programs

Principal State Agencies Involved.   (1) Illinois Archeological Survey, 137 Davenport Hall, University of Illinois, Urbana, Illinois 61801. (2) University of

Illinois, Department of Anthropology, Urbana, Illinois 61801. (3) Southern Illinois University Museum, Carbondale, Illinois 62901. (4) Illinois State Museum, Spring and Edwards Streets, Springfield, Illinois 62706.

State Funds Allocated Annually for Research. Salaries equivalent to approximately eight archeologists plus approximately $40,000 (including state funds utilized for archeological research outside of the state).

Discussion. The Illinois Archeological Survey is an organization made up of all practicing professional archeologists working within the state, including those at the three institutions just listed. Its members meet several times each year to coordinate research efforts by the active institutions, and it serves as the central coordinating agency for site records. The Survey serves as the formal contracting agent with the Highway Department for the highway salvage program. It also publishes results of research, though the institutions also have individual publication programs. Whichever institution actually handles the field work assumes primary responsibility for the data and materials. The office of the Survey (including minor research funds) is permanently supported by the University of Illinois.

Archeological Legislation

Citation. Ill. Stat. Ann., Sections 133c1 through 133c6 (Smith-Hurd Supp. 1970). Laws of 1907, p. 374; Laws of 1925, p. 498.

Principal Provisions. The 1907 law encourages the state's political subunits to engage in research pursuant to historical and archeological remains with the intention of publishing the findings at reasonable public expense. The 1925 law authorizes the acquisition of state parks, including sites relating to "Indian History." The more recent legislation reserves archeological resources on state property to the state unless permission is obtained in writing from the appropriate state department; such departments may grant permission to competent persons. Deeds given by the state may reserve rights to archeological resources. The Illinois State Museum is to review applications and counsel the departments.

Comments. The only thing wrong with the 1907 law is that it is no longer, if it was ever, brought into use to help preserve the state's archeological resources. There are current efforts to achieve a more effective set of laws. The recent law is relatively standard for state lands.

INDIANA

State-Supported Archeological Research Programs

Principal State Agencies Involved. (1) Indiana University, Glen A. Black Laboratory of Archaeology, and Department of Anthropology, Bloomington, Indiana 47401. (2) Ball State University, Department of Anthropology, Muncie, Indiana 47306. (3) Indiana State Museum, 202 North Alabama, Indianapolis, Indiana 46304.

State Funds Allocated Annually for Research. Salaries equivalent to one or two archeologists plus approximately $5000, most of which is allocated to a summer field session for training students.

Discussion. Actually, in years past, the Indiana Historical Society (a quasi-public organization operating with private funds) has been the primary institution fostering archeology in the state, but the state universities and to some extent the Indiana State Museum are now attempting to develop programs. Approximately $1000 a year is made available for archeological survey work by the Indiana Historical Society. Other than that, the present research activity is principally via the university field sessions and the archeologists on the university staffs, who operate with limited time and funds.

Archeological Legislation

None.

Comments. An act concerned with historical and cultural preservation [Ind. Ann., Stat., Sections 48-9001 through 48-9011 (1967)] was passed, evidently in response to the Historic Preservation Act, but it refers primarily to cities of the first class and, unlike the federal act, studiously avoids any mention of archeology.

IOWA

State-Supported Archeological Research Programs

Principal State Agencies Involved. (1) State University of Iowa, State Archaeologist, Iowa City, Iowa 52240. (2) Iowa State University, Department of Sociology and Anthropology, Ames, Iowa 50010. (3) State Department of Archives and History, State Museum, Des Moines, Iowa 50300.

State Funds Allocated Annually for Research. Salaries equivalent to between one and two archeologists plus approximately $35,000.

Discussion. An Iowa Archaeological Advisory Board of ten members was established in 1964. Its functions are to review the activities of the state archeologist, discuss policies and programs, aid in preparation of the annual budget for archeological research (to be submitted to the legislature via the State University of Iowa), and coordinate archeological research activities in the state. This board has not been active to date.

The state archeologist is a member of the staff of the Department of Sociology and Anthropology at the State University of Iowa. The state archeological program is funded and administered through the university Division of Research and Administration with the assistance of a faculty advisory committee. A full-time and a part-time assistant state archeologist, who are basically responsible for the fairly extensive highway salvage program, are also on the program staff at the State University of Iowa. In addition, the state program has recently concluded agreements with two private colleges (Luther College in northeast Iowa and Parsons College in southeast Iowa) establishing state regional research centers at these two schools. The two colleges each agree to make staff time of one or more professional archeologists and laboratory facilities available to the state program, which in turn provides a certain amount of research funds and equipment. The agreement provides for an annual administrative review, and any collections made by the centers revert to the State University of Iowa should the centers be discontinued. Limited time and funds occasionally are made available by Iowa State University and the State Museum.

Archeological Legislation

Citation. Iowa Code Ann., Title 12, Section 303.6; Iowa Code Ann., Title 12, Sections 304.1 through 304.7 (1949). Iowa Code Ann., Title 5, Sections 111.2, 111.35, 111.41, and 111.57 (1949); Iowa Code Ann., Title 5, Sections 111A.1 and 111A.7 (Supp. 1970); Iowa Code Ann., Title 12, Sections 305A.1 through 305A.6 (Supp. 1969).

Principal Provisions. The curator of the Department of History and Archives shall receive and arrange for exhibit of archeological material; the State Conservation Committee shall investigate archeological specimens; the County Conservation Board shall give consideration to archeological features when acquiring land for recreational purposes; and the state archeologist (a member of the faculty of the Department of Sociology and Anthropology at the State University of Iowa) shall have primary responsibility for discovery, location, and excavation of sites and the recovery and preservation of remains and shall coordinate all such activities in the state. No person may destroy or remove "natural attractions" (which in context could be construed to include archeological material) from lands of the State Conservation Commission. Highway archeological salvage utilizing federal funds is specifically authorized.

Comments. Except for the law creating the state archeologist, the laws pertaining to archeology treat it in a manner peripheral to the law's main intent. In general the laws show little coordination and their effectiveness is thereby decreased. The establishment of a cooperative program with private colleges in the state which draws on their resources to the benefit of the state program while providing the colleges with research funds is a unique and interesting arrangement worthy of study by others.

Some archeologists in Iowa indicated that they felt that Iowa's laws (Iowa Code Ann., Sections 714.21 through 714.24) prohibiting disturbance of human remains were broadly enough worded to cover archeological remains and so, I suppose, they are, as are such laws in most if not all states. The point is, would a court so construe it? Legal authorities in Arkansas, which has a law essentially similar in content, felt that the courts would not so apply the law. Furthermore, there is no provision for relief from the provisions of this law by archeologists. If the Iowa courts construe the law to apply equally to aboriginal burials, then the archeologist who excavates an archeological grave is subject to prosecution. Some clarification would seem in order.

KANSAS

State-Supported Archeological Research Programs

Principal State Agencies Involved. (1) Kansas State Historical Society, 10th and Jackson Streets, Topeka, Kansas 66612. (2) University of Kansas, Department of Anthropology, Lawrence, Kansas 66044.

State Funds Allocated Annually for Research. Salaries equivalent to four or five archeologists for full-time research plus approximately $15,000.

Discussion. The Kansas State Historical Society employs three archeologists whose principal responsibilities are research and museum interpretation, while archeologists on the staff of the University of Kansas carry out some research in conjunction with summer student training, federal contract research, or on their own. In January 1971 the historical society and the highway commission entered into an agreement for highway salvage of sites endangered by construction with state or state and federal funds.

Archeological Legislation

Citation. Kan. Gen. Stat. Ann., Sections 74-5401 through 74-5408 (1967).

Principal Provisions. This legislation establishes a Kansas Antiquities Commission composed of the secretary of the State Historical Society (chairman), the heads of the departments of anthropology of the University of Kansas, Kansas State University, and Wichita State University, and the state archeologist on the staff of the State Historical Society (secretary).

No one may excavate, remove material from, or vandalize a site or area on land owned or controlled by the state without specific authorization. Such permits may be granted for limited periods by the secretary of the Antiquities Commission to educational or research institutions or other public organizations which submit satisfactory written requests and which have adequate staffs and physical facilities to conduct such research.

State agencies in Kansas with archeological research staffs and adequate facilities shall ipso facto have permission to conduct such excavations. Artifacts recovered from any such excavations shall revert to the state if they are no longer needed by the excavating agency and the state wishes to retain them. Investigators are required to report sites discovered, and any violation of the act is a misdeameanor.

KENTUCKY

State-Supported Archeological Research Programs

Principal State Agencies Involved. (1) University of Kentucky, Museum of Anthropology, Lexington, Kentucky 40506. (2) University of Louisville, Archaeological Survey, Louisville, Kentucky 40208. (3) University of Western Kentucky, Department of Anthropology, Bowling Green, Kentucky 42101.

State Funds Allocated Annually for Research. The salary of less than one archeologist full time plus approximately $10,000.

Discussion. The three institutions listed are informally organized into a Kentucky Archaeological Survey, which serves as a coordinating body whose primary function is intrastate communication. Each institution is administratively independent with respect to initiating and carrying out salvage projects which it proposes to the various state or federal agencies.

Archeological Legislation

Citation. Ky, Rev. Stat. Ann., Sections 164.705 through 164.735 (1967).

Principal Provisions. This act is an antiquities act only and designates the Department of Anthropology of the University of Kentucky as an agency empowered to grant permits to excavate on state, county, or locally owned lands. This act repealed all previous legislation.

Comments. All institutional and individual members of the Kentucky Archaeological Survey have been granted "open permits." Such permits are granted to professional archeologists and institutions upon written request to the Department of Anthropology, University of Kentucky, Lexington, Kentucky.

LOUISIANA

State-Supported Archeological Research Programs

Principal State Agencies Involved. (1) Louisiana State University, Department of Geography and Anthropology, and the Coastal Studies Institute, Baton Rouge, Louisiana 70803.

State Funds Allocated Annually for Research. Salary equivalent to one archeologist plus approximately $3500 (including the state portion of highway salvage money).

Discussion. One archeologist employed by Louisiana State University devotes most of his time to research though funds are presently dependent almost entirely upon highway salvage projects. Archaeologists at other state institutions do some research but largely with nonstate funds.

Archeological Legislation

Citation. La. Rev. Stat., Chapter 8, Sections 521 through 527 (Supp. 1968).

Principal Provisions. This law establishes the Louisiana Historical Preservation and Cultural Commission. It appears to have been established, at least in part, as a result of and in accord with the guidelines of the Historic Preservation Act. The thirteen-member commission is charged with encouraging in a variety of ways the preservation of Lousiana historic and archeological resources, but it is largely a coordinating and advisory body rather than one established to initiate a full-fledged research program. It is authorized to encourage research by others and to place markers on important sites and objects. An archeologist is chairman of this commission's review committee.

Comments. In essence, Louisiana has no true archeological legislation. Archeology is included under this commission's purview but, like similar commissions established in other states as a result of the Historic Preservation Act, the actual effect on archeological research is likely to be slight, at least at first, unless additional legislative and/or practical action is taken.

MAINE

State-Supported Archeological Research Programs

Principal State Agencies Involved. (1) University of Maine, Department of Sociology and Anthropology, Orono, Maine 04473. (2) Maine State Park and Recreation Commission, Division of Historic Sites, State Street, Augusta, Maine 04330. (3) Maine State Museum, State House, Augusta, Maine 04430.

State Funds Allocated Annually for Research. A portion of the salary of one archeologist plus approximately $1000.

Discussion. The archeologist on the staff of the University of Maine does some work with state funds, and informal arrangements have been made with the State Highway Department so that both the university and the state museum are notified of highway activities. The Division of Historic Sites has hired an archeologist on occasion, part time. As all artifacts and materials gathered from state land come under the permanent custody of the state museum, it is now in a position to establish and maintain a centralized repository of data and materials.

Archeological Legislation

Citation. Me. Rev. Stat. Ann., Title 27, Chapter 13, Sections 371 through 374 (Supp. 1969).

Principal Provisions. All archeological materials on state lands are declared to be state property, including all underwater materials in the coastal waters or under any lakes and ponds greater than ten acres (for these fall under state jurisdiction in Maine). The director of the Museum and the senior archeologist at the University of Maine, in conjunction, may grant permits for excavation on state lands, but anything recovered remains under the permanent custody of the state museum. The permit must also be approved by the state agency having jurisdiction over the land. Failure to carry out the provisions of the permit (established by the state museum and the senior archeologist rather than by law) can result in revocation of the permit and forfeiture of materials. Materials recovered can be placed under long-term loan by the state museum.

Comments. The abundance of lakes of varying sizes and the possibility of underwater-diving activity makes these aspects of the law of particular pertinence in Maine.

MARYLAND

State-Supported Archeological Research Programs

Principal State Agencies Involved. (1) Maryland Geological Survey State Archaeologist, The Johns Hopkins University, Baltimore, Maryland 21218. (2) University of Maryland, Department of Anthropology, College Park, Maryland 20742. (3) The Maryland Historical Trust, Box 1704, Annapolis, Maryland 10404. (4) St. Mary's City Commission, St. Mary's City, Maryland.

State Funds Allocated Annually for Research. The salaries of three to four archeologists plus approximately $10,000.

Discussion. A Division of Archaeology within the Maryland Geological Survey was first funded in 1969. It is concerned with coordination of amateur and professional research in both historic and prehistoric archeology. In 1969 also, the Department of Anthropology at the University of Maryland made an initial move toward the development of an archeological research program oriented toward both historic and prehistoric archeology. The Maryland Historical Trust has included archeological research in some of its restoration projects since 1966, and experienced amateur archeologists and professional restoration architects have participated in these projects.

In addition to the three agencies listed, the St. Mary's City Commission, a state-funded agency, began archeological research during 1968 at the site of St. Mary's City, the first colonial settlement in Maryland. It employs one archeologist full time.

Archeological Legislation

Citation, Md. Ann. Code, Article 66c, Sections 110B through 110L (Supp. 1968).

Principal Provisions. This legislation protects archeological resources on state-owned or state-controlled land though specifically exempting the State Roads Commission. The Maryland Geological Survey may grant permits for excavation on state lands to "properly qualified" persons or institutions and may promulgate rules and regulations. It declares that all archeological objects and materials on state land are state property and shall be deposited for permanent preservation in a reputable museum, institution of higher learning, or other recognized scientific or historical institution or society. There is a statement of legislative intent that excavations on private property should conform to the spirit of this act, and citizens are encouraged to report sites to the Geological Survey or other responsible authority.

A Division of Archaeology is established within the Geological Survey, the administrative head of which shall be the state archeologist, who shall be a professional archeologist appointed by the Geological Survey Commission. Assistants and other employees also are authorized. There is also established a standing advisory committee consisting of five members "with skill and knowledge in archeological matters" to be appointed by the Geological Survey Commission for an indefinite term. The committee is to meet at least four times a year, and the state archeologist is charged with attending all such meetings. The committee is to advise the Geological Survey on archeological matters and to formulate rules and regulations regarding archeology. The functions and purposes of the Division of Archaeology are set forth in some detail and include the obligation to sponsor and engage in direct fundamental research, to cooperate in the excavation of sites under state control, to recover and protect objects of archeological significance, to cooperate with interested parties or individuals and make materials available to museums or other institutions for demonstrating the archeological history of the state, to disseminate archeological information by reports, and to enforce any laws regulating archeological sites or objects on state land. Finally, the Geological Survey Commission is empowered to accept gifts and endowments for the purposes for which the program was established.

Comments. A perfectly adequate set of regulations has established the office of state archeologist. If the office becomes funded to the extent that it can be adequately staffed and develop a program, it should be come an effective initiating and coördinating agency with respect to the state's archeological resources.

MASSACHUSETTS

State-Supported Archeological Research Programs

None.

Archeological Legislation

Citation. Mass. Gen. Laws Ann. Chapter 9, Sections 26 and 27 (1963); Mass. Gen. Laws Ann., Chapter 40, Section 8D, 1963); Mass. Gen. Laws Ann., Chapter 79, Section 5A (1963).

Principal Provisions. This legislation establishes a Massachusetts Historical Commission consisting of the state secretary or his appointee (chairman), the commissioner of natural resources, commissioner of commerce, two persons appointed by the governor, and seven persons appointed by the state secretary with one representative from each of the following: the Bay State Historical League, Massachusetts Historical Society, Society for the Preservation of New England Antiquities, the American Antiquarian Society, the Trustees of Reservations, the New England Historic Genealogical Society, and The Massachusetts Archeological Society, Incorporated.

"The commission may request the chairman to examine certain sites and structures in the commonwealth and to make recommendations concerning their historical significance. Any such site or structure deemed by the commission to be of substantial historical significance to the commonwealth may, with the written consent of the person or persons claiming ownership, and such others having recorded interests, as the commission shall deem necessary, be certified by the commission as an historic landmark and a list of such certified historic landmarks shall be maintained and published annually by the state secretary. . . . No such certification shall take effect until a notice of such certification has been recorded in the registry of deeds in the county where such certified landmark is situated. The commission may establish standards for the care and management of such certified landmarks, and may withdraw such certification for failure to maintain such standards provided that a notice of such withdrawal shall be recorded as aforesaid. No certified historic landmark shall be altered in such a manner as would seriously impair its historical values without permission of the commission. . . . Before granting such permission the commission shall hold a public hearing. The commission may grant such permission or may withhold permission for any period up to one year during which time the commission shall consult with civic groups, public agencies and interested citizens to ascertain what action, if any, ought to be taken to preserve such landmark, and shall make recommendations for its preservation to the commonwealth or its political subdivisions, to historical societies or to other interested civic organizations. The superior court shall have jurisdiction in equity to enforce the provisions of this section and, on petition of any party in interest, may alter, amend or revoke the order of the commission." A certified landmark may not be taken by eminent domain except by leave of the general court.

There is also legislative provision for the establishment of city or town historical commissions.

Comments. This landmark law evidently is working quite well. Since certified landmarks are protected from eminent domain, the commission is in a strong position when working with the highway department or other public agencies concerned with modifying the landscape. By being in a position to work closely with all of the concerned agencies at an early stage, and by the presence of recognized authorities on the commission, it has been possible for this to become a powerful and effective law. Legislation to establish a state archeologist is currently (early 1971) under consideration.

The Massachusetts law deserves close study and emulation by others. For a more complete discussion of it, see "Cooperation in Preservation in Massachusetts" by Richard W. Hale, Jr., *Historic Preservation,* Vol. 17, No. 4, 1965, pp. 152-155.

MICHIGAN

State-Supported Archeological Research Programs

Principal State Agencies Involved. (1) University of Michigan, Museum of Anthropology and Department of Anthropology, Ann Arbor, Michigan 48104. (2) Michigan State University, Museum and Department of Anthropology, East Lansing, Michigan 48823. (3) Mackinac Island State Park Commission, The Museum, Michigan State University, East Lansing, Michigan 48823.

State funds Allocated Annually for Research. Salaries equivalent to approximately five archeologists plus perhaps $35,000, though the annually changing nature of this research and the varying number of institutions involved makes it difficult to set any accurate figure.

Discussion. The Historical Commission, though charged with responsibility to collect material relative to Michigan Indian tribes, does not have an archeologist on its staff and carries out no archeological research. The principal field work in the state is carried out by one or another of the archeologists employed for teaching and research by the various state institutions of higher learning, in particular the two institutions listed, though personnel of other state institutions such as Western Michigan University, Wayne State University, and Grand Valley State College are also developing programs. No one state agency is in a position to actively coordinate a statewide program; however, the Conference on Michigan Archaeology, a nonprofit corporation composed of professional archeologists and other qualified professional people, is consulted by the Department of Natural Resources on archeological matters on state land.

In recent years the Mackinac Island State Park Commission has employed one staff archeologist and provided funds for research at Mackinac Island and Ford Michilimackinac.

Archeological Legislation

Citations. Mich. Comp. Laws, Sections 299.51 through 299.55 (1948); Mich. Comp. Laws, Section 399.4 (1913).

Principal Provisions. Sections 299.51 through 299.55 reserve to the state all rights to explore or excavate all archeological sites or materials on lands owned or controlled by the state and under certain conditions reserve all such rights to the state in all deeds given by the state. A permit (to be granted without charge) from the director of the Department of Natural Resources is required before excavation on state land, and consent of the landowner is necessary before removal of any archeological material from private land.

The enabling legislation of the Michigan Historical Commission has been interpreted as including the duty to collect and preserve archeological objects, but it has no active program to this end. It, as well as all other agencies, is subject to the permit law.

Recently, acting under authority of the antiquity act, the Department of National Resources has started requiring permits for underwater work on state-owned bottomlands of Lake Superior, Michigan, Huron, St. Claire, and Erie. A report must be made at the end of each year (under penalty of not being issued a subsequent permit), and the state reserves the right to claim any salvaged object within one year of this being reported. Reimbursement of salvage costs will be considered.

MINNESOTA

State-Supported Archeological Research Programs

Principal State Agencies Involved. (1) Minnesota Historical Society, St. Paul, Minnesota 55101. (2) University of Minnesota, Department of Anthropology, and State Archaeologist, Minneapolis, Minnesota 55455.

State Funds Allocated Annually for Research. Salaries equivalent to three archeologists plus approximately $25,000.

Discussion. The Minnesota Historical Society is concerned primarily with historical sites and receives funds for this directly from the legislature. Prehistoric archeological research is handled or coordinated by the state archeologist, who is on the staff of the Department of Anthropology of the University of Minnesota. (The state archeologist has teaching duties in addition to research responsibilities.) The funds for this research are channeled through the Minnesota Outdoor Recreation and Resources Commission, which in turn is financed by a special levy of 1 ¢ additional state tax on cigarettes. A line item budget request is submitted by the state archeologist to the commission, and the approved figure is then presented to the legislature.

Highway salvage archeology is administered by the Minnesota Historical Society under contract with the highway department.

Archeological Legislation

Citation. Minn. Stat. Ann., Sections 138.31 through 138.41 (1963); Minn. Stat. Ann. Sections 138.51 through 138.64 (1965). (See pages 215-220 for complete text.)

Principal Provisions. In the Field Archaeology Act (Minn. Stat. Ann., Sections 138.31 through 138.41) the state reserves to itself the exclusive right and privilege of field archeology on state lands and declares that it is legislative intent that field archeology on private lands be discouraged and sites reported to the state archeologist. All persons, other than the state archeologist, must obtain permits from the director of the Minnesota Historical Society to do field archeology on state land, and the society and the state archeologist must administer and enforce the act. The State Archaeologist must be a professor of archeology on the staff of the University of Minnesota and is appointed by the director of the historical society for a four-year term. The state archeologist is charged with carrying out research, cooperating with the state agencies, retrieving and protecting sites and materials on state land and encouraging their preservation on private land, disseminating knowledge through publications, and, assisted by the director of the historical society, formulating license provisions and approving their issuance. Normal licensing procedures may be abridged in an emergency and less qualified persons approved for the work. Licenses may be renewed or revoked. Normally, the state reserves title to all objects recovered on state land, with the state archeologist as custodian. If a license or emergency license names another custodian, title to the objects and data revert to the state if such custodian fails to care for them properly or make them available to students of archeology. Nonresident schools and scientific institutions may also be licensed to excavate, and disposition of materials shall be determined by the licensing agents when it is issued. The state archeologist, with the approval of the director of the historical society, may barter or dispose of objects in his custodianship. He must make annual reports, and he or the director of the historical society may issue rules and regulations to carry out the act. Other departments are required to cooperate but must not be unduly burdened.

The Historic Sites Act (Minn. Stat. Ann., Sections 138.51 through 138.64) sets forth a registry of state historic sites (including archeological ones) and declares that neither the state nor any of its instrumentalities may alter the physical features or historic characters of said sites without prior approval of the Minnesota Historical Society.

Comments. All in all, the Field Archaeology Act is a thoughtfully worded law which, with care and reasonableness, covers nearly all probable contingencies with respect to state land. It should be carefully studied by anyone interested in antiquities legislation. More adequate funding of a positive state program could make this a model state.

MISSISSIPPI

State-Supported Archeological Research Programs

Principal State Agencies Involved. (1) State Department of Archives and History, Box 571, Jackson, Mississippi 39533. (2) University of Mississippi, Department of Sociology and Anthropology, University, Mississippi 38677. (3) Mississippi State University, Department of Sociology and Anthropology, State College, Mississippi 39762.

State Funds Allocated Annually for Research. Salaries equivalent to two to three archeologists plus approximately $5000.

Discussion. Three archeologists have been employed by the State Department of Archives and History (one, the director, is with the department half time and with Mississippi State University half time). Research funds are limited, but, in addition to those just indicated, the legislature has made available $60,000 of state funds which can be used to match grants from other private or federal sources—an interesting innovation worthy of note. Some research is accomplished by the archeologists at the universities on their own and in connection with student training.

Archeological Legislation

Citation. Miss. Code, Sections 6192-101 through 6192-123.

Principal Provisions. This act declares that it is a public policy and a public interest of the state to locate, protect, and preserve all sites, objects, buildings, and locations of historical, archeological, educational, and scientific interest located in, on, or under any of the lands of the State of Mississippi, including the tidelands, submerged lands, and the bed of the sea within the state's jurisdiction. The Board of Trustees of the Department of Archives and History is given the authority to administer the act. Its records shall be subject to inspection by any citizen when accompanied by a member of the board or authorized employee. The duties of this committee are to determine the site of and designate state archeological landmarks or to remove such designations, to contract or otherwise provide for the discovery and salvage operations covered under the act, to issue permits for such investigations, and to protect and preserve the archeological resources of the state. It is to be the legal custodian of all items recovered under the act.

The act declares that all sunken or abandoned ships and their contents, and all sites, objects, buildings, artifacts, and locations of historical, archeological, scientific, or educational interest located on, in, or under state lands, including tidelands and submerged lands, riverbeds, and sea bottoms which are owned by or are within the jurisdiction of the State of Mississippi are declared by the act to be state archeological landmarks and as such may not be taken, altered, damaged, destroyed, salvaged, or excavated without a permit from the board of trustees. A site on private land determined by a majority vote of the board to be of sufficient importance also may be designated, with the landowner's written consent, a state archeological landmark, and such designation will be recorded on the deeds of the property. All such state archeological landmarks made by majority vote may have such designation removed if they are determined to be of no further historical, archeological, educational or scientific value, and if on private land, such notification shall also be recorded on the deed.

The board may enter into contracts with qualified institutions or individuals for the discovery and salvage of treasure imbedded in the earth, sunken or abandoned ships or wrecks of the sea, parts thereof, and their contents. These may provide for fair compensation of the salvager in terms of percentage of the reasonable cash value of the objects recovered or, at the discretion of the board, a fair share of the objects recovered. The amount constituting a fair share is to be determined by the board, and the reasonable cash value is to be determined by an expert appraisal or by representatives of the contracting parties. Violation of the contract by the salvager will result in termination of the contract and superior title to all objects recovered is claimed by the State of Mississippi until they are released by the board.

The board may also issue permits for excavation or other investigation on state archeological landmarks, and these also may provide for the permittee to retain a portion of the materials recovered and for the termination of the permit if the terms are violated. All investigations carried out under permit will be done under the supervision of the board, and the board is the legal custodian of all antiquities recovered and is empowered to promulgate rules and regulations relative to this act.

The board is authorized to expend monies available to it for the purchase of the salvager's share of recovered items which the board has determined should remain the property of Mississippi. It may also accept funds from a third party with which to purchase such specimens, with the proviso that the third party will receive the items purchased but must make them available for public viewing and must resell them to the board at any time the board should request, at no change in price.

It is declared legal for the board to restore antiquities for private individuals, but this shall be done under the rules and regulations promulgated by the board, with all costs to be paid by the private party. Forgery of an archeological or other object that derives value from its antiquity, with the intent of misrepresenting it, is declared illegal, as is intentionally defacing or vandalizing Indian pictographs or archeological sites. It is declared illegal to injure or remove historical artifacts or structures on state property and on private property unless with the consent of the landowner.

The attorney general and any citizen are specifically given power to take legal action under this act, and all administrative offices and state agencies are authorized and directed to cooperate with and assist the board. Law enforcement agencies and officers are also authorized and directed to assist.

Comments. This law was patterned almost word for word after the Texas law passed slightly earlier, and both draw upon the Arkansas legislation.

Aside from differences in terminology the Mississippi law does not restrict its coverage to pre-twentieth-century ships, as does the Texas act, and it specifically includes their contents (as in reality does the Texas law by inclusion of the term "artifacts"). The Mississippi act specifically extends to any citizen, as well as the attorney general, the power to take action under the act.

MISSOURI

State-Supported Archeological Research Programs

Principal State Agencies Involved. University of Missouri, Director of American Archaeology, and Department of Anthropology, 15 Switzler Hall, Columbia, Missouri 65201.

State Funds Allocated Annually for Research. Salaries equivalent to seven archeologists plus approximately $60,000.

Discussion. Missouri has one of the oldest and best established centralized state-supported archeological research programs in the country. The organizational arrangements are not so clear-cut as to inspire direct emulation in all details, but they have been worked out over a period of years and evidently are well adapted to the local situation. Basically, the archeological research funds are handled as a separate budget within the College of Arts and Sciences. The director of American archaeology establishes the basic budget in coordination with the director of archeological research activities, the director of the Archaeological Research Center and Field School, the director of the River Basin Surveys, and the director of the Archaeological Survey of Missouri, all but the last named of whom are also members of the Department of Anthropology. The budget is then submitted through the dean of the College of Arts and Sciences. The State Park Board (which administers sites developed into parks) and the highway department contract archeological work through the university and through the director in charge of that particular activity. The governor has appointed an advisory committee on archeology to the park board with the director of Archaeological Research Activities as an *ex officio* member. There is a permanently established field school at a large site in one of the state parks. A visitors' center at that park is jointly supported by the university and the State Park Board.

Archeological Legislation

Citation. Mo. Ann. Stat., Section 560.473 (Supp. 1970).

Principal Provisions. Destruction or collection of archeological material on state park land is prohibited.

Comments. This is a perfectly practical but severely limited preservation law since, for example, it does not even apply similar protection to other state lands.
Another act (not cited) transfers land in Van Meter State Park from the State Park Board to the University of Missouri to be used for archeological research. This has led to a cooperative and continuing program of research between the board and the university at this location, and, to some extent, elsewhere.

MONTANA

State-Supported Archeological Research Programs

Principal State Agencies Involved. (1) University of Montana, Department of Anthropology, Missoula, Montana 59801. (2) Montana State University, Department of Anthropology, Bozeman, Montana 59715.

State Funds Allocated Annually for Research. A portion of the salary of one archeologist plus less than $1000.

Discussion. A limited amount of archeological research is being done by archeologists at the universities, but this is almost totally supported by federal or private money with minimal state contributions.

Archeological Legislation

Citation. Mont. Rev. Codes Ann., Sections 75-1202 through 75-1206 (1967).

Principal Provisions. The commissioner of the State Land Office is authorized on recommendation of the State Historical Society with the approval of the commissioner of public lands to declare prehistoric structures or objects on state-owned or state-controlled lands to be state monuments.

Permits, to be issued by the commissioner of public lands on recommendation of the Board of Trustees of the State Historical Society, are required for excavation or gathering of archeological materials in the state (whether on public or private land is not stated). Such investigation must be for the benefit of educational or scientific institutions and not less than fifty percent of the materials collected shall remain in the state unless the commissioner of public lands accepts a smaller amount. It is forbidden to export archeological materials from the state except those gathered under a permit from the commissioner of public lands or under provisions of the federal statutes. Appropriation, excavation, or defacement of archeological materials on state land without a permit is a misdemeanor, and law officers and county attorneys are enjoined to enforce this provision.

Comments. It is not clear what, if any, penalty is provided except for the last provision outlined, and, in general, the wording is unclear. The provision prohibiting export is patently impossible to enforce. It is not clear whether the permit provision is intended to extend to private land or not.

NEBRASKA

State-Supported Archeological Research Programs

Principal State Agencies Involved. (1) Nebraska State Historical Society, 1500 R Street, Lincoln, Nebraska 68508. (2) University of Nebraska, Laboratory of Anthropology, and Department of Anthropology, Lincoln, Nebraska 68508. (3) University of Nebraska State Museum, Lincoln, Nebraska 68508.

State Funds Allocated Annually for Research. The salaries of two archeologists plus approximately $20,000.

Discussion. The Nebraska State Historical Society has a long-standing program of archeological research and allocates specific salary and maintenance funds from its budget for this work, which is directed by an archeologist on the staff. There is no specific authorization for this program in the state statutes, but it is recognized in the Society's constitution as one of its functions. There is specific authorization for a highway salvage program, which the Society has begun. The Department of Anthropology, University of Nebraska, supports a field school out of regularly appropriated funds, which is directed by a faculty member, but no other faculty member is released for archeological research on a continuing basis. The state museum has allocated no funds regularly but has supported specific archeological projects in the past. All three agencies have agreements with the State Highway Department, and the anthropology department and the museum contract with the federal government for salvage projects. What coordination exists among the three is on a strictly personal basis.

Archeological Legislation

Citation. Legislative resolution of 1935; Neb. Rev. Stat., Section 39-1363 (1959).

Principal Provisions. The Conservation and Survey Division of the University of Nebraska is given authority to regulate and control collections of materials, including archeological materials, within the state borders, but this is by legislative resolution and lacks the force of law. The second citation authorizes the Department of Roads to enter into highway salvage agreements.

Comments. General intent is shown, but it is rather poorly defined, never employed, and does not have the force of law. The specific authorization for highway salvage and for the expenditure of state funds for this purpose is necessary in many states and certainly marks a step in the right direction.

NEVADA

State-Supported Archeological Research Programs

Principal State Agencies Involved. (1) Nevada Archeological Survey, University of Nevada, Reno, Nevada 89507. (2) University of Nevada, Las Vegas, Nevada 89109. (3) Nevada State Museum, Reno, Nevada 89507.

State Funds Allocated Annually for Research.   Salaries equivalent to approximately one person full time plus approximately $1000.

Discussion.   A considerable increase in the state effort for archeological research and employment of two or more persons full time for this purpose is on the drawing boards for the next biennium. At the present time very minor amounts of research are being carried out by the individuals on the staffs of the three institutions involved. All archeological research, including that done by out-of-state institutions, is coordinated by the Nevada Archeological Survey office located on the Reno campus of the University of Nevada.

Archeological Legislation

Citation.   Nev. Rev. Stat., Sections 381.200 through 381.260 (1953).

Principal Provisions.   Excavation or exploration of archeological sites and materials on state or federal land is prohibited without a permit from the Board of Directors of the Nevada State Museum (and federal authorities where appropriate). Other state agencies may be designated by the board to issue permits (this refers particularly to the Nevada Historical Society). To qualify for a permit, the work must be done for an educational or scientific institution for public benefit and by trained persons. Reasonable rules may be prescribed and upon issuance of a permit, appropriate state officials and local law enforcement personnel shall be notified and shall be responsible for enforcement. All excavations and artifactual materials may be examined by such persons. Vandalism is prohibited (whether federal and state lands are included is not stated). A report is required, and fifty percent of the material is to be retained by the state museum unless the board decides otherwise. If the Nevada Historical Society issues the permit, it shall retain the fifty percent, or, if it is also the permit holder, one hundred percent. Permits are limited to one year (but can be renewed if the work has been diligently prosecuted) and to a reasonable area, and may not be issued if the site or structure can be preserved as a public park. Failure to initiate work within six months voids the permit. The act shall not interfere with collecting arrowheads not a part of a prehistoric site nor the taking of photographs. Materials taken without a permit shall be forfeited to the Nevada State Museum.

Comments.   The legal situation is somewhat clouded by the necessity for taking into consideration several state agencies. While it is not necessarily bad to have several responsible agencies, this can be a potential danger point.

NEW HAMPSHIRE

State-Supported Archeological Research Programs

None regularly funded by the state.

Discussion. Franklin Pierce College has begun doing occasional small highway salvage projects which, of course, does involve matching money from the state highway department.

Archeological Legislation

None.

NEW JERSEY

State-Supported Archeological Research Programs

Principal State Agencies Involved. Department of Education, State Museum (Bureau of Research-Archeology), Post Office Box 1868, Trenton, New Jersey 08625.

State Funds Allocated Annually for Research. The salaries of approximately one and a half archeologists plus $8000.

Discussion. The State Museum moved into a new building several years ago and at that time a considerable sum was spent on equipment and facilities, which are now available to further archeological research. In the past archeological research has been carried out by archeologists attached to the Archeology Section of the Bureau of Research of the State Museum, but currently (early 1971) there is no one on the museum staff specifically to do archeological research. The State Museum is the contracting agency for federal programs.

Archeological Legislation

None.

Comments. There is no specific legislation, but by agreement with the agencies having jurisdiction over state land any sites situated thereon are protected and reserved for investigation by the State Museum.

NEW MEXICO

State-Supported Archeological Research Programs

Principal State Agencies Involved. (1) Museum of New Mexico, Laboratory of Anthropology, Post Office Box 2087, Sante Fe, New Mexico 87501. (2) University of New Mexico, Department of Anthropology, Albuquerque, New Mexico 87106. (3) Eastern New Mexico University, Department of Anthropology, Paleo-Indian Institute, Portales, New Mexico 88130.

State Funds Allocated Annually for Research. Salaries equivalent to four archeologists full time plus approximately $20,000.

Discussion. The Laboratory of Anthropology has an active program which, drawing on long-standing basic state support, has been able to develop and attract outside support from a number of sources. Laboratory personnel were instrumental in initiating the now nationwide program of highway salvage archeology, and this continues on both state and federal road construction projects. More recently, they have been attempting to initiate and coordinate the efforts of various state and federal agencies toward an integrated program of research involving archeology, geology, and other sciences. The results of this program, if it is carried through, should provide the basic data necessary for effective planning in the areas of recreation planning, watershed management, forest and grasslands control, urban planning, area redevelopment projects, dam construction, and certain economic developments.

Personnel from Eastern New Mexico University are active in research in the state, though largely with nonstate funds. The Department of Anthropology at the University of New Mexico conducts an annual summer training session but otherwise allocates no funds for research.

Archeological Legislation

Citation. N.M. Stat. Ann., Sections 4-27-4 through 4-27-16 (1969).

Principal Provisions. Repeals most sections of previous act concerning antiquities. Creates a Cultural Properties Review Committee of seven members consisting of the state archeologist (who is the curator-in-charge of the Laboratory of Anthropology of the Museum of New Mexico), state historian (who is the deputy for archives of the New Mexico State Records Center), and five other professional members to be appointed by the governor. The appointed members must be professionally recognized in the American Southwest with specialized knowledge of New Mexico. No more than two members may be appointed from any one of these fields. The committee may issue, with the concurrence of the state archeologist, permits for the excavation of sites on state lands to reputable museums, universities, colleges, or other historical, scientific, or educational institutions, or societies approved by the committee. All materials shall be the property of the state, and the Museum of New Mexico shall be the state depository, although prior arrangements may be made to place the materials in some other state institutions. The committee shall identify, document, and register cultural properties within the state which it considers to be of historical, archeological, scientific, architectural, or other significance. Where a cultural property is on private land, and the landowner accepts the care and preservation responsibilities of a "registered cultural property," the landowner's property taxes shall be reduced in the amount that he expends for restoration, preservation, and maintenance of the cultural property.

Comments. The Cultural Properties Review Committee is also the data-gathering body which nominates properties for the National Register under the Historic Preservation Act of 1966. In accordance with the latter act, nominations are channeled through the state liaison officer, in this case the state planning officer of the New Mexico State Planning Office. The Museum of New Mexico is responsible for the administration, development, and maintenance of all registered cultural properties and thus works closely with the state planning office, which is responsible for the preparation of a comprehensive, statewide historic sites preservation plan. The tax-exemption provisions for registered cultural properties on private land is worthy of note and emulation.

NEW YORK

State-Supported Archeological Research Programs

Principal State Agencies Involved. New York State Education Department, Anthropological Survey of the New York State Museum and Science Service, State Education Building, 31 Washington Avenue, Albany, New York 12210.

State Funds Allocated Annually for Research. Salaries equivalent to approximately two archeologists plus from approximately $15,000 to $20,000.

Discussion. The Anthropological Survey is directed by the state archeologist, an employee of the education department, who prepares the basic budget. The Survey is principally a research organization and is the contracting agent for the highway salvage program. It also is responsible for administering the antiquities act and serves as a central clearing house for data. The branches of the State University of New York at Buffalo, Oswego, Binghamton, and Albany also conduct some archeological research with state funds.

Archeological Legislation

Citation. N.Y. Educ. Law, Section 233 (McKinney 1970), N.Y. Conservation Law, Section 831-4 (1971 suppl.).

Principal Provisions. The state museum is established as the proper repository for all state collections. The commissioner of education is empowered and directed to make appropriate contracts to establish a highway salvage program. A permit from the commissioner of education is required before a person may excavate, appropriate, or damage any objects of archeological interest on lands owned by the state. Violations shall be reported to the commissioner, and discovery of objects on state land shall also be reported to him. Permits to work on land under this jurisdiction may be granted by the respective state departments with the approval of the commissioner of education.

The 1971 act empowers the state historic trust to designate any Indian cemetery not on an Indian reservation as a place of historic interest and prohibits destruction, alteration, conversion, or impairment of such a cemetery without written permission from the historic trust.

Comments. The regulations of the Commission of Education, Article XXXI, Section 241, set forth the details with respect to obtaining permits. Permits may be issued for one year by the assistant commissioner for the New York State Museum and Science Service to qualified educational and scientific institutions or to professionally competent individuals. All discoveries of archeological sites and materials shall be reported to the state museum. Permits may be revoked at any time. The conservation law, to my knowledge, is the first attempt to make specific provision for the protection of Indian cemeteries. It would appear to apply to all non-reservation land.

NORTH CAROLINA

State-Supported Archeological Research Programs

Principal State Agencies Involved. (1) State Department of Archives and History, Division of Historic Sites, Post Office Box 18, Raleigh, North Carolina 27202. (2) University of North Carolina, Research Laboratory of Anthropology, Chapel Hill, North Carolina 27514.

State Funds Allocated Annually for Research. Salaries equivalent to approximately five archeologists plus approximately $25,000.

Discussion.   North Carolina has a dual organization for archeological research. The Division of Historic Sites, an administrative division of the North Carolina State Department of Archives and History, is responsible for historic sites archeology, while the Research Laboratory of Anthropology, which is administratively responsible to the University of North Carolina, is responsible for all prehistoric archeology within the state. The departmental archeologist of the Division of Historic Sites and his assistant devote a major portion of their time to research on historic sites, and the division administers several developed archeological sites, which have been designated state historic sites. The research laboratory has two subdivisions. The first, under the state archeologist, who is also director of the research laboratory, has two archeologists, who devote their full time to research over the state, including prehistoric sites which are state historic sites. The second subdivision, with two archeologists who combine teaching and research, is oriented toward student research and the teaching of archeological techniques.

Archeological Legislation

Citation.   N.C. Gen. Stat., Sections 70-1 through 70-4 (1935); N.C. Gen. Stat., Sections 121-1 through 121-13.1 (1955).

Principal Provisions.   Private landowners are urged to refrain from destruction of archeological materials and to obtain the cooperation and assistance of persons qualified to make archeological explorations. All persons with archeological material in their possession are urged to commit them to a public institution for safekeeping. Any persons in charge of construction or excavation on state lands shall report any archeological material to the director of the state museum or the director of the State Department of Archives and History. Excavation or removal or destruction of archeological material on state or state-controlled land without a permit from the director of the state museum or director of the State Department of Archives and History is prohibited. The State Department of Archives and History is authorized to acquire properties of archeological significance and to make reasonable rules for the use of such properties by the public. It shall have the power to obtain such sites by condemnation. Employees of the department may be designated special peace officers to enforce the regulations concerning such sites and shall have the power of arrest.

Comments.   Adequate, workable control of state lands seems to be provided.

NORTH DAKOTA

State-Supported Archeological Research Programs

Principal State Agencies Involved. (1) State Historical Society of North Dakota, Liberty Memorial Building, Bismarck, North Dakota 58501. (2) University of North Dakota, Department of Sociology and Anthropology, Grand Forks, North Dakota 58202.

State Funds Allocated Annually for Research. The salary of one archeologist plus approximately $1000 (generally as matching money for specific projects).

Discussion. There is no state program as such. The State Historical Society of North Dakota does contract with federal agencies to do salvage archeology, but at present state contributions are limited to whatever matching funds are required for these specific projects. No funds are regularly provided by the university, though some small grants are made for individual projects.

Archeological Legislation

Citation. N.D. Rev. Code, Section 55-02-07 (Supp. 1965); N.D. Cent. Code, Sections 55-03-1 through 55-03-07 (1965); N.D. Cent. Code, Sections 55-10-01 through 55-10-10 (1967).

Principal Provisions. Any archeological site or artifacts found on land owned by the state or its political subdivisions or that otherwise comes into its custody shall be protected, excavated, and stored under direction of, or in the manner prescribed by, the superintendent of the State Historical Society Board. An annual license from this board is required for investigation or excavation of archeological material on any land in North Dakota ($5.00 for one site, $2.50 for each additional site; renewal $2.00). Such permits shall be for only single sites or locations, though supplementary permits for additional sites may be granted. A permit shall be issued only to qualified persons. If the site is on state land, all objects and records shall be deposited with the State Historical Society, and if on private land, a permit will not be issued until it is agreed that copies of all notes and maps shall be delivered to the State Historical Society. In every case a final report is required. Permits for state land may be revoked at any time if the superintendent of the State Historical Society feels that work is not being done properly. Private landowners may excavate on their own land, and the owner may issue written permission for others to excavate thereon without a state permit being required. When any state lands are sold, the title to all archeological materials shall be retained by the state or municipal subdivisions. Conviction or violation results in forfeiture of materials.

Sections 55-10-01 through 55-10-10 define and (and list) "state historic sites" and "state archaeological sites," which can be on public or private land. If any state agency acquires such a site, the State Historical Society must be notified, and no state agency may alter such a site without approval from the superintendent of the board of the Society. All state and governmental subdivisions are required to cooperate with the Society in preserving these sites.

Comment. By requiring the landowners' written consent this law accomplishes much the same thing as the more normal trespass regulations in some other states. The annual licensing fee of $5.00 for the first site and $2.50 for each subsequent site hardly seems a realistic means of defraying the costs of any supervision of such permits. Efforts to amend this fee provision have not been successful.

OHIO

State-Supported Archeological Research Programs

Principal State Agencies Involved. The Ohio Historical Society, Division of Archaeology, Columbus, Ohio 43210.

State Funds Allocated Annually for Research. The salaries of two archeologists plus approximately $13,000.

Discussion. The Ohio Historical Society is a private agency of the State of Ohio but operates as the official history commission under several Ohio codes. Its operating expenses are provided by state, federal, and private funds, and it is the official custodian of the state's historical properties, including several archeological sites. An annual allocation is made from the Society's budget for archeological research.

Archeological Legislation

Citation. Ohio Rev. Code Ann., Sections 149.30 through 149.301 (1969).

Principal Provisions. In addition to establishing the Ohio Historical Society's public functions, it provides the authority for the Society to acquire and administer archeological sites, and authorizes condemnation proceeding to obtain them if necessary. The Ohio Historic Site Preservation Advisory Board is established; it is to be appointed by the governor with advice and consent of the state senate. Archeologists may be included on this board (federal guidelines relating to the Historic Preservation Act require their presence). The board shall assist the Society in its preservation program and in suggesting appropriate legislation.

OKLAHOMA

State-Supported Archeological Research Programs

Principal State Agencies Involved. (1) University of Oklahoma, State Archaeologist, Department of Anthropology, Norman, Oklahoma 73069. (2) University of Oklahoma Research Institute, Oklahoma River Basin Survey, Norman, Oklahoma 73069.

State Funds Allocated Annually for Research. The salary of one archeologist plus $5000.

Discussion. The University of Oklahoma established in 1968 the position of state archeologist, the funds for which are requested from the legislature by the provost as a part of the university budget. The program is administered by the provost. The River Basin Survey is the official agency for salvage work done under contract with the National Park Service. The only state funds available to the Survey are the costs involved in the provision of space and facilities.

Archeological Legislation

Citation. Okla. Stat. Ann., Title 70, Chapter 50, Section 3309 (1965); Okla. Stat. Ann. Title 74, Chapter 9A, Section 241 (Supp. 1970).

Principal Provisions. A license, to be issued by the chairman of the Department of Anthropology, is required of all persons (other than persons sponsored or controlled by the Department of Anthropology) excavating or investigating an archeological site or material on all land, private, federal, or state, in Oklahoma, and fifty percent of all materials gained must be deposited with the Museum of Science and History of the University of Oklahoma. Such license shall be for one site only and issued only subsequent to investigation by the chairman. The person, if qualified, pays a $50.00 fee and agrees to deposit fifty percent of the materials at the University of Oklahoma. Additional licenses for other sites require a fee of $25.00, as do renewals for another year. A license may be revoked at any time if the chairman feels the work is being done improperly. False labeling of archeological material or features or sale of such falsely labeled objects is prohibited. Violation of this section will result in forfeiture.

The 1970 legislation officially established the Oklahoma Archeological Survey under the Board of Regents of the University of Oklahoma and charges the Survey with a reasonably standard but perfectly adequate set of responsibilities.

Comments. This 1935 law was amended in 1965 to remove the paleontological coverage initially provided, to exempt work sponsored or controlled by the Department of Anthropology from its provisions, and to include private land in the requirement that fifty percent of the material be deposited with the university (previously only the licensing provision had applied to private land). Unless they are willing to test the issue of state rights vs. federal rights relative to federal land within state boundaries, it is unlikely that the provision requiring deposit of fifty percent of the material found on federal land could be applied, and even the licensing requirement might be subject to question. Extension of the deposition provision to private land also is subject to serious question as to its constitutionality, though presumably the state does have licensing power. The investigation requirements, if conscientiously adhered to by applicants, could rapidly cause serious administrative complications. The fees required to support this investigation, although more realistic than those of North Dakota, are still inadequate, and availability of staff time for such work would also be a serious problem. Of course, the wording is such that if an investigation is not made, a license cannot be issued, and the applicant is left with no apparent recourse, at least within the provisions of the act.

OREGON

State-Supported Archeological Research Programs

Principal State Agencies Involved. (1) University of Oregon, Department of Anthropology, and Oregon State Museum of Anthropology, Eugene, Oregon 97403. (2) Oregon State University, Corvallis, Oregon 97330. (3) Portland State University, Portland, Oregon 97208.

State Funds Allocated Annually for Research. Salaries equivalent to one to two archeologists plus an average of approximately $3000.

Discussion. There is no regularly funded program of archeological research in Oregon. One member of the staff of the Oregon State Museum of Anthropology (which is a part of the Museum of Natural History at the university) spends approximately one-third time on research. No museum funds are specifically budgeted for archeological research, though limited travel funds and equipment are so used. Archeologists in the Department of Anthropology and the other state universities also occasionally conduct archeological research both within and without the state on an individual project or field school basis with state funds.

Archeological Legislation

Citation. Ore. Rev. Stat., Section 273.705 (1967); Ore. Rev. Stat., Section 273.711 (1967); Ore. Rev. Stat., Section 352.090 (1967); Ore. Rev. Stat., Section 273.715 (1967).

Principal Provisions. Permits to excavate and remove archeological materials from land owned or controlled by the state must be secured from the Division of Public Lands and the president of the University of Oregon. Permits shall be regularly granted to reputable educational and scientific organizations with a view toward promoting knowledge, provided half of said material shall be state property unless a lesser amount is agreed to. Recognized institutions of higher learning in the state may conduct archeological research on state land and retain possession of the material, provided they present a complete catalog to the Oregon State Museum of Anthropology within six months. Material gained by institutions or universities without permit becomes state property and is deposited with the Oregon State Museum of Anthropology. The Oregon State Museum of Anthropology is designated the official repository of state-owned archeological materials, and the University of Oregon assumes full responsibility for its custody.

A new "beach bill" (not cited) authorizes the issuance of permits for individuals to dig sites on state-owned beaches. This law appears to be in conflict with the state's basic antiquity legislation, and at least suggests that the responsible state agencies will not be expected to enforce the antiquities law.

PENNSYLVANIA

State-Supported Archeological Research Programs

Principal State Agencies Involved. (1) Pennsylvania Historical and Museum Commission, Box 232, Harrisburg, Pennsylvania 17108. (2) Pennsylvania State

University, Department of Anthropology, University Park, Pennsylvania 16802. (3) University of Pennsylvania, University Museum, and Department of Anthropology, Philadelphia, Pennsylvania 19104.

State Funds Allocated Annually for Research. Salaries equivalent to approximately four full-time archeologists plus approximately $20,000.

Discussion. The Pennsylvania Historical and Museum Commission is the primary state agency supporting archeological research. Administratively, the archeologists attached to the commission have been placed in the Bureau of Museums, Section of Archaeology, and one carries the title State Archaeologist. This section also conducts historic sites archeology for the commission's Bureau of Historic Sites and Properties. The major portion of the state funds available for archeological research is channeled through the Section of Archaeology as salaries for field crews and via specifically negotiated contracts or grants-in-aid. Some of it is used in coordination with various federal programs (for example, Job Corps), which supplement the amounts available. The highway department is beginning to cooperate with the museum on salvage, and the museum is beginning to encourage cooperation by the major utility companies. The two universities carry out research outside of Pennsylvania, which is largely but not entirely supported by nonstate funds. Pennsylvania State University personnel devote some time to research within the state with limited state funds.

Archeological Legislation

Citation. Pa. Stat. Ann., Title 71, Section 716 (1963); Pa. Stat. Ann., Title 18, Section 4863 (1963).

Principal Provisions. The Pennsylvania Historical and Museum Commission is established with the duty (among others) to carry out prehistoric and historic sites archeology and report this work to the public. Manufacturing, selling, or offering for sale spurious archeological specimens is forbidden.

RHODE ISLAND

State-Supported Archeological Research Programs

None.

Archeological Legislation

None.

SOUTH CAROLINA

State-Supported Archeological Research Programs

Principal State Agencies Involved. University of South Carolina, Institute of Archaeology and Anthropology, Columbia, South Carolina 29208.

State Funds Allocated Annually for Research. Salaries of four archeologists plus approximately $25,000.

Discussion. The institute, founded as a separate state agency in 1963, has now been taken into the university and reports directly to the vice president for advanced studies and research. The director of the institute, who shall be the professor of American archeology and anthropology on the university faculty who has the longest tenure in that capacity at the rank of assistant professor or higher, is also the state archeologist. A basic line-item appropriation is made to the university each year for the basic operation of the institute; in addition, specific project funds are available from local (including county), state, and federal sources. Only the basic state appropriation is included in the figure for state funds given here.

Archeological Legislation

Citation. S.C. Code, Section 9-331 (1969); S.C. Code, Sections 54-321 through 54-328 (1969).

Principal Provisions. One act (S.C. Code, Section 9-331) is the enabling legislation for the institute. The second act has reference to underwater materials. Title to all underwater objects within one marine league of mean low-watermark which have been unclaimed for ten years is claimed for the state, and the institute is declared to be the responsible state agency which may issue permits. These permits may require payment of a fee and retention of all or part of the material by the state, may allow sale of objects recovered by the licensee or the institute, and may include other "reasonable conditions." The licensee is responsible for obtaining any federal permission required. Any funds received by the institute from this source may be used for its operation. State and local law-enforcement agencies are empowered to assist.

Comments. As yet there is not adequate staff to implement the underwater act, but these are being requested. The details of the responsibilities of the state archeologist, the time he may be off or teach elsewhere, are spelled out in unusual detail. In general this type of detail is better left to administrative decision rather than incorporated into state law.

SOUTH DAKOTA

State-Supported Archeological Research Programs

Principal State Agencies Involved. (1) South Dakota State Archaeological Commission, South Dakota State Historical Society, Pierre, South Dakota 57501. (2) University of South Dakota W. H. Over Dakota Museum, Vermillion, South Dakota 57069.

State Funds Allocated Annually for Research. A portion of the salary of one archeologist plus occasional small sums for specific projects.

Discussion. In 1947 the South Dakota State Archaeological Commission was established, composed of the secretary of the State Historical Society, the director of the W. H. Over Dakota Museum, and the director of the Museum of the South Dakota School of Mines and Technology. In 1970 the composition of the commission was changed to the secretary of the society plus a person appointed by the president of each of the two schools rather than specifying the museum directors. Funds can be (but have not been) appropriated directly to the commission by the legislature. The divisive interests of the commissioners (none of whom need be archeologists) is always a potential source of difficulty in such arrangements, and in this instance the arrangement does not appear yet to have led to the development of an active state program, though occasional salvage projects have been undertaken with funds from other agencies. The museum at the University of South Dakota does conduct some research with special funds made available by the university to the museum archeologist for individual projects, and it, more than any other agency, serves as a central repository for data.

Archeological Legislation

Citation. S.D. Code, Sections 1-20-1 through 1-20-16 (1970).

Principal Provisions. Sections 1-20-1 through 1-20-6 created the Archaeological Commission and empowered it to investigate archeological sites and materials in the state (by implication on private, state, and federal land), especially where they are to be flooded as a result of work by the United States Army Corps of Engineers and the Bureau of Reclamation. The field work shall be done by qualified individuals, with proper records kept and results published. Volunteers may be utilized. All material resulting from the work shall be state property, with representative collections going to the state museum at Pierre, the University of South Dakota museum, and the School of Mines and Technology, while the remainder, if any, may be sent with the state to other public (preferably state) institutions.

Permits are required before any investigation of archeological sites or materials can be made on any public lands in South Dakota. Application for permit is to be made to the State Historical Society setting forth (1) the location of the site to be investigated and (2) the qualification and scientific fitness of the applicant. Each application is to be accompanied by the filing fee of $5.00 (institutions of higher learning in South Dakota are exempted from the fee). Supplementary permits for investigation of other sites cost $2.50 each. No permits shall be issued until the site has been inspected by the Society and the fitness of the investigator determined, and the investigator has agreed to deliver one-half of material recovered to the state. Each permit terminates at the end of the calendar year but may be renewed ($2.00) within thirty days. It may be revoked at any time by the Society for unlawful or improper investigation. Fees are to be deposited in the state treasury in the archeological fund and shall be used to investigate applications and inspect sites. Nothing contained in this chapter should be construed to limit or prohibit any persons owning land in this state from exploring or excavating for archeological material on his own land. Where land is sold, conveyed, transferred, or leased by the state or any political subdivision thereof, the title to any archeological materials, whether on or below the surface, shall be retained by the state. Violation of the act is a misdemeanor. Punishment is forfeiture of all archeological materials and a fine of not more than $100. In case of failure to pay the fine the person shall be imprisoned in the county jail for not more than thirty days. The violation shall be considered to have been committed in the county where the investigation took place.

Comments. The South Dakota law was patterned after the North Dakota law as it was originally drafted. The permit fees are totally unrealistic, as they are too small to finance the inspections required.

While a commission and regulatory provisions are established, no real program of positive action was provided for and none has developed, an example of the uselessness of the negative regulatory approach unless it is backed by a positive program of state-supported research and development.

TENNESSEE

State-Supported Archeological Research Programs

Principal State Agencies Involved. (1) Department of Conservation, Division of Archaeology, Nashville, Tennessee. (2) University of Tennessee, Department of Anthropology, Knoxville, Tennessee 37916. (3) Memphis State University, Anthropological Research Center, Memphis, Tennessee 38111.

State Funds Allocated Annually for Research. The salary equivalent to approximately one to two archeologists full time plus approximately $5000.

Discussion. Essentially, no state funds are available for general archeological research other than the salary of one person attached to the Department of Conservation and several persons part time at the University of Tennessee and Memphis State University. The University of Tennessee has served as the contracting agent for federal salvage programs, including highway salvage. Memphis State conducts a field school partially supported by state funds. On at least one occasion the Department of Conservation has provided for archeological research and now has a state archeologist on its staff. The University of Tennessee in cooperation with Memphis State and the Tennessee Archaeological Society maintains a central file of information.

Archeological Legislation

Citation. Tenn. Code Ann., Chapter 468, Sections 1 through 19 (Supp. 1970).

Principal Provisions. This law creates a Division of Archaeology in the Department of Conservation to be headed by a state archeologist. The division is authorized to initiate and maintain a statewide program in archeology, including locating and excavating sites, carrying out other fundamental research, publication of its findings as well as display of them, and other educational activities. It stipulates that it is not the purpose of the division to preempt, replace, or otherwise interfere with archeological research programs conducted by state institutions of higher learning but rather to stimulate and supplement such programs whenever possible. An Advisory Council to the commissioner of conservation and the state archeologist is created to be appointed by the governor and to be composed of three anthropologists representing the University of Tennessee, Memphis State University, and Vanderbilt University, respectively, one representative each from the Tennessee Archaeological Society and the Tennessee Historical Commission, and one member from the public at large. Members serve for five years and may be reappointed. The council will advise in all policy matters relating to the Division and employment of personnel and is to organize and set forth rules and operational procedures. Both the Advisory Council and state archeologist have to submit annual reports to the governor and the Tennessee General Assembly.

All objects gathered by or given to the state archeologist are state property but are available to the public and may be loaned if in the public good. The state reserves to itself exclusive rights to the archeological materials on state property.

Only persons authorized by the division may excavate on any state land. Permits may be issued, but all artifacts, photographs, and records obtained by permittee remain the property of the state and shall be maintained in public repositories. Vandalism and mutilation of archeological remains on state property is prohibited. All state agencies must cooperate with the division, and they are urged to have any of their employees notify the division of the discovery or location of sites or artifacts and endeavor to prevent their destruction. It is the responsibility of state agencies to make the provisions of the act known to contractors operating on their land. Upon written notice from the state archeologist, the director of the Property Service Division shall reserve from sale any state lands, including lands forfeited to the state for nonpayment of taxes, on which sites or artifacts are located or may be found, and subsequent to adequate examination, these lands will then be released by the state archeologist. It is declared an act of trespass and a misdemeanor to go on any private property for the purpose of excavating or removing artifacts without obtaining the owner's express permission.

Significant archeological sites may be so designated by the Tennessee Historical Commission and placed on the Tennessee Register of Historic Sites but only with the written consent of the state agency or private landowner having jurisdiction over the site. Such permission may be revoked giving thirty days notice. The division may enter into contracts with any corporations or organizations for the purpose of salvaging archeological remains. The State Highway Department is authorized and directed to enter into appropriate contracts and agreements with the Bureau of Public Roads and to expend both state and federal funds for archeological salvage. The division is authorized to accept gifts and grants and is authorized to assist and support the program of the Tennessee Archaeological Society to the extent that the purposes of the two coincide, and the Archaeological Society is requested to assist and cooperate with the division.

Sections 16 and 17 of this act, which surely were added to the bill when it was being considered on the floor of the state senate or house, are best quoted in their entirety:

SECTION 16: "The State Archaeologist shall authorize upon written request any citizen of the State or group of citizens of the State permission to excavate or surface hunt for artifacts. Artifacts found under this section shall become the property of the citizen, however, the State Archaeologist may require any record, description, photograph, or other significant data concerning the artifacts to be sent to the State Archaeologist. No artifacts found under this section shall be removed from the State for more than three hundred and sixty-four days in one year."

SECTION 17: "The provisions of this act shall not apply to the following counties having the following populations according to the Federal Census of

1960 or any subsequent Federal Census: not less than 55,000 or more than 56,000; not less than 4,700 or more than 4,800; not less than 11,000 or more than 11,511."

Comments. The first fifteen sections of this act obviously are patterned after the Arkansas antiquities act. The subsequent two sections are perhaps the most astonishing bits of antiquities legislation presently to be found in any state. Section 16 essentially invalidates any protective provisions of the first fifteen sections, as well as adding a removal provision which is completely unrealistic and impossible to enforce. Section 17 apparently was added by individual legislators attempting to preserve some particular county pothunters' paradise from any state interference or supervision. This legislation constitutes a clear example of what can happen when archeological legislation is introduced and no shepherd (see pages 34-36) is available to see it through the legislative process. It is possible, of course, that a shepherd might not be able to prevent developments such as Sections 16 and 17, but in most instances I think it would be possible to do so. In this particular instance the crowning touch was applied when the engrossing clerk failed to include the appropriation of $30,000 for the Division of Archaeology, which had been approved by the state senate and house, in the copy of the bill which was sent to the governor. Evidently no one was around to catch this slight oversight. As a consequence, the program was not funded for some time, though in late 1970 the governor did make some funds available, which have enabled the program to get started.

TEXAS

State-Supported Archeological Research Programs

Principal State Agencies Involved. (1) Texas Historical Survey Committee, State Archeologist, Post Office Box 12276, Capitol Station, Austin, Texas 78711. (2) University of Texas, Department of Anthropology, Division of Research in Anthropology and Texas Memorial Museum, Austin, Texas 78712. (3) Texas Western College, El Paso Centennial Museum, El Paso, Texas 79902. (4) West Texas State University, Panhandle-Plains Museum, Canyon, Texas 79015. (5) Texas Technological College Museum, Lubbock, Texas 79409. (6) State Parks and Wildlife Commission, Austin, Texas 78901.

State Funds Allocated Annually for Research. Salaries equivalent to approximately nine archeologists full time plus approximately $15,000.

Discussion. The rather small amount of funds available for research (relative to the number of research personnel) may be misleading, for actually at the University of Texas a considerable amount has been invested in archeological research in terms of space and facilities. Instead of a well-balanced program, however, the emphasis to date at the University of Texas has been on furnishing a well-staffed and fully equipped research base. Well over half of the research personnel in Texas are located here, and considerable sums have recently been expended improving the already good basic laboratory facilities. However, an average of well under $1000 per man of operating funds is provided university staff members, a figure which seems generous only when compared to that available for archeological research at the other educational institutions. The theory evidently has been that given a good solid base, the contract funds will roll in, a theory which seems partly borne out in fact. However, the other side of the coin is that without adequate state funds for at least a few people the statewide research program can never be a cohesive well-rounded one. Personnel must work where there is contract money available rather than where they can make the most efficient use of their time measured in terms of the value of the scientific data obtained relative to time and funds invested. The archeologists at the other three state education isntitutions have only extremely limited time or funds at their disposal for research.

The establishment in September 1965 of the position of state archeologist attached to the State Building Commission (and now transferred to the Texas Historical Survey Committee), and the establishment of an Antiquities Committee in 1969 were major steps in correcting the state program's basic imbalance. The function of the state archeologist, in theory at least, is to develop the statewide overview, to inventory and evaluate the state's archeological resources, and to seek, acquire, preserve, and develop the most outstanding localities. This research should provide the specific data needed to enable the individual institutions to present a strong case for a better balanced attack on the total archeological problem. Should this approach succeed, Texas could find itself with one of the better programs of archeological research in the country. The hiring of an archeologist to handle archeological research on lands coming under the supervision of the State Parks and Wildlife Commission is another hopeful sign, as is the fact that the highway department has recently employed an archeologist to undertake highway salvage.

Archeological Legislation

Citation. Tex. Rev. Civ. Stat., Article 6145-9 (Supp. 1969). (See pages 220-230 for complete text.)

Principal Provisions. This act declares that it is a public policy and a public interest of the state to locate, protect, and preserve all sites, objects, buildings, pre-twentieth-century shipwrecks, and locations of historical, archeological, educational, and scientific interest located in, on or under any of the lands of the State of Texas, including the tidelands, submerged lands, and the bed of the sea within the state's jurisdiction. It creates an Antiquities Committee to be composed of seven members, namely, the director of the State Historical Survey Committee, the director of the State Parks and Wildlife Department, the commissioner of the General Land Office, the state archeologist, one professional archeologist from a recognized museum or institution of higher learning in Texas, one professional historian with experience in Texas history and culture, and the director of the Texas Memorial Museum at the University of Texas. Each of these is to be a resident of Texas and is to be appointed by the governor of Texas with the advice and consent of the state senate. The duties of this committee are to determine the site of and designate state archeological landmarks or to remove such designations, to contract or otherwise provide for the discovery and salvage operations covered under the act, to issue permits for such investigations, and to protect and preserve the archeological resources of the state. It is to be the legal custodian of all items recovered under the act.

The act declares that all sunken or abandoned pre-twentieth-century ships and their contents, and all sites, objects, buildings, artifacts, and locations of historical, archeological, scientific, or educational interest located on, in, or under state lands, including tidelands, submerged riverbeds, and sea bottoms which are owned by or within the jurisdiction of the State of Texas, are to be state archeological landmarks and as such may not be taken, altered, damaged, destroyed, salvaged, or excavated without a permit from the Antiquities Committee. A site on private land determined by a majority vote of the Antiquities Committee to be of sufficient importance also may be designated, with the landowner's written consent, a state archeological landmark, and such designation shall be recorded in the deed of the property. All such state archeological landmarks made by majority votes may have such designation removed if they are determined to be of no further historical, archeological, educational, or scientific value, and, if on private land, such notification shall also be recorded on the deed.

The Antiquities Committee may enter into contracts with qualified institutions or individuals for the discovery and salvage of treasure imbedded in the earth, sunken or abandoned ships or wrecks of the sea, parts thereof, and their contents. These contracts may provide for fair compensation of the salvager in terms of percentage of the reasonable cash value of the objects recovered or, at the discretion of the Antiquities Committee, a fair share of the objects recovered. The amount constituting a fair share is to be determined by the committee, and the reasonable cash value is to be determined by an expert appraisal or by representatives of the contracting parties. Violation of the contract by the salvager will result in termination of the contract, and superior title to all objects recovered is claimed by the State of Texas until they are released by the Antiquities Committee.

The Antiquities Committee may also issue permits for excavation or other investigation on state archeological landmarks, and these also may provide for the retention by the permittee of a portion of the materials recovered and for the termination of the permit if the terms are violated. All investigations carried out under permit will be done under the supervision of the Antiquities Committee, and the committee is the legal custodian of all antiquities recovered and is empowered to promulgate rules and regulations relative to this act.

The Antiquities Committee is authorized to expend monies available to it for the purchase of the salvager's share of recovered items which the committee has determined should remain the property of Texas. It may also accept funds from a third party with which to purchase such specimens with the proviso that the third party will receive the items purchased but must make them available for public viewing and must resell them to the Antiquities Committee at any time the committee should request at no change in price.

It is declared legal for the committee to restore antiquities for private individuals, but it shall be under the rules and regulations promulgated by the committee and all costs shall be paid by the private party. Forgery of archeological or other objects which derive value from their antiquity with the intent of misrepresenting them is declared illegal, as is intentionally defacing or vandalizing Indian pictographs or petroglyphs. Damaging archeological sites or damaging or removing archeological objects without the consent of the owner is forbidden.

The attorney general and any other citizen are specifically given power to take legal action under this act, and all administrative office and state agencies are authorized and directed to cooperate with and assist the Antiquities Committee. Law enforcement agencies and officers are also authorized and directed to assist.

Comments. This carefully thought-out law covers most of the standard situations as well as some special to Texas and other coastal states where salvaging of shipwrecks is a special problem. In this one aspect, there might be some legal complication with respect to any federally owned vessels for, though the State of Texas has claimed ownership of all pre-twentieth-century vessels, the federal government does not disclaim ownership of such vessels regardless of the time which has passed. One other area is not clear. Once the landowner has entered into an agreement with the Antiquities Committee for a site on his property to be designated as a landmark, has he given up all control of that site? This would seem to be indicated, for the act specifically spells out that only the Antiquities Committee can authorize work, any modification, or any excavation of such a landmark, and there is no proviso for the private landowner being an exception to this. If this is the case, this easement statute is unlike the Arkansas scientific easement statute, which specifies that the landowner and the state agency both have veto power over who does work at the site on the property.

The rules and regulations promulgated under the committee's authority are reasonably standard but adequate. It is reiterated that all objects remain state property, including copies of all field notes or other records, and publication is required.

UTAH

State-Supported Archeological Research Programs

Principal State Agencies Involved. (1) University of Utah, Department of Anthropology, Anthropology Museum, and Statewide Archaeology Survey, Salt Lake City, Utah 84112. (2) Utah State Park Board, Boulder, Utah 84716.

State Funds Allocated Annually for Research. Salaries equivalent to one or two archeologists plus approximately $5000, nearly all of which is specifically for work on highway rights-of-way.

Discussion. The director of archeological research at the university Department of Anthropology is also responsible for both the Statewide Archaeology Survey and the Anthropology Museum. These serve as the principal contracting agencies for federally and privately sponsored research and have some funds for conducting survey work and for publications. The curator of the museum devotes a major portion of his time to research. The archeologist attached to the State Park Board and stationed at Anasazi State Park carries out some archeological research at the state park.

Archeological Legislation

Citation. Utah Code Ann., Section 63-11-2 (1969).

Principal Provisions. Archeological excavation or exploration on state or federal land is prohibited without a permit from the Division of Parks and Recreation. The Board of Parks and Recreation Commission is authorized to promulgate for division enforcement appropriate regulations to protect ruins and relics. No archeological material may be removed from public lands (by implication this includes federal land) without permission of the division and the board, and they may require that a portion remain in the state. Violation invokes forfeiture as well as other penalties.

Comments. Except for the extension of the law to federal land, this law closely resembles the Idaho law. The desire to extend state control to federal lands in a state like Utah is understandable, but, even if this is adjudged constitutional, the law as it is presently worded would appear potentially to conflict with the federal statutes wherein exportation is not forbidden. Some states (for example, Montana) recognize this and make specific exemption for any conflicts with federal statutes. There are no legislative qualifications or other restrictions set forth with respect to whom permits may be granted.

VERMONT

State-Supported Archeological Research Programs

Principal State Agencies Involved. University of Vermont, Department of Sociology and Anthropology, 31 South Prospect Street, Burlington, Vermont 05401.

State Funds Allocated Annually for Research. None specifically allocated for this purpose.

Discussion. An archeologist of the Department of Sociology and Anthropology has been attempting since 1968 to collect data on sites in the state but without any specific state support. The Vermont Historical Society, which receives state appropriations, has done minor archeological work in the past but has no active program.

Archeological Legislation

None.

Comments. There is an act [Vt. Stat. Ann., Tit. 22, Chapter 7, Sections 341 through 346 (1961)] establishing a board to be concerned with historic sites and buildings which is authorized to cooperate with "State and local organization with similar objectives," but there has been no indication that any archeology has been included.

VIRGINIA

State-Supported Archeological Research Programs

Principal State Agencies Involved. (1) Virginia State Library, 1101 Capital

Square, Richmond, Virginia 23219. (2) Virginia Historic Landmarks, Ninth Street Office Building, Richmond, Virginia 25219.

State Funds Allocated Annually for Research. Salaries equivalent to one to two archeologists full time plus approximately $2000.

Discussion. Minor amounts of state funds are expended for the archeologically related activities of the Landmarks Commission and through the activities of an archeologist on the Virginia State Library staff. The latter individual coordinates most of the archeological activity in the state (the majority of which is privately funded or done by volunteers), and his office also has served as the contracting agent for federally sponsored programs.

Archeological Legislation

Citation. Va. Code Ann., Sections 10-135 through 10-145.1 (1966); Va. Code Ann., Sections 10-146 through 10-150 (1966).

Principal Provisions. The legislation creates in the Executive Department of the government the Landmarks Committee of nine members with the power (among others) to conduct a survey of state or nationally significant structures or sites, including archeological sites. Tax assessments shall be reduced for certified landmarks and historic districts. The commission may seek and obtain from landowners restrictions upon the use of certified landmarks. These shall be recorded on the deed and these too shall serve to reduce the tax assessment. The commission also has the power of eminent domain. Within the structure of the commission is a Research Center for Historical Archaeology (not yet funded) to be located at or near the College of William and Mary, with a commissioner of historical archaeology in charge. He and his staff are charged with carrying out research and providing educational training in the field.

Comments. This was an unusually prompt state reaction to the federal Historic Preservation Act and one which went beyond what that act requires in that it established an agency to take state initiative in carrying out archeological research at least in the area of historical archeology. Hopefully, this or some other means can be found to include all archeological research, and adequate funds will soon be made available to make the program effectively operative. A 1970 law to create a Science Museum of Virginia ultimately may provide an adequate state base for archeological research in Virginia.

WASHINGTON

State-Supported Archeological Research Programs

Principal State Agencies Involved. (1) University of Washington, Department of Anthropology, Seattle, Washington 98105. (2) Washington State University, Department of Anthropology, Pullman, Washington 99163.

State Funds Allocated Annually for Research. Salaries equivalent to five archeologists full time plus approximately $30,000.

Discussion. At least one person at each institution devotes full time to research. Both universities contract with the State Highway Department, and, in addition, limited university funds are available for research purposes.

Archeological Legislation

Citation. Wash. Rev. Code, Sections 27.44.00 through 27.44.020 (1964); Wash. Rev. Code, Section 27.48.010 (1964).

Principal Provisions. Willfully removing or injuring a cairn or grave or a glyptic or painted record of any prehistoric tribe is prohibited, unless the record from such shall be destined for exhibit or perpetual preservation in a recognized manner and permission has been granted by the president of the University of Washington or Washington State University or a designated faculty member.

The storage, preservation, and exhibit of (among other things) "artifacts and relics" is declared to be a public project for which public funds may be spent.

Comments. Perhaps this is adequate for what it covers, but it does not cover much.

WEST VIRGINIA

State-Supported Archeological Research Programs

Principal State Agencies Involved. West Virginia Geological Survey, Section of Archeology, Post Office Box 879, Morgantown, West Virginia 26505.

State Funds Allocated Annually for Research. The salaries of two archeologists plus from $3000 to $4000.

Discussion. Although the funds available seem unusually limited, it actually is very hard to determine any exact figure in this instance. The operation of the Section of Archaeology's research program is subsumed almost entirely under the general program and budget of the West Virginia Geological Survey. Funds and assistance are drawn not only from there but also from the Department of Welfare (labor) and the State Road Commission (for equipment, though no regular highway salvage program is in operation). The senior archeologist serves on the State Antiquities Commission. The work of the two archeologists is full-time research except for the normal administrative details attendant upon any such program, and a small amount of teaching by one of them.

Archeological Legislation

Citation. W. Va. Code Ann., Sections 5-12-1 through 5-12-5 (Supp. 1970).

Principal Provisions. This legislation creates a West Virginia Antiquities Commission of nine members: the chief of the Division of Parks and Recreation in the Department of Natural Resources, the state historian and archivist, the director of the State Geological and Economic Survey, the head of the Section of Archeology, the president of the West Virginia Historical Society, the president of the West Virginia Historical Association of College and University Teachers, and three representatives of the public at large who are appointed by the governor with the advice and consent of the state senate.

The commission meets at least twice a year and makes an annual report. It is empowered to locate and recommend for acquisition historical sites, to direct archeological research, to determine archeological needs and priorities, and to receive gifts, bequests, and funds in the name of the state. Archeological sites on state land, or on private land when investigation and development rights have been acquired by the state, shall not be disturbed except with the commission's permission. The West Virginia Antiquities Fund is created in which all monies appropriated for the purpose of the program are to be deposited.

The commission is authorized "to recommend the acquisition, development, and preservation of our State's historic archeological sites and treasures."

Comments. Though a basic intent has been shown and a beginning made, a fully funded program has not yet developed.

WISCONSIN

State-Supported Archeological Research Programs

Principal State Agencies Involved. (1) State Historical Society of Wisconsin,

Wisconsin Archaeological Survey and Anthropology Section of the Museum Division, 816 State Street, Madison, Wisconsin 53706. (2) University of Wisconsin, Department of Anthropology, Madison, Wisconsin 54306. (3) University of Wisconsin-Milwaukee, Department of Anthropology, Milwaukee, Wisconsin 53211.

State Funds Allocated Annually for Research, Salaries equivalent to approximately two archeologists full time plus an average of from $2000 to $5000 are provided, although this fluctuates considerably depending upon individual projects, in particular upon highway salvage work.

Discussion. Wisconsin, even earlier than Illinois, found it desirable to organize the archeologists working within the state into an incorporated body, the Wisconsin Archaeological Survey. The Survey is legally an affiliate of the Historical Society but, like Illinois, it is an organization of individuals, not of the institutions they represent. It is supported by contributions from those institutions, both general and in support of specific projects, rather than by any direct legislative action. Nominally, all field research in the state is done under the auspices of the Survey. It serves as the official consultant to state agencies. As a voluntary coordinating agent for what work is undertaken with state funds, the Survey apparently has served quite well.

The two universities do some research in Wisconsin with state funds on an individual basis but have no state research programs as such.

Wisconsin's highway salvage program has a long (since 1959) and successful history. They are able to survey all state and federally funded roads and carry out excavations as necessary.

Archeological Legislation
Citation. Wis. Stat. Ann., Section 27.012 (Supp. 1969).

Principal Provisions. The state reserves to itself the exclusive right of field archeology on state land; persons doing field archeology on private land are encouraged to abide by the provisions of the Wisconsin Field Archaeology Act; looting of all archeological remains is "strongly discouraged." Persons knowing of sites are requested to contact the state archeologist, but the act as a whole is not intended to burden people using state property for proper and lawful purposes.

Only the state archeologist (a professional archeologist residing in Wisconsin, appointed by the director of the State Historical Society of Wisconsin) or individuals licensed by the director of the State Historical Society may engage in field archeology on sites owned by the state. The state archeologist sponsors and engages in field work within the state, cooperates with other state agencies, encourages preservation of sites on private property, protects objects on state sites endangered by public construction, cooperates with the State Historical Society and public and private institutions of higher education in protecting and preserving archeological objects and data, encourages dissemination of data, approves permits for qualified persons, and otherwise carries out and enforces the act.

The director of the State Historical Society may give permits, which can include restriction to a specific site, to qualified persons approved by the state archeologist; permission must also be obtained from the state agency controlling the land (which cannot be denied without good cause). If the permit is requested for work on private land (strongly urged but not mandatory), there must be the written consent of the landowner. There are no fees. Normal procedure can be waived in an emergency. Permits may be revoked for good cause. Ownership of all objects is reserved to the state, but custodianship by others is permitted subject to revocation for good cause. All state agencies are to cooperate with the state archeologist. A board is established to review decisions of the director consisting of a member of the Wisconsin Archaeological Society, a member of the Wisconsin Archaeological Survey, and a member of the Board of Curators of the State Historical Society (each to be chosen by his own organization). This board shall submit its recommendations to the board of curators of the State Historical Society for final discussion. Property held in trust for purposes of preserving archeological sites for public use by nonprofit organizations may be exempt from real or personal property taxes if approved by the county board of the county concerned. It is prohibited to make falsely or to alter any object so that it appears to have value because of antiquity or to transfer such with intent to defraud.

Comments.   This law, like the Minnesota law, is one of an increasing number of thoughtfully worded attempts by states to provide maximum practical regulatory protection to a state's archeological resources. One interesting feature is that this law is worded so that permits to conduct field archeology cannot be issued to institutions but only to individuals. The provisions which permit tax relief for archeological sites held in public trust by nonprofit organizations are worthy of note, as is that allowing waiver of permit conditions in an emergency.

WYOMING

State-Supported Archeological Research Programs

Principal State Agencies Involved.   (1) University of Wyoming, Department of

Anthropology, Laramie, Wyoming 82070. (2) Wyoming Recreation Commission, Laramie, Wyoming 82070.

State Funds Allocated Annually for Research. An archeologist's summer salary and well under $1000 annually.

Discussion. Only a very limited amount of work is undertaken with funds made available from the departmental budget. The bulk of funds are obtained from outside grants. In 1967 a summertime position of state archeologist was established in the Recreation Commission (which falls within the the Executive Department) to be staffed by an archeologist at the university. Only limited maintenance funds have yet been available to the state archeologist, but through his efforts the highway department and large private companies are beginning to become concerned.

Archeological legislation

Citations. Wyo. Stat. Ann., Sections 36-11 through 36-13 (1959); Wyo. Stat. Ann., Section 36-44.6d (Supp. 1969).

Principal Provisions. A permit from the State Board of Land Commissioners is required prior to archeological investigation on state or federal land, and the board is authorized to promulgate rules for such investigation. No archeological material shall be removed from the state without the board's approval, and the board may require that a portion remain in the state.

The office of state archeologist is created with full responsibilities to carry out and publish archeological research and to cooperate with others in protecting the state's archeological resources.

EXAMPLES OF ARCHEOLOGICAL LEGISLATION

Examples of State and Local Archeological Legislation

ARIZONA

Arizona Antiquities Act of 1960

AN ACT Relating to Archaeological, Paleontological and Historical Features of This State; Providing for the Preservation of Antiquities Within Arizona; Amending Sections 41-771 and 41-772, Arizona Revised Statutes, and Amending Title 41, Chapter 4, Article 4, Arizona Revised Statutes, by Adding Sections 41-773 to 41-776, Inclusive.

41-771. Archaeological Discoveries: Restrictions as to Who May Explore

No person, except when acting as a duly authorized agent of an institution or corporation referred to in Section 41-772, shall excavate in or upon any historic or prehistoric ruin, burial ground, archaeological or vertebrate paleontological site, or site including fossilized footprints, inscriptions made by human agency, or any other archaeological, paleontological or historical feature, situated on lands owned or controlled by the State of Arizona, or any agency thereof.

41-772. Permits to Explore

A. Only educational institutions, public museums or nonprofit corporations organized for scientific and research purposes, may pursue any activity prescribed in Section 42-771.

B. No such activity may be undertaken until a permit is first secured therefor from the Director of the Arizona State Museum.

C. Permits shall be granted by the Director for such periods of time and under such regulations as he may from time to time determine to institutions or corporations, which are qualified to conduct such activities for the benefit of museums, universities, colleges, or other recognized scientific or educational institutions, or for the purpose of propagating the knowledge to be gained, and which shall undertake to preserve permanently all objects, photographs, and records in public repositories under their own supervision or control, or the supervision or control of other similar institutions or corporations.

41-773. Prohibiting Unnecessary Defacing of Site or Object

No person, institution, or corporation shall deface or otherwise alter any site or object embraced within the terms of sections 41-771 and 41-772, except in the course of activities pursued under the authority of a permit granted by the Director of the Arizona State Museum.

41-774. Duty to Report Discoveries

A person in charge of any survey, excavation, or construction on any lands owned or controlled by this state, by any public agency or institution of the state, or by any county or municipal corporation within the state shall report promptly to the Director of the Arizona State Museum the existence of any archaeological, paleontological, or historical site or object discovered in the course of such survey, excavation, or construction, and shall take all reasonable steps to secure its preservation.

41-775. Unlawful Reproduction of Original Archaeological Specimen

No person shall reproduce, retouch, rework, or forge any archaeological, paleontological, or historical object, deriving its principal value from its antiquity, or make any object, whether copied or not, or falsely label, describe, identify, or offer for sale or exchange any object, with intent to represent the same to be an original and genuine archaeological, paleontological, or historical specimen, nor shall any person offer for sale or exchange any object with knowledge that it has previously been collected or excavated in violation of any of the terms of this article.

41-776. Violation; Penalty

Any person, institution or corporation violating any provision of this article is guilty of a misdemeanor punishable by a fine not exceeding five hundred dollars or by imprisonment in the county jail for not to exceed six months, or both, and in addition, shall forfeit to the Arizona State Museum all articles and material discovered, collected, excavated, or offered for sale or exchange, together with all photographs and records relating to such objects.

Arizona State Museum Rule No. 1
Conditions upon Which Permits are Issued to Conduct Archaeological and Paleontological Work on State Lands in Arizona
Uniform Rules and Regulations

Prescribed by the Director of the Arizona State Museum to carry out the provisions of an act entitled "AN ACT Relating to Archaeological, Paleontological and Historical Features of This State; Providing for the Preservation of Antiquities Within Arizona: Amending Sections 41-771 and 41-772, Arizona Revised Statutes, and Amending Title 41, Chapter 4, Article 4, Arizona Revised Statutes, by Adding Section 41-773 to 41-776, Inclusive." (Laws of Arizona 1960, Ch. 38.)

1. Jurisdiction over ruins, archaeological sites, historic and prehistoric monuments and structures, objects of antiquity, historic landmarks, and other objects of historic or scientific interest, which occur on land owned or controlled by the State of Arizona, shall be exercised under Sec. 41-772 of the act by the Director of the Arizona State Museum.

2. No permit for the removal of any ancient monument or structure which can be permanently preserved under the control of the State of Arizona *in situ,* and remain an object of interest, shall be granted.

3. Permits for the examination of ruins, the excavation of archaeological sites, and the gathering of objects of antiquity will be granted, by the Director of the Arizona State Museum, to reputable museums, universities, colleges or other scientific or educational institutions, or to their duly authorized agents.

4. No exclusive permit shall be granted for a larger area than the applicant can reasonably be expected to explore fully and systematically within the time limit named in the permit.

5. Each application for a permit should be filed with the Director of the Arizona State Museum, and must be accompanied by a definite outline of the proposed work, indicating the name of the institution making the request, the date proposed for beginning the field work, the length of time proposed to be devoted to it, and the person who will have immediate charge of the work. The application must also contain an exact statement of the character of the work, whether examination, excavation, or gathering, and the public museum in which the collections made under the permit are to be permanently preserved. The application must be accompanied by a sketch plan or description of the

particular site or area to be examined, excavated, or searched, so definite that it can be located on the map with reasonable accuracy.

Uniform Rules and Regulations

6. No permit will be granted for a period of more than three years, but if the work has been diligently prosecuted under the permit, the time may be extended for proper cause upon application.

7. Failure to begin work under a permit within six months after it is granted, or failure to diligently prosecute such work after it has been begun, shall make the permit void without any order or proceeding by the Director of the Arizona State Museum.

8. Applications for permits in various areas of the state may be referred, respectively, to the Museum of Northern Arizona, the Heard Museum, Pueblo Grande Laboratory, the Amerind Foundation, or to such other organization as may be desirable, for recommendation.

9. Every permit shall be in writing and copies shall be transmitted to the regional institution concerned (of those named in paragraph 8 above) and to the state officer in charge of the land involved. The permittee will be furnished with a copy of these rules and regulations.

10. At the close of each season's field work the permittee shall make a typed report in duplicate to the Director of the Arizona State Museum, in such form as he may prescribe, and shall prepare in duplicate a catalogue of the collections and of the photographs made during the season, indicating therein such material, if any, as may be available for exchange.

11. Institutions and persons receiving permits for excavation shall, after completion of the work, restore the lands upon which they have worked to their customary condition, to the satisfaction of the state officer in charge.

12. All permits shall be terminable at the discretion of the Director of the Arizona State Museum.

13. An officer in charge of land owned or controlled by the State of Arizona may at all times examine the permit of any person or institution claiming privileges granted in accordance with the act and these rules and regulations, and may fully examine all work done under such permit. These prerogatives extend also to the Director of the Arizona State Museum and to his duly authorized representatives.

14. Any object of antiquity taken, or collection made, on lands owned or controlled by the State of Arizona, without a permit, as prescribed by the act and by these rules and regulations, or there taken or made, contrary to the rules and regulations, may be seized wherever found and at any time, by the proper state officer or by any person duly authorized by the Director of the Arizona State Museum, and disposed of as the Director of the Arizona State Museum shall determine, by deposit in the proper public depository in the State of Arizona or otherwise.

15. Every collection made under the authority of the act and these rules and regulations shall be preserved in the public museum designated in the permit and shall be accessible to the public. No such collection shall be removed from such public museum without the written authority of the Director of the Arizona State Museum, and then only to another public museum, where it shall be accessible to the public; and when any public museum, which is a depository of any collections made under the provisions of the act and these rules and regulations, shall cease to exist, every such collection in such public museum shall thereupon revert to the state collections and be placed in the depository within the State of Arizona designated by the Director of the Arizona State Museum.

ARKANSAS

Act 82 of 1959, Acts of Arkansas

AN ACT to Create an Arkansas Program of Archeological Research, and for Other Purposes.

WHEREAS, Arkansas is a State rich in archeological resources which, if properly excavated, catalogued and preserved, can add immeasurably to the knowledge of our history and our heritage; and

WHEREAS, the preservation of our antiquities is of value and interest not only to the citizens of Arkansas but to persons from other states who visit Arkansas as well; and

WHEREAS, many historic sites and archeological treasures are either unsurveyed and undiscovered, due to lack of a coordinated and adequate program, or are, in fact, in danger of being lost to posterity by reason of unscientific exploitation, highway construction, flooding from reservoirs in connection with building of dams, and by other means;

NOW THEREFORE, this legislative body recognizes the need for a state-wide program of archeological research and enacts this measure for the achievement of that purpose.

Be It Enacted by the General Assembly of the State of Arkansas:

SECTION 1. The Board of Trustees of the University of Arkansas is hereby designated agent of the State of Arkansas for the purpose of conducting a program of archeological research as hereinafter described.

SECTION 2. The University of Arkansas shall initiate, operate, and maintain a program in archeology which shall include, but not be limited to, the following areas of action:

(a) Excavation of historical sites, ruins, and mounds for the purpose of securing data and objects relating to early man in Arkansas;

(b) Fundamental research in Arkansas archeology and the encouragement of public cooperation in the preservation of Arkansas antiquities;

(c) Research in and study of anthropology, geology, and related social and physical sciences, both prior to excavation and thereafter in order to plan in aid of discovery of sites and artifacts and their proper assessment once discovered;

(d) Publication of findings in terms of their scientific, popular, and cultural values;

(e) Display and custodianship of relics, artifacts, sites and other tangible results of the program;

(f) Educational activities providing a stimulus to archeological efforts and the encouragement of archeological societies, parks, and museums.

SECTION 3. The University of Arkansas is to make available for study in connection with this program the holdings of its Museum which contains the world's best and most extensive collection of Arkansas archeological material, and the valuable collection of archeological and related literature held by its Library. Housing, in the nature of laboratory and office space, shall be assigned by the University for this activity, and the cooperation of University personnel in other related fields of activity shall be extended to the program herein created; provided, that the University of Arkansas' responsibility to initiate, operate, and continue to maintain an archeological program exceeding the scope of its present operations in that field shall be and is hereby made dependent upon the biennial appropriation of additional State funds (which amounts are now available to the University of Arkansas) for said purpose. All funds received from any source for this program shall be held by, expended by, and distributed through regular University of Arkansas · business channels, but used only in support of the activity herein described.

SECTION 4. All other state agencies, departments, and institutions, as well as county and city officials, are hereby directed to cooperate in the activities described in order that a State-wide focus shall be given the implementation of the program created by this measure.

SECTION 5. All artifacts, fossils, relics, and other personal property discovered, donated or otherwise acquired in pursuance of this program shall be the property of the State of Arkansas held in trust by the University of Arkansas. That institution shall to the extent possible make these items available for scientific use, or public display by appropriate public bodies at places throughout the State; provided, complete authority is hereby granted to exchange and barter such items, for other such items deemed of equal value, with persons, non-profit organizations, and public agencies both within and without Arkansas, in order that representative collections may be assembled and that study and analysis be enhanced.

SECTION 6. In recognition of the fact that archeological materials and antiquities are destroyed or damaged in connection with the construction of public works such as highways and dams, the program created hereby shall include salvage work in advance of or co-existent with public construction, and advice directed to the avoidance of waste of archeological sites and materials. Authority is hereby granted to the University of Arkansas to cooperate with individuals and State and federal agencies in surveying and excavating archeological sites, and full power to contract with such persons or agencies relative to these matters is hereby extended.

SECTION 7. The State Highway Commission is hereby authorized and directed to enter into appropriate contracts and cooperative agreements with the University of Arkansas and the U. S. Bureau of Public Roads and to expend funds, both State and Federal, in aid of archeological salvage and archeological preservation on all or any part of the lands and rights of way now or hereafter coming into its control in order that the beneficial purposes of this Act shall be achieved.

SECTION 8. The Board of Trustees of the University of Arkansas is hereby authorized to accept grants, bequests, devises, gifts, and donations for purposes of a State program in archeological research and to expend same to that end. Its full power to accept and hold title to interests in land for said purposes is hereby recognized. Said Board is hereby empowered to make a reasonable charge for publications and expend the proceeds for this program.

SECTION 9. All laws and parts of laws in conflict herewith are hereby repealed.

SECTION 10. It is hereby determined by the General Assembly that archeological materials, sites, mounds, and relics are being lost through thoughtless destruction by untrained excavators as well as through the construction of public dams and highways; that early preventive action is required and that immediate educational efforts should be made in order that the heritage of an earlier age not be lost; that a comprehensive State program of archeology will result in findings which will be of interest and value not only to the citizens of this State but to those who visit Arkansas as well; that the best method of accomplishing these objectives and preventing the losses referred to is by creation of a State program of archeological research. Therefore, an emergency is hereby declared to exist and this Act being necessary for the preservation of the public peace, health, safety, and welfare shall be in full force and effect from and after its passage and approval.

Act 39 of 1967, Acts of Arkansas

AN ACT to Designate the Program of Archeological Research and Discovery Provided for in Act 82 of 1959 as the Arkansas Archeological Survey; to Implement and Expand Said Program by Providing for the Appointment of a Director of the Survey and a State Archeologist; to Prescribe a Procedure whereby Any Public Institution of Higher Learning in Arkansas May Participate in the Program; to Authorize the Survey to Mutually Assist and Cooperate with the Arkansas Archeological Society in Furthering the Purposes of Public Archeological Education; and for Other Purposes.

Be It Enacted by the General Assembly of the State of Arkansas:

SECTION 1. The Program of archeological research and discovery being carried on under the supervision of the Board of Trustees of the University of Arkansas pursuant to the provisions of Act 82 of 1959, shall be continued pursuant to and in accordance with the provisions of said Act 82 of 1959, and the provisions of this Act, and said program is hereby designated and shall hereafter be referred to as the Arkansas Archeological Survey. The Board of Trustees of the University of Arkansas shall continue to be the administrative agent for the Survey, and the purposes and aims of the Survey shall continue to be as set forth in Act 82, but it is the specific intent of this Act to enlarge and broaden the program and to authorize and encourage all public institutions of higher learning in Arkansas to participate therein in the manner provided herein.

SECTION 2. The Board of Trustees of the University of Arkansas shall appoint a Director of the Arkansas Archeological Survey from the Anthropologists on the staff of the University who shall be responsible for the over-all administration and coordination of the Survey, and who shall serve at the pleasure of the Board of Trustees of the University. The Director shall perform these duties and any others as may be set by the Board of Trustees of the University of Arkansas and not from funds appropriated for the Arkansas Archeological Survey.

The Board of Trustees of the University of Arkansas shall appoint a State Archeologist who shall have a Doctor of Philosophy Degree in Anthropology, or the equivalent in training and experience, and such other full or part time employees as may be required to carry on the program, all of whom shall possess such qualifications as may be prescribed by the Board of Trustees. The State Archeologist shall be a full-time employee of the Survey and he and all other full or part-time employees of the Survey, except the Director, shall receive compensation not to exceed the maximum authorized for each position by the General Assembly from funds appropriated for the Survey. Funds appropriated for the Arkansas Archeological Survey shall be by specific appropriation separate and distinct from funds appropriated for the University of Arkansas, and shall be used exclusively for the purposes of the Survey. All expenditures of funds appropriated for the Arkansas Archeological Survey shall be made in accordance with and subject to the State purchasing laws, the State travel laws and regulations, and other laws and regulations applicable thereto.

SECTION 3. The Arkansas Archeological Survey shall initiate, operate, and maintain a program in archeology which shall include, but not be limited to, the following areas of action:

(a) Excavation of historical sites, ruins, and mounds for the purpose of securing data and objects relating to early man in Arkansas;

(b) Fundamental research in Arkansas archeology and encouragement of public cooperation in the preservation of Arkansas antiquities;

(c) Research in and study of anthropology, geology, and related social and physical sciences, both prior to excavation and thereafter in order to plan and aid in discovery of sites and artifacts and their proper assessment once discovered;

(d) Publication of findings in terms of their scientific, popular, and cultural values;

(e) Display and custodianship of relics, artifacts, sites and other tangible results of the program;

(f) Educational activities providing a stimulus to archeological efforts and the encouragement of archeological societies, parks, and museums.

SECTION 4. All public institutions of higher learning in Arkansas desiring to participate in the program provided for in Act 82 of 1959, and this Act, may contract with the University of Arkansas for Survey archeologists to be assigned to and in residence at the contracting institutions. Any such institutions desiring to be assigned a Survey archeologist in residence at the institution shall agree to provide the University under contract an amount not less that the equivalent of twenty-five percent (25%) of the salary of the archeologist upon a nine (9) month basis, and when such contract is entered into by the University of Arkansas and a cooperating institution, the Survey archeologist may be assigned to and based at the cooperating institution for the contract period which shall normally be twelve (12) months unless a shorter period is provided in the contract. During the portion of the Survey archelogist's time contracted for by a cooperating institution, he may perform research, teaching, or other related functions as may be directed by the cooperating institution in accordance with the terms of the contract, provided such other functions shall not be such as to interfere with the effective performance of his duties as a Survey archeologist.

The University of Arkansas shall ·enter into contracts with cooperating institutions for the assignment of Survey personnel to the extent that such assignments are consistent with the purposes and aims of the Survey, and insofar as funds and personnel permit such contracts to be made or renewed.

SECTION 5. The Arkansas Archeological Survey shall serve as the repository for copies of all archeological field notes, photographs, publications, or other records obtained through the use of State funds by whatever agency. All archeological objects found through the efforts of the Survey shall be deposited at the University of Arkansas Museum, provided, archeological objects obtained by Survey archeologists while under contract to and assigned to a cooperating institution may, upon request of the cooperating institution, be assigned to the custody of such institution if appropriate and adequate safeguards are provided.

SECTION 6. The Arkansas Archeological Survey shall hold title to and have primary responsibility for all archeological objects and materials obtained pursuant to this program, or otherwise accruing to the Survey and it shall be the responsibility of the Director of the Survey to see that all archeological material is properly and adequately safeguarded, and available at all reasonable times to interested scientists, and to the public insofar as funds and good scientific practices permit. The Director of the Survey may, whenever it is consistent with good scientific practices and in the furtherance of the aims and purposes of the Survey as stated in this Act and Act 82 of 1959, approve of and permit the loan of such objects and materials to a state museum in Arkansas, to educational or scientific institutions or organizations, or other institutions or organizations for purposes of research or public education.

SECTION 7. The University of Arkansas and cooperating institutions shall provide appropriate housing to the extent that it is available in the nature of laboratory and office space for Arkansas Archeological Survey personnel without cost to the Survey, and said personnel shall be deemed employees of the University of Arkansas.

SECTION 8. The Arkansas Archeological Survey is hereby authorized to assist and support the programs of the Arkansas Archeological Society to the extent that the purposes and aims of the two coincide.

SECTION 9. The Arkansas Archeological Society is hereby requested to annually review and evaluate the programs and activities of the Arkansas Archeological Survey and to provide written reports of such evaluation to the Director of the Survey, each state-supported institution of higher learning and such other interested institutions and agencies that may request the same.

SECTION 10. The provisions of this Act shall be supplemental to Act 82 of the General Assembly of Arkansas of 1959, and shall not repeal or modify any provisions of said Act 82 except as specifically provided herein.

SECTION 11. In the event that any provisions of this Act are declared unconstitutional, or the applicability thereof to any person or circumstances is held invalid, the constitutionality of the remainder of this Act and applicability thereof to other persons and circumstances shall not be affected.

Act 58 of 1967, Acts of Arkansas

AN ACT for the Protection and Preservation of Arkansas' Archeological Heritage, its Antiquities, Artifacts and Sites, and for Other Purposes.

WHEREAS, the public has an interest in preservation of all antiquities, historic ruins, sites, artifacts, and similar places and things for their scientific and historical information and value; and

WHEREAS, the public has a right to the knowledge to be derived and gained from a scientific study of these materials; and

WHEREAS, the most recent past has seen the neglect, desecration and destruction of sites and the removal without adequate records of archeological objects and artifacts with a resulting loss to our people of knowledge concerning their heritage; and

WHEREAS, prehistoric and historic remains, sites, and objects of antiquity are rightfully and properly the subject of coordinated and organized activities exercised on behalf of the general welfare of the public as a whole in order that they may be preserved, studied, exhibited, and evaluated;

NOW, THEREFORE

Be It Enacted by the General Assembly of the State of Arkansas:

SECTION 1. Definitions: As used in this Act, the words hereinafter set forth shall be defined as follows:

A. Artifacts: All relics, specimens, or objects of an historical, prehistorical, archeological or anthropological nature, which may be found above or below the surface of the earth, and which have scientific or historic value as objects of antiquity, as aboriginal relics, or as archeological specimens.

B. Site: All aboriginal mounds, forts, earthworks, village locations, burial grounds, historic or prehistoric ruins, mines or caves, which are or may be the source of artifacts; or any place where individual artifacts, defined herein, may be found.

C. Field Archeology: The study of the traces of human culture at any land or water site by means of surveying, digging, sampling, excavating, or removing sub-surface objects, or going on a site with that intent.

SECTION 2. Legislative Intent: The State of Arkansas reserves to itself the exclusive right and privilege of field archeology on sites owned or controlled by the State, its agencies, departments, and institutions, in order to protect and preserve archeological and scientific information, matter, and objects. All such information and objects deriving from State lands shall be utilized solely for scientific or public educational purposes and shall remain the property of the State.

It is a declaration and statement of legislative intent that field archeology on privately owned lands should be discouraged except in accordance with both the provisions and spirit of this Act; and persons having knowledge of the location of archeological sites are encouraged to communicate such information to the Arkansas Archeological Survey.

SECTION 3. Cooperation by State Agencies and Other Governmental Subdivisions: All State agencies, departments, institutions, and commissions, as well as all counties and municipalities, shall cooperate fully with the Arkansas Archeological Survey in the preservation, protection, excavation, and evaluation of artifacts and sites; and to that end, where any site or artifacts may be found or discovered on property owned or controlled by the State or by any county or municipality, the agency, bureau, commission, governmental subdivision, or county or municipality, having control over or owning such property or preparing to excavate or perform work upon such property or currently performing work of any type upon such property is urged to notify the Arkansas Archeological Survey of the discovery and location of such site or artifacts and shall cooperate to the fullest extent practicable with the Arkansas Archeological Survey to preserve and prevent the destruction of such site or artifacts and to allow the Arkansas Archeological Survey to assist in and effect the removal of such artifacts by means designed to preserve and permit the study and evaluation of such artifacts; and the provisions of this Act shall be made known to contractors by the State agencies doing the contracting.

SECTION 4. Landmarks: An archeological site of significance to the scientific study or public representation of Arkansas aboriginal past may be publicly designated by the Arkansas Archeological Survey as a "State Archeological Landmark" provided that no sites shall be so designated without the express written consent of the State agency having jurisdiction over the land in question or, if it is on privately owned land, of the owner thereof. Once so designated excavation for the purpose of recovery or the recovery of artifacts from such sites by persons other than the Arkansas Archeological Survey or their duly designated agents shall be a misdemeanor.

SECTION 5. Reservation from Sale of State Lands of Archeological Importance: Upon written notice to the Commissioner of State Lands given by the Arkansas Archeological Survey, the Commissioner of State Lands shall reserve from sale any State lands, including lands forfeited to the State for non-payment of taxes, on which sites or artifacts are located or may be found, as designated by the Arkansas Archeological Survey; provided, however, that the reservation of such lands from sale may be confined to the actual location of the site or artifacts. When such sites or artifacts have been explored, excavated or otherwise examined to the extent desired by the Arkansas Archeological Survey, said Survey shall then file with the Commissioner a statement releasing such lands and permitting the sale of same.

SECTION 6. Trespass: It shall be deemed an act of trespass and misdemeanor for any person, natural or corporate, to remove artifacts and antiquities of the kind described herein from the private land of any owner thereof without his permission being first obtained.

SECTION 7. Vandalism: In order that sites and artifacts on state owned or controlled land shall be protected for the benefit of the public, it is hereby made a misdemeanor for any person, natural or corporate, to write upon, carve upon, paint, deface, mutilate, destroy, or otherwise injure any objects of antiquity, artifacts, Indian painting, or sites and all such acts of vandalism shall be punished as misdemeanors according to the provisions of this Act.

SECTION 8. Violations: All acts expressly declared herein to be illegal, prohibited, or deemed misdemeanors shall, upon conviction of the person for engaging in the conduct thus prescribed, be punished as misdemeanors and the person guilty thereof shall be fined not less than fifty dollars ($50.00) nor more than five hundred dollars ($500.00) or imprisoned in the city or county jail for not less than one month or more than six months or both. It is hereby made the duty of the Prosecuting Attorney for the district wherein the offense is committed to prosecute alleged offenders to the full extent of the law.

SECTION 9. Severability: If any provision of this Act or the application thereof to any person or circumstance is held invalid, such invalidity shall not affect other provisions or applications of the Act which can be given effect without the invalid provisions or application and to this end the provisions of this Act are declared to be severable.

HAWAII

Relating to Historic & Archaeological Sites and Permits to Examine and Excavate Ruins Thereon, Pursuant to Act 254, Session Laws of Hawaii 1967 and Section 14-10.2, 14-10.3, Chap. 276, Revised Laws of Hawaii 1955

SECTION 1. These rules and regulations are intended to implement Act 254, Session Laws of Hawaii 1967 and Section 14-10.2, 14-10.3, and Chapter 276 Revised Laws of Hawaii 1955, for the detailed and efficient control and administration over historic and archaeological sites, ruins, historic and prehistoric monuments and structures, object of antiquity, historic landmarks, and other objects of historical or scientific interest situated on public lands owned or controlled by the State of Hawaii.

SECTION 2. As used in this regulation:

"State" shall mean the State of Hawaii.

"Department" shall mean the Department of Land and Natural Resources, State of Hawaii.

"Board" shall mean the Board of Land and Natural Resources, State of Hawaii.

"Chairman" shall mean the Chairman of the Board of Land and Natural Resources, State of Hawaii, or his authorized representatives.

"Division" shall mean the Division of State Parks, Department of Land and Natural Resources, State of Hawaii.

"Director" shall mean the Director of the Division of State Parks, Department of Land and Natural Resources, State of Hawaii, or his authorized representatives.

"Permittee"—a museum, university, college or other recognized scientific or education institutions to which a permit is issued, its representative, agent, servant or employee.

SECTION 3. No permit for the removal of any ancient monument or structure which can be permanently preserved under the control of the State *in situ* and remain an object of interest shall be granted.

SECTION 4. Permits for the examination of ruins, the excavation of archaeological sites, the gathering of objects of antiquity or for statewide survey, reconnaissance and emergency excavations may be granted by the Board to reputable museums, universities, colleges or other recognized scientific or educational institutions.

SECTION 5. No such activity shall be undertaken until a permit is first secured from the Board.

SECTION 6. No permit for excavation shall be granted for a larger area than the applicant can reasonably be expected to explore fully and systematically within the time limit named in the permit.

SECTION 7. Each application for a permit shall be made on the form furnished by the Department and must be accompanied by a definite outline of the proposed work, the name of the institution making the request, the data proposed for commencement of the field work, the length of time proposed to be devoted to it and the person who will have immediate charge of the work. The application must also contain an exact statement of the character of the work, whether examination, excavation or gathering of objects, and the museum or institution in which the collections made under the permit are to be permanently preserved. Applications for permits shall be referred to the Director for recommendations. Names and addresses of any supervisory staff members not included on the application form shall be furnished to the Department upon their addition.

SECTION 8. Permits shall be on a month-to-month basis and shall not extend for a period of more than one year from the date of issuance, provided, however, that a permit may be renewed for such additional period beyond one year as the Board may for good cause allow.

SECTION 9. Permits shall be subject to the following terms and conditions:

a. Permits shall be revocable at any time at the discretion of the Board, upon delivery of notification in writing to the permittee of such revocation.

b. Failure to commence work under the permit within six (6) months after it is granted or failure to diligently prosecute such work after it has been begun, shall automatically terminate the permit.

c. Every field representative of a permittee shall carry an I.D. card bearing his photo on his person at all times and shall produce the same for inspection upon request by the Director.

d. The permittee shall mark all field vehicles and campsites within the permitted areas with signs reading as follows: "Archaeological Field Work under State of Hawaii Permit No. ____." Such signs may be obtained from the Division and shall be installed by the permittee prior to the commencement of any field study called for under the permit.

e. The use and enjoyment of the permitted areas shall not be in support of any policy which discriminates against anyone based upon race, creed, color or national origin.

f. The permittee shall not commit, suffer and permit to be committed any waster, nuisance, strip or unlawful, improper and offensive use of the permitted areas, or any part thereof.

g. The permittee shall comply with all the requirements of all municipal, state and federal authorities and observe all municipal, state and federal statutes pertaining to the said premises, now in force or which may hereinafter be in force.

h. The State shall not be liable at any time for any damage or injury to persons or property which may arise by reason of the use and occupancy of the permitted areas, or the carelessness, negligence or improper conduct of the permittee, its representatives, agents, employees or licensees.

i. The permittee shall at the expiration or sooner termination of a permit peaceably and quietly surrender and deliver possession of the permitted areas to the State, in good order and condition to the satisfaction of the Director.

j. Prior to the commencement of any activity within a permitted area, the permittee shall notify the Director of the commencement date of such contemplated activity and the estimated time of completion.

SECTION 10. The permittee shall submit the following reports to the Director at such times as hereinafter mentioned:

a. Project report within two (2) weeks after completion of a survey, reconnaissance or emergency salvage excavation.

b. Project report, in duplicate, to be filed quarterly on the progress of work, except in the case of a survey for exploration and examination.

c. Preliminary project report, in duplicate, within six (6) weeks after the completion of field work.

d. Final project report, in duplicate, within one (1) year after the expiration date of the permit.

e. Three copies of the publication of the project within six (6) months after the filing date of the final report. If no publication is forthcoming within said six (6) months period, the State shall have the right to publish the same.

SECTION 11. A permittee shall report promptly to the Director of the existence of ruins and archaeological sites, historic or prehistoric ruins or monuments, objects of antiquity, historic landmarks, historic and prehistoric structures and other objects of historic and scientific interest discovered in the course of any survey, excavation, reconnaissance or construction and shall take all reasonable steps to secure its preservation.

SECTION 12. Disinterment of human remains shall be made in accordance with the provisions of Chapter 276, Revised Laws of Hawaii 1955, the violation of which shall subject the person so offending to a fine of not more than $1,000.00 or imprisonment at hard labor of not more than two years.

SECTION 13. Every collection, together with the original field notes, records and photographs pertaining thereto, made under authority of law and these rules and regulations shall be preserved in the museum or institution designated in the permit and shall be accessible to all qualified persons.

SECTION 14. Any person who appropriates, excavates, injures, or destroys any historic or prehistoric ruin or monument, or any object of antiquity, situated on lands owned or controlled by the State of Hawaii, without the permission of the Board of Land and Natural Resources shall be fined not more than $500.00 or imprisoned not more than ninety (90) days or both, and in addition, shall forfeit to the State of Hawaii all articles and material discovered, collected, excavated or offered for sale or exchange, together with all photographs and records relating to such objects.

Hawaii Act 216 of 1969

A BILL FOR AN ACT Relating to the Preservation and Protection of Prehistoric and Historic Sites and Archeological Remains. *Be It Enacted by the Legislature of the State of Hawaii:*

SECTION 1. Chapter 9 of the Revised Laws of Hawaii 1955 is amended by adding a new section to read as follows;

"Sec. 9- . *Archeological investigation, recording and salvage; appropriations.* Whenever any public construction or improvement of any nature whatsoever is undertaken by any government agency on lands which are controlled or owned by the State or by any county and which are sites of historic or prehistoric interest and value, or locations of prehistoric or historic remains, one per cent of the appropriations for such public construction or improvement, or so much thereof as may be necessary, shall be expended by the department of land and natural resources for the archeological investigation, recording and salvage of such sites or remains when it is deemed necessary by the department."

SECTION 2. Section 14-8 of the Revised Laws of Hawaii 1955 is amended to read as follows:

"Sec. 14-8. *Prehistoric and historic sites and remains.*

(a) The department of land and natural resources shall locate, identify, and preserve in suitable records information regarding prehistoric and historic sites, locations, and remains. The information shall be submitted to the director of taxation who shall clearly designate on all tax maps of the State, the location of all prehistoric or historic sites, or locations and remains. The department shall cooperate with other state agencies and owners of private prehistoric or historic sites.

(b) Before any public construction or improvement of any nature whatsoever is undertaken by the State, the city and county of Honolulu, or any of the counties, or any governmental agency or officer, the head of such agency or such officer shall first examine the current tax map of the area to be affected by such public construction or improvement to determine whether any heiaus, ancient burial places, or sites, or remains of prehistorical or historical interest are designated on such map. If so designated, the proposed public construction or improvement shall not be commenced, or, in the event it has already begun, continued, until the head of such agency or such other officer shall have advised the department of the proposed public construction or improvement and shall have secured the concurrence of the department or, as hereafter provided, shall have secured the written approval of the governor.

If the concurrence of the department is not obtained after ninety days after the filing of a request therefor with the department by, or after the filing of a notice of objections by the department with, the agency or officer seeking to proceed with any project, such agency or officer may apply to the governor for permission to proceed notwithstanding the nonconcurrence of the department and the governor may take such action as he deems best in overruling or sustaining the department.

(c) Before any construction, alteration, or improvement of any nature whatsoever is undertaken or commenced on a designated private prehistoric or historic site by any person, he shall give to the department three months notice of intention to construct, alter, or improve the site.

After the expiration of the three-month notification period, the department shall either commence condemnation proceedings for the purchase of the site or remains, permit the owner to proceed with his construction, alteration or improvement, or undertake or permit the recording and salvaging of any historical information deemed necessary to preserve Hawaiian history, by any qualified agency for this purpose.

Any person who violates the provisions of the first paragraph of this subsection shall be fined not more than $1,000 or imprisoned not more than ninety days, or both."

SECTION 3. Chapter 14 of the Revised Laws of Hawaii is amended by adding a new section to read as follows:

"Sec. 14-8.5. *Excavation and removal of prehistoric and historic remains on private lands.* Before any prehistoric or historic remains are excavated or removed from private lands by the department of land and natural resources, the department or its designated investigators shall first secure the written approval of the owner of such lands. Whenever the value of the private prehistoric or historic site is diminished by the excavation or removal of prehistoric or historic remains by the department of land and natural resources, the owner of the site shall be compensated for the loss, at a monetary sum mutually agreed upon by the department and the owner or at a monetary sum set by the court."

SECTION 4. Section 14-10.2 of the Revised Laws of Hawaii 1955 is amended to read as follows:

"Sec. 14.10.2. *Permits to examine ruins, excavate and gather objects on public lands.* Permits for the examination of ruins, excavation of archeological sites, and the gathering of objects of antiquity upon lands owned or controlled by the state or any county, may be granted by the department of land and natural resources to persons or institutions which they deem properly qualified to conduct such examination, excavation, or gathering, subject to such rules and regulations as the department may prescribe; provided, that the examination, excavations, and gatherings are undertaken for the benefit of public museums, universities, colleges, or other recognized public scientific or educational institutions, with a view to increasing the knowledge of such objects and that the gatherings may be made for permanent preservation in public museums if so deemed by the department."

SECTION 5. Section 14-10.3 of the Revised Laws of Hawaii 1955 is amended to read as follows:

"Sec. 14-10.3. *Penalties.* It shall be unlawful for any person to take, appropriate, excavate, injure or destroy any prehistoric or historic ruin or monument or object of antiquity, situated on lands owned or controlled by the State without the permission of the department of land and natural resources. Any person who violates this section shall be fined not more than $1,000 or imprisoned not more than ninety days, or both.

Any prehistorical and historical objects and remains which have been taken without a permit shall be seized, deposited and preserved in public museums by the department of land and natural resources."

SECTION 6. Chapter 14 of the Revised Laws of Hawaii 1955 is amended by adding a new section to read as follows:

"Sec. 14- . *Reproduction of prehistorical or historical objects; representation as originals; penalties.* It shall be unlawful to reproduce or forge a prehistorical or historical object with the intent to represent it as an original. Any person who violates this section shall be fined not more than $1,000 or imprisoned not more than ninety days, or both."

SECTION 7. Chapter 99 of the Revised Laws of Hawaii is amended by adding a new section to read as follows:

"Sec. 99- . *Reservation of rights to prehistoric and historic remains on leased public lands.* The board of land and natural resources shall, in leases of public lands retain the rights to all prehistoric and historic remains found on such lands."

SECTION 8. The Revisor of Statutes may reword and renumber the references in this Act and make such other formal or verbal changes as may be necessary to conform with the Hawaii Revised Statutes.

SECTION 9. This Act shall take effect upon its approval.

Hawaii Act 236 of 1969

A BILL FOR AN ACT Relating to the Establishment of a Non-Profit Corporate Foundation Enabling Acceptance of Funds and Gifts

Be It Enacted by the Legislature of the State of Hawaii:

SECTION 1. *Statement of Purpose.* The purpose of this Act is to create a non-profit corporation for historic preservation, restoration, presentation, museum activities, and support programs; and in cooperation with and in assistance to the department of land and natural resources and other state agencies to receive sites, buildings, and objects significant in Hawaii's history and culture, to preserve and administer them for public benefit; to accept, hold, and administer gifts, securities, grants, scholarships, endowments, private bequests or other property of whatsoever character for a comprehensive historical preservation and/or museum's program.

This agency shall be the depository of all resources which are made available or offered of desirable land, historical collections, and donations made by groups and persons as gifts to the state to help insure the Hawaiian heritage.

SECTION 2. *Establishment of the Hawaii Foundation for History and the Humanities; board of trustees.* There is hereby created an educational, non-profit corporation to be known as the Hawaii Foundation for History and the Humanities which shall be headed by a board of trustees.

The board shall consist of fifteen (15) members of which the following shall serve as ex officio voting members of the board:

(1) President of the University of Hawaii,
(2) Chairman of the board of land and natural resources,
(3) Director of planning and economic development,
(4) Chairman of the state foundation on culture and arts.

The remaining members shall be chosen by the members of the Hawaii Foundation from its membership at any regular meeting of the Hawaii Foundation except that the initial members of the Board shall be appointed by the Governor of Hawaii. Each member of the Board other than ex officio members shall serve for a term of five years from the expiration of his predecessor's term, except that the members first appointed shall serve for terms of from one to five years as designated by the Governor at the time of appointment.

A vacancy in the Board shall be filled for the balance of the unexpired term as prescribed in the rules and regulations of the Foundation. The Chairman of the Board shall be elected by a majority vote of the members of the Board. No compensation shall be paid to members of the Board of Trustees for their services as such members, but they may be reimbursed for travel and actual and reasonable expenses necessarily incurred by them in attending Board meetings and performing other official duties on behalf of the Hawaii Foundation at the direction of the Board.

Membership shall be open to any resident of Hawaii upon payment of such reasonable fees as the board of trustees may prescribe.

SECTION 3. *Powers and duties.* The Hawaii Foundation for History and the Humanities shall have the following powers and duties:

(1) to have succession until dissolved by Act of the Hawaii State Legislature, in which event title to the properties of the Hawaii Foundation, both real and personal, shall, insofar as consistent with existing contractual obligations and subject to all other legally enforceable claims or demands by or against the Hawaii Foundation, pass to and become vested in the State of Hawaii;

(2) to sue or be sued in its corporate name;

(3) to adopt, alter, and use a corporate seal;

(4) to adopt a constitution and to make such bylaws, rules and regulations, not inconsistent with the laws of the State of Hawaii, as it deems necessary for the administration of its functions, including among other matter, bylaws, rules and regulations governing visitation to historic properties, museums and other facilities under its control, administration of corporate funds, and the organization and procedure of the Board of Trustees.

(5) to accept, hold and administer funds and properties from private or governmental agencies for the purposes for which the Hawaii Foundation is created and in accordance with such conditions as the transferring agency or the legislature may prescribe under the law.

(6) to accept, hold, and administer gifts and bequests of money, securities, or other personal property of whatsoever character, in trust, for the purposes for which the Hawaii Foundation is created. Unless otherwise restricted by the terms of the bequest of gift, the Hawaii Foundation is authorized to sell, exchange, or otherwise dispose of, and to invest or reinvest in such investments as it may determine from time to time the moneys, securities, or other property given or bequeathed to it. The principal of such corporate funds, together with the income therefrom and all other revenues received by it from any source whatsoever, shall be placed in such depositories as the Hawaii Foundation shall determine and shall be subject to expenditure by the Hawaii Foundation for its corporate purposes;

(7) to acquire by gift, devise, purchase, and to hold in trust real property for the state and for the people of Hawaii unless otherwise restricted by the terms of the gift or devise, to encumber, convey, or otherwise dispose of any real property, or any estate or interest therein with the exception that no designated historic site or monument may be encumbered, conveyed, or disposed of without Legislative approval, as may be necessary and proper in carrying into effect the purposes of the Hawaii Foundation;

(8) to conduct research, studies and investigations in the fields of history and the humanities, and to make, publish, and distribute the results thereof;

(9) to coordinate and correlate activities and projects of the Hawaii Foundation with the work of the University of Hawaii, the department of land and natural resources, the Hawaii Foundation on Culture and the Arts and other state agencies to further the purposes of this Act;

(10) to review the work of the department of land and natural resources and

to collaborate with it on its functions under chapter 6, Hawaii Revised Statutes, pertaining to historical objects and sites, and to review such surveys and historic preservation plans as may be required, and to approve properties for nomination to the National Register as provided for in the Historic Preservation Act of 1966, Public Law 89-665;

(11) to enter into contracts and to execute all instruments necessary and appropriate to carry out the purposes of the foundation;

(12) to designate particular places, as places of historic interest, and to take such action, including erection of a sign or marker, as may be appropriate for public recognition and appreciation of such site;

(13) to approve all designations of particular places as places of historical interest.

SECTION 4. *Development of Support Programs.* The Hawaii Foundation shall develop a continuing comprehensive museum and museum activities support program which shall include, but not be limited to:

(1) providing matching grants-in-aid to governmental or private agencies for projects which fulfill the purposes of this Act;

(2) providing technical assistance and staff development and training opportunities: and

(3) assisting in the training of competent museum personnel and in the development of employment and career opportunities in museum and related fields.

SECTION 5. *Annual report.* The Hawaii Foundation for History and the Humanities shall submit an annual report to the governor, the state senate, and the state house of representatives. The report shall include, but not be limited to, the total number and amount of gifts received, payroll disbursements, contracts entered into, and progress and accomplishments made during the year.

SECTION 6. *Creation of state trust for historic preservation.* The Hawaii Foundation for History and the Humanities shall in cooperation with the State Foundation on Culture and the Arts develop a plan for creation of a state trust for historic preservation, the purpose of which will be to provide coordination of the efforts of both foundations in the field of history, and shall present such plan to the legislature at its next session.

SECTION 7. This Act shall take effect upon its approval.

MINNESOTA

The Minnesota Field Archaeology Act of 1963

AN ACT Relating to Field Archaeology and Providing Penalties for Violations thereof; Repealing Minnesota Statutes 1961, Sections 84.37 to 84.41.

Be It Enacted by the Legislature of the State of Minnesota:
SECTION 1. (138.31) Minnesota field archaeology act of 1963: definitions.
Subdivision 1. As used in sections 1 to 13, the terms defined in this section have the meaning given them.
Subdivision 2. "State site" or "state archaeological site" means a land or water area, owned by or subject to the paramount right of the state, county, township or municipality where there are objects or other evidence of archaeological interest. This term includes all aboriginal mounds and earthworks, ancient burial grounds, prehistoric ruins, and other archaeological features on state land or on land subject to the paramount rights of the state.
Subdivision 3. "Site" or "archaeological site" has the same meaning as "state site" or "state archaeological site."
Subdivison 4. "Object" means a natural or man made article, implement, skeleton, bone, or other items of archaeological interest.
Subdivision 5. "Field archaeology" means the study of the traces of human culture at any land or water site by means of surveying, digging, sampling, excavating, or removing objects, or going on a site with that intent.
Subdivision 6. "Director of the historical society" means the director of the Minnesota historical society.
Subdivision 7. "Historical society" means the Minnesota historical society.
Subdivision 8. "The university" means the university of Minnesota.
Subdivision 9. "Schools" means universities, colleges, and junior colleges, whether publicly or privately owned.
Subdivision 10. "Scientific institutions" means museums, historical societies, foundations for archaeological study, state agencies, and scholarly groups with professional standing and physical facilities for the display, study, and preservation of objects of archaeological interest.
Subdivision 11. "Archaeological methods" means scientific procedures used in field archaeology by recognized professional authorities on archaeology.
Subdivision 12. "Data" means filed notes, photographs, maps, and other records relating to field archaeology.
Subdivision 13. "Custodian" means any school or scientific institution which has the physical possession of objects of archaeological significance or data belonging to the state.

SECTION 2. *(138.32) Legislative Intent.* The state of Minnesota reserves to itself the exclusive right and privilege of field archaeology on state sites, in order to protect and preserve archaeological and scientific information, matter, and objects.

It is a declaration and statement of legislative intent that field archaeology on privately owned lands should be discouraged except in accordance with both the provisions and spirit of sections 1 to 14; and persons having knowledge of the location of archaeological sites are encouraged to communicate such information to the state archaeologist.

SECTION 3. *(138.33) Unlicensed field archaeology prohibited.* No person other than the state archaeologist and individuals duly licensed by the director of the Minnesota historical society shall engage in any field archaeology on any state site.

SECTION 4. *(138.34) Administration of the act.* The Minnesota state historical society shall act as the agency of the state to administer and enforce the provisions of this act. Some enforcement provisions are shared with the state archaeologist.

SECTION 5. *(138.35) State archaeologist.* Subdivision 1. *Appointment.* The state archaeologist shall be a professional archaeologist on the staff of the university and shall be appointed by the director of the Minnesota historical society for a four year term.

Subdivision 2. *Duties of state archaeologist.* The duties of the state archaeologist shall include the following:

(a) To sponsor, engage in, and direct fundamental research into the archaeology of this state and to encourage and coordinate archaeological research and investigation undertaken within the state.

(b) To cooperate with other agencies of the state which may have the authority in areas where sites are located, or which may have the responsibility for marking sites, or arranging for their being viewed by the public.

(c) To protect to the extent possible and to encourage the preservation of archaeological sites located on privately owned property.

(d) To retrieve and protect objects of archaeological significance discovered by field archaeology or discovered during the course of any public construction or demolition work, and to the extent possible, those discovered during the course of any other construction or demolition work.

(e) To obtain for the state other objects of archaeological significance, and data relating thereto.

(f) To cooperate with the historical society, the University, and other custodians to preserve objects of archaeological significance, together with the data relating thereto.

(g) To disseminate archaeological facts through the publication of reports of archaeological research conducted within the state.

(h) To approve licensing of qualified persons to engage in field archaeology, as provided in section 6, and to otherwise carry out and enforce sections 1 to 13.

SECTION 6. *(138.36) Licenses.* Subdivision 1. *Content; issuance.* The director of the historical society and the state archaeologist shall formulate and issue such provisions for licenses as are required to carry out and enforce sections 1 to 13.

Subdivision 2. *Power to issue.* The director of the Minnesota historical society, acting as an agent of the state, may issue a license to a qualified person approved by the state archaeologist to engage in field archaeology on a specified state site. The director of the Minnesota historical society may also issue a license to a qualified person, either in connection with the right to engage in field archaeology on a specified site, or alone, to engage in purely preliminary or exploratory activities in a specified area where a site is thought to exist. If a state site or an area to be described in a license is under the jurisdiction of any other agency of the state, or, if the field archaeology to be licensed may interfere with a project of any other agency, the applicant for a permit shall obtain the approval of that agency. No agency shall withhold approval without good cause.

Subdivision 3. *Emergency licenses.* The director of the historical society or the state archaeologist may waive or abridge provisions of sections 1 to 13 in an emergency in which objects of interest to the state are found in the course of construction or demolition work, or in other situations in which time is of the essence to save objects or gather data. The director of the historical society or the state archeologist may issue short form emergency licenses to persons not otherwise qualified to enable them to salvage objects or gather data in the time available.

Subdivision 4. *Renewal of licenses.* The director of the Minnesota historical society may renew any license for another calendar year. The application for renewal shall be made in the form and contain the information required by the state archaeologist.

Subdivision 5. *Revocation and suspension.* The director of the historical society or the state archaeologist may revoke or suspend a license because of the improper conduct of the licensee, the use of improper or substandard methods, or other good cause.

SECTION 7. *(138.37) Ownership, custody and use of objects and data.*

Subdivision 1. *Title to objects and data.* The state reserves to itself the title to all objects found and data gathered in field archaeology, except as provided in subdivisions 2 and 3. Although a license may name a custodian other than the state archaeologist, title to the objects and data nevertheless is reserved to the state, and physical possession of them reverts to the state if the custodian named ceases to exist, or if the state archaeologist finds that the custodian is not properly caring for them or keeping them conveniently available for study by students of archaeology.

Subdivision 2. *Field archaeology on behalf of nonresident schools and scientific institutions.* The director of the Minnesota historical society, with the approval of the state archaeologist, may agree for the state with an agency of another state, or with a school or scientific institution of another state, to permit qualified persons acting for the nonresident agency, school, or institution to be licensed to engage in field archaeology in this state. Under such an agreement, the director of the historical society and the state archaeologist shall, at the time the license is issued, determine the disposition of the objects found.

Subdivision 3. *Disposal of and acquisition of objects.* If the best interests of this state are deemed served thereby, the state archaeologist, with the approval of the director of the historical society, may barter one or more objects belonging to this state for one or more objects belonging to another state, a private person, or any school, scientific institution, or other body having title thereto; and the state archaeologist, with the approval of the director of the historical society, may dispose of one or more objects belonging to this state. The state archaeologist and director of the Minnesota historical society may accept on behalf of the state any gift of an object, of data, or of any deed to a privately owned site if they deem the gift valuable to the state under the provisions of sections 1 to 13; they may also accept any gift of money to be used for one or more of the purposes covered by sections 1 to 13, but shall be held strictly accountable to the state for the use made of any such gift of money.

SECTION 8. *(138.38) Reports of state archaeologist.* The state archaeologist shall consult with and keep the director of the historical society informed as to significant field archaeology, projected or in progress, and as to significant discoveries made. Annually, and also upon leaving office, the state archaeologist shall file with the director of the historical society a full report of his activities including a summary of the activities of his licensees, from the effective date hereof or from the date of the last full report of the state archaeologist.

SECTION 9. *(138.39) Rules and regulations.* The director of the historical society may make and issue such rules and regulations, not inconsistent with law, as may be required to carry out the provisions of sections 1 to 13. In making such rules and regulations, they shall consult with other agencies of the state whose activities may be affected thereby.

SECTION 10. *(138.40) Cooperation of state agencies; disclaimer of intent to burden public.* The department of conservation, the departments of highways, and all other state agencies whose activities may be affected shall cooperate with the historical society and the state archaeologist to carry out the provisions of sections 1 to 13 and the rules and regulations issued thereunder, but sections 1 to 13 are not meant to burden persons who wish to use state property for recreational and other lawful purposes or to unnecessarily restrict the use of state property.

SECTION 11. *(138.41) Penalties.* Subdivision 1. *Willful violations.* Whoever violates section 3, or willfully defaces, injures, destroys, displaces, or removes any object or data belonging to the state, or willfully interferes with evidence or work on any state site or other site for which a license has been issued, or willfully violates any other provision of sections 1 to 14, or the rules and regulations issued by the director of the historical society, upon conviction shall be punishable by a fine of not more than $100 or imprisonment for not more than 90 days, or both.

Subdivison 2. *Other penalties.* The director of the Minnesota historical society may suspend or revoke the license of any licensee, or refuse another license, or initially refuse a license to any person who has violated a provision of sections 1 to 13, whether the violation is willful or not. Also, the director may refuse to name a school or a scientific institution as the custodian of objects or data under any license or agreement whatever, if that school or scientific institution has failed in its duty to care for and preserve objects or data belonging to the state or has failed to make such objects or data conveniently available to students of archaeology.

SECTION 12. *Laws Repealed.* Minnesota Statutes 1961, Sections 84.37, 84.38, 84.39, 84.40, and 84.41 are repealed. This repeal does not affect any right in specific property heretofore acquired under section 84.39.

SECTION 13. *Title.* Sections 1 to 13 may be cited as "the Minnesota field archaeology act of 1963."

SECTION 14. *Effective date.* Sections 1 to 13 are effective July 1, 1963.

TEXAS

Texas Antiquity Act of 1969

AN ACT Establishing and Adopting an Antiquities Code for the State of Texas; Setting Forth the Public Policy of the State with Respect to Archeological and Historical Sites and Items; Creating an Antiquities Committee of Seven Members; Providing for the Organization, Compensation, Duties, Powers, and Procedures of the Antiquities Committee; Empowering the Antiquities Committee to Enter into Contracts for Research and Salvage Activities on State Archeological Landmarks; Creating and Defining State Archeological Landmarks; Providing for the Designation of Certain Sites on Private Lands as State Archeological Landmarks with the Consent of the Owner thereof; Providing that the Antiquities Committee may Declare a State Archeological Landmark of No Further Historical, Archeological, Educational or Scientific Value; Providing for a System of Permits and Contracts for the Salvage of Treasures Imbedded in the Earth and the Excavation or Study of Archeological and Historical Sites and Objects; Providing the Antiquities Committee with the Power to Promulgate Reasonable Rules and Regulations Concerning Salvage and Other Study of State Archeological Landmarks; Empowering the Antiquities Committee To Determine the Disposition and Repository of Objects and Artifacts Recovered by Such Salvage and Study Operations; Providing for a Means of Fair Compensation to the Salvager Operating under Permit from the Antiquities Committee; Empowering the Antiquities Committee To Accept Gifts, Devises, and Bequests, and To Otherwise Purchase and Acquire from the Permittee Objects Deemed by the Antiquities Committee To Be Important Enough To Remain the Property of the State of Texas; Making It Unlawful To Forge or Duplicate an Archeological Artifact or Object with Intent To Deceive or To Offer said Object for Sale; Making It Unlawful To Intentionally Deface Aboriginal or Indian Rock Art;

Making It Unlawful To Enter the Enclosed Lands of Another without Permission and Intentionally Take, Damage, or Destroy Any Archeological or Historical Site, Structure, or Monument on Private Lands; Providing a Penalty for Violations of This Act; Providing Injunctive Relief for Violation of This Act and Providing for Venue thereof; Defining Personnel To Enforce This Act; Making It Unlawful for Any Person Not the Owner and without Authority To Injure or Destroy Any Historical Structure, Monument, Marker, Medallion, or Artifact; Providing a Saving Clause; Repealing Laws in Conflict and Designated Prior Laws; and Declaring an Emergency.

Be It Enacted by the Legislature of the State of Texas:

SECTION 1. This Act shall be known, and may be cited, as the "Antiquities Code of Texas."

SECTION 2. It is hereby declared to be the public policy and in the public interest of the State of Texas to locate, protect, and preserve all sites, objects, buildings, pre-twentieth century shipwrecks, and locations of historical, archeological, educational, or scientific interest, including but not limited to prehistoric and historical American Indian or aboriginal campsites, dwellings, and habitation sites, archeological sites of every character, treasure imbedded in the earth, sunken or abandoned ships and wrecks of the sea or any part or the contents thereof, maps, records, documents, books, artifacts, and implements of culture in any way related to the inhabitants, prehistory, history, natural history, government, or culture in, on or under any of the lands in the State of Texas, including the tidelands, submerged lands, and the bed of the sea within the jurisdiction of the State of Texas.

SECTION 3. There is hereby created a committee known as the Antiquities Committee, to be composed of seven (7) members, namely: The Director of the State Historical Survey Committee, the Director of the State Parks and Wildlife Department, the Commissioner of the General Land Office, the State Archeologist, and the following citizen members, to wit: one professional archeologist from a recognized museum or institution of higher learning in Texas, one professional historian with expertise in Texas history and culture, and the Director of the Texas Memorial Museum of The University of Texas; each citizen member to be a resident of the State of Texas and to be appointed by the Governor with the advice and consent of the Senate, who shall serve for a term coexistent with the Governor appointing him and until his successor shall have been appointed and qualified. Each citizen member of the Antiquities Committee is entitled to receive a per diem allowance for each day spent in performance of his duties and reimbursement for actual and necessary travel expenses incurred in the performance of his duties, as provided by the General Appropriations Act. The Antiquities Committee shall select one of its members as the Chairman. The Antiquities Committee may employ such personnel as are necessary to perform the duties imposed upon such Committee, to the extent such employment is provided for by the General Appropriations Act.

Employees of the Antiquities Committee shall be deemed to be employees of the Texas State Historical Survey Committee. The Antiquities Committee shall keep a record of its proceedings which shall be subject to inspection by any citizen of Texas desiring to make an examination in the presence of a member of the Antiquities Committee or an authorized employee of such Antiquities Committee. Four members of the Antiquities Committee shall constitute a quorum for the conducting of business.

SECTION 4. The duties of the Antiquities Committee shall be to determine the site of, and to designate, State Archeological Landmarks and to remove from such designation certain of such sites as hereinafter provided, to contract or otherwise provide for the discovery and salvage operation herein covered and to consider the requests for, and issue the permits hereinafter provided for, and to protect and preserve the archeological resources of Texas. The Antiquities Committee shall be the legal custodian of all items hereinafter described which have been recovered and retained by the State of Texas and shall maintain an inventory of such items showing the description and depository thereof.

SECTION 5. All sunken or abandoned pre-twentieth century ships and wrecks of the sea and any part or the contents thereof and all treasure imbedded in the earth, located in, on or under the surface of lands belonging to the State of Texas, including its tidelands, submerged lands and the beds of its rivers and the sea within the jurisdiction of the State of Texas are hereby declared to be State Archeological Landmarks and are the sole property of the State of Texas and may not be taken, altered, damaged, destroyed, salvaged or excavated without a contract or permit of the Antiquities Committee.

SECTION 6. All other sites, objects, buildings, artifacts, implements, and locations of historical, archeological, scientific, or educational interest, including but expressly not limited to, those pertaining to prehistoric and historical American Indian or aboriginal campsites, dwellings, and habitation sites, their artifacts and implements of culture, as well as archeological sites of every character that are located in, on or under the surface of any lands belonging to the State of Texas or by any county, city, or political subdivision of the state are hereby declared to be State Archeological Landmarks and are the sole property of the State of Texas and all such sites or items located on private lands within the State of Texas in areas that have been designated as a "State Archeological Landmark" as hereinafter provided, may not be taken, altered, damaged, destroyed, salvaged, or excavated without a permit from, or in violation of the terms of such permit of, the Antiquities Committee.

SECTION 7. Any site located upon private lands which is determined by majority vote of the Antiquities Committee to be of sufficient archeological, scientific or historical significance to scientific study, interest or public representation of the aboriginal or historical past of Texas may be designated by the Antiquities Committee as a "State Archeological Landmark." It is specifically provided, however, that no such site shall be so designated upon private land without the written consent of the landowner or landowners in recordable form sufficiently describing the site so that it may be located upon the ground. Upon such designation the consent of the landowner shall be recorded in the deed records of the county in which the land is located. Any such site upon private land shall be marked by at least one marker bearing the words "State Archeological Landmark" for each five (5) acres of area.

SECTION 8. Upon majority vote of the Antiquities Committee any State Archeological Landmark, on public or private land, may be determined to be of no further historical, archeological, educational, or scientific value or not of sufficient value to warrant its further classification as such; and upon such determination may be removed from such designation and in the case of sites located on private land that have theretofore been designated by instrument of record, the Antiquities Committee is authorized to cause to be executed and recorded in the deed records of the county where such site is located an instrument setting out such determination and releasing the site from the provisions hereof.

SECTION 9. The Antiquities Committee shall be authorized to enter into contracts with other state agencies or institutions and with qualified private institutions, corporations, or individuals for the discovery and salvage of treasure imbedded in the earth, sunken or abandoned ships or wrecks of the sea, parts thereof and their contents. Such contracts to be on forms approved by the Attorney General. The contracts may provide for fair compensation to the salvager in terms of a percentage of the reasonable cash value of the objects recovered, or at the discretion of the Antiquities Committee, of a fair share of the objects recovered; the amount constituting a fair share to be determined by the Antiquities Committee taking into consideration the circumstances of each such operation, and the reasonable cash value may be determined by contract provision providing for appraisal by qualified experts or by representatives of the contracting parties and their representative or representatives. Such contract shall provide for the termination of any right in the salvager or permittee thereunder upon the violation of any of the terms thereof. Superior title to all objects recovered to be retained by the State of Texas unless and until they are released to the salvager or permittee by the Antiquities Committee. No person, firm, or corporation may conduct such salvage or recovery operation herein described without first obtaining such contract. All such contracts and permits shall specifically provide for the location, nature of the activity, and the time period covered thereby, and when executed are to be recorded by the person, firm, or corporation obtaining such contract in the office of the County Clerk in the county or counties where such operations are to be conducted prior to the commencement of such operation.

SECTION 10. The Antiquities Committee shall be authorized to issue permits to other state agencies or institutions and to qualified private institutions, companies, or individuals for the taking, salvaging, excavating, restoring, or the conducting of scientific or educational studies at, in, or on State Archeological Landmarks as in the opinion of the Antiquities Committee would be in the best interest of the State of Texas. Such permits may provide for the retaining by the permittee of a portion of any recovery as set out for contracting parties under Section 9 hereof. Such permit shall provide for the termination of any rights in the permittee thereunder upon the violation of any of the terms thereof and to be drafted in compliance with forms approved by the Attorney General. All such permits shall specifically provide for the location, nature of the activity, and time period covered thereby. No person, firm, or corporation shall conduct any such operations on any State Archeological Landmark herein described without first obtaining and having in his or its possession such permit at the site of such operation, or conduct such operations in violation of the provisions of such permit.

SECTION 11. All salvage or recovery operations described under Section 9 hereof and all operations conducted under permits or contracts set out in Section 10 hereof must be carried out under the general supervision of the Antiquities Committee and in accordance with reasonable rules and regulations adopted by the Antiquities Committee and in such manner that the maximum amount of historic, scientific, archeological, and educational information may be recovered and preserved in addition to the physical recovery of items. The Antiquities Committee shall be the legal custodian of all antiquities recovered, and is specifically authorized and empowered to promulgate such rules and regulations and to require such contract or permit conditions as to reasonably affect the purposes of this Act.

SECTION 12. The Antiquities Committee is hereby authorized to expend such sums, from any appropriations hereafter made for such purposes, as it may deem advisable to purchase from the salvager or permittee of such salvager's or permittee's share, or portion thereof, of items recovered which in the opinion of the Antiquities Committee should remain the property of the State of Texas. The Antiquities Committee is authorized and empowered to accept gifts, grants, devises, and bequests of money, securities, or property to be used in the purchase of such items from the salvager or permittee. Further, in this respect, the Antiquities Committee may enter into contracts or agreements with such persons, firms, corporations, or institutions, as it might choose, whereby such persons, firms, corporations, or institutions, for the privilege of retaining possession of such items, may advance to the Antiquities Committee money necessary to procure from the salvager or permittee such items as the Antiquities Committee might determine should remain the property of the State of Texas upon the condition that at any time the Antiquities Committee may choose to repay to such person, firm, corporation, or institution such sum so advanced, without interest or additional charge of any kind, it may do so and may recover possession of such items; and provided, further, that during the time the said items are in the possession of the person, firm, corporation, or institution advancing the money for the purchase thereof they shall be available for viewing by the general public without charge or at no more than a nominal admission fee, and that such items may not be removed from the State of Texas except upon the express authorization of the Antiquities Committee for appraisal, exhibition, or restorative purposes.

SECTION 13. The restoration of antiquities for private parties is authorized and shall be under the rules and regulations promulgated by the Antiquities Committee, and all costs incurred in such restoration, both real and administrative, shall be paid by the private party.

SECTION 14. No person shall intentionally reproduce, replicate, retouch, rework, or forge any archeological or other object which derives value from its antiquity, with intent to represent the same to be original or genuine and with intent to deceive or offer any such object for sale or exchange.

SECTION 15. No person shall intentionally and knowingly deface any American Indian or aboriginal paintings, hieroglyphics, or other marks or carvings on rock or elsewhere which pertain to early American Indian or aboriginal habitation of the country.

SECTION 16. No person, not being the owner thereof, and without the consent of the owner, proprietor, lessee, or person in charge thereof, shall enter or attempt to enter upon the enclosed lands of another and intentionally injure, disfigure, remove, excavate, damage, take, dig into, or destroy any historical structure, monument, marker, medallion, or artifact, or any prehistoric or historic archeological site, American Indian or aboriginal campsite, artifact, burial, ruin, or other archeological remains located in, on or under any private lands within the State of Texas.

SECTION 17. Any person violating any of the provisions of this Act shall be guilty of a misdemeanor, and upon conviction shall be punished by a fine of not less than Fifty Dollars ($50.00) and not more than One Thousand Dollars ($1,000.00) or by confinement in jail for not more than thirty (30) days, or by both such fine and confinement. Each day of continued violation of any provision of this Act shall constitute a distinct and separate offense for which the offender may be punished.

SECTION 18. In addition to, and without limiting the other powers of the Attorney General of the State of Texas, and without altering or waiving any criminal penalty provision of this Act, the Attorney General of the State of Texas shall have the power to bring an action in the name of the State of Texas in any court of competent jurisdiction for restraining orders and injunctive relief to restrain and enjoin violations or threatened violations of this Act, and for the return of items taken in violation of the provision hereof, and the venue of such actions shall lie either in Travis County or in the county in which the activity sought to be restrained is alleged to be taking place or from which the items were taken. Any citizen in the State of Texas shall have the power to bring an action in any court of competent jurisdiction for restraining orders and injunctive relief to restrain and enjoin violations or threatened violations of the Act, and for the return of items taken in violation of the provisions hereof, and the venue of such actions shall lie in the county in which the activity sought to be restrained is alleged to be taking place or from which the items were taken.

SECTION 19. The chief administrative officers of all state agencies are authorized and directed to cooperate and assist the Antiquities Committee and the Attorney General in carrying out the intent of this Act. All law enforcement agencies and officers, state and local, are authorized and directed to assist in enforcing this Act and in carrying out the intent hereof.

SECTION 20. It shall be unlawful for any person, not being the owner thereof, and without lawful authority, to wilfully injure, disfigure, remove or destroy any historical structure, monument, marker, medallion, or artifact.

SECTION 21. The Sections of this Act and each provision and part thereof are hereby declared to be severable and independent of each other, and the holding of a Section, or part thereof, or the application thereof to any person or circumstance, to be invalid, ineffective or unconstitutional shall not affect any other Section, provision or part thereof, or the application of any Section, provision, or part thereof, to any other person and circumstance.

SECTION 22. All laws in conflict herewith and laws codified as Chapter 32, Acts of the 42nd Legislature, 1st Called Session, 1931 (Article 147a, Vernon's Texas Penal Code); Chapter 1, General Laws, page 60, Acts of the 46th Legislature, Regular Session, 1939 (Article 147b, Vernon's Texas Penal Code); Chapter 153, Acts of the 58th Legislature, 1963 (Article 147b-1, Vernon's Texas Penal Code); Chapter 193, Acts of the 58th Legislature, 1963 (Article 147b-2, Vernon's Texas Penal Code), are hereby repealed.

SECTION 23. The fact that irreparable damage and harm is rapidly being done to the archeological and historical heritage of the State of Texas and its citizens, and that historical and archeological sites, and treasures on public lands are without adequate legal protection and supervision and are being destroyed and damaged without lawful authority, create an emergency and imperative public necessity that the Constitutional Rule requiring bills to be read on three several days in each House be suspended, and this Rule is hereby suspended; and this Act shall take effect and be in force from and after the date of its passage, and it is so enacted.

State of Texas Antiquities Committee Rules and Regulations

The Antiquities Committee was created by the Antiquities Code of Texas, Senate Bill No. 58, Acts of the 61st Legislature, Second called Session, 1969, and codified as Article 6145-9 in Vernon's Civil Statutes. The Antiquities Committee is specifically empowered to "promulgate reasonable rules and regulations concerning salvage and other study of state archeological landmarks" as well as having other powers specifically outlined in the Antiquities Code of Texas. State archeological landmarks include "all sites, objects, buildings, pre-twentieth century shipwrecks and locations of historical, archeological, educational or scientific interest including, but not limited to, prehistoric and historic American Indian or aboriginal campsites, dwellings and habitation sites, archeological sites of every character, treasure embedded in the earth, sunken or abandoned ships and wrecks of the sea, or any part of the contents thereof; maps, records, documents, books, artifacts, and implements of culture in any way related to the inhabitants, prehistory, history, natural history, government, or culture, in, on or under, any of the lands of the State of Texas." Section 6 of the Code provides that historical and archeological sites on lands belonging to any county, city, or political subdivision of the state of Texas are State Archeological Landmarks and may not be taken, altered, damaged, destroyed, salvaged or excavated without a permit from the Texas Antiquities Committee. Also protected under the Antiquities Code of Texas are specially designated archeological landmarks on private property as well as all "American Indian or aboriginal paintings, hieroglyphics, or other marks or carvings on rock or elsewhere which pertain to early American or aboriginal habitation of the country." The Antiquities Committee is further empowered to "provide for a system of permits and contracts for salvage of treasures embedded in the earth and the excavation or study of archeological and historical sites and objects."

The following rules and regulations have been adopted by the Antiquities Committee of the State of Texas on the ninth day of February, 1970:

1. Investigations undertaken on state archeological landmarks must be oriented toward solving a particular research problem, in preparation of a site for public interpretation, or for the purpose of salvaging information and specimens from a site threatened with immediate destruction.

2. The Texas Antiquities Code specifies that all investigations must be carried out "in such a manner that the maximum amount of historic, scientific, archeological and educational information may be recovered and preserved." Such investigations must therefore involve the exclusive use of scientific techniques of excavation, recovery, recording, preservation, and analysis normally used in archeological investigations. Use of any new or unusual techniques must be approved in advance by the Texas Antiquities Committee.

3. Permits to conduct investigations of any nature on state archeological landmarks, as defined in the Texas Antiquities Code, will be issued exclusively by the Texas Antiquities Committee under the conditions provided in these Rules and Regulations. Permits will be issued by the Texas Antiquities

Committee to scientific and educational institutions, non-profit corporations and organizations, and governmental agencies which have demonstrated their ability to carry out proper archeological investigations and whose staffs include one or more professional archeologists who will supervise the project. Permits may also be issued to individuals and private corporations who: (a) retain a professional archeologist to be in direct charge of the project from field investigation through preservation of collections and analysis of data to publication of results. A professional archeologist is one who has a graduate degree in archeology or anthropology from an accredited institution of higher education, or the equivalent as approved by the Antiquities Committee, with a minimum of two field seasons under competent supervision and who has published results of archeological investigations in scholarly journals; (b) provide proof that adequate funds, equipment, facilities, and personnel are available to properly conduct the investigation as proposed to the Antiquities Committee, and to publish the results.

State or local archeological societies wishing to conduct investigations on state archeological landmarks must be sponsored by a scientific or educational institution or reputable museum, whose staffs include a professional archeologist who will supervise the project.

Permits for limited investigations may also be issued to particularly qualified individuals who, in the judgement of the Texas Antiquities Committee, are qualified to undertake and complete a specific project of limited scope, under the supervision of a professional archeologist.

4. All specimens, artifacts, materials and samples plus a duplicate copy of original field notes, maps, drawings, and photographs resulting from the investigations remain the property of the State of Texas, with certain exceptions left to the discretion of the Texas Antiquities Committee in Article 9 of the Texas Antiquities Code. The Antiquities Committee will determine the final disposition of all artifacts, specimens, materials and data recovered by investigations on state archeological landmarks which remain the property of the state.

5. Investigators who receive permits, shall be responsible for cleaning, cataloging, and preserving all collections, specimens, samples, and records, and for the publication of results of the investigation.

6. No permit will be granted for a period of more than one year, but if the work has been diligently prosecuted under the permit, the time may be extended upon application showing good cause.

7. Four categories of permits, oriented toward specific types of investigation, are issued by the Antiquities Committee:

a. *Survey and Reconnaissance*

This permit is for the purpose of searching a specific area for sites and includes visual examination of the surface, plus use of specialized equipment such as magnetometers and metal detectors. Under this permit, investigation is limited to recording site locations, mapping, photography, and controlled surface collecting.

b. *Testing*

This permit allows detailed examination of a particular site including systematic test excavations.

c. *Excavation*

This permit covers full investigation and extensive excavation of a particular locality.

d. *Recording Rock Art*

This permit covers the copying of Indian or aboriginal petroglyphs, pictographs, hieroglyphics, or other forms of rock art. Recording techniques which involve application of brushes, heat, chemicals, water, chalk, or other preparations to the rock surfaces are prohibited unless specifically authorized by the Antiquities Committee.

8. Any institution, corporation, organization, museum, or individual desiring a permit for investigation of an archeological landmark should file an application with the Texas Antiquities Committee, P.O. Box 12276, Capitol Station, Austin, Texas 78711, at least three months prior to the proposed beginning date of the project. Special circumstances may require that a permit be issued on short notice when a site is threatened with immediate destruction in which case the Chairman may poll the Committee for an immediate decision. When a permit is issued for emergency salvage of a site threatened with destruction, the same rules and regulations apply as with all other permits. The application should include:

a. A statement of the purpose of the investigation

b. An outline of the proposed work

c. Proposed beginning date for the field work and the length of time which will be devoted to field work

d. The proposed date of publication of the results of the investigation

e. Name and address of the person and his professional qualifications who will be in immediate charge of the project

f. An accurate sketch plan of the particular site or area to be investigated and a map showing the latitude and longitude

g. Location where the specimens, material, and data will be kept during the analysis of results of the investigation

h. Evidence of adequate funds, personnel, equipment and facilities to properly complete the proposed investigation

9. When a permit is issued, it will contain all special regulations governing the particular investigation; it will be approved by a majority of the Antiquities Committee; and it will be signed by the Chairman and by the permittee. Anyone carrying out an investigation of a state archeological landmark will have a copy of the permit available at the site of the investigation during all working hours.

10. Institutions, museums, organizations, corporations and persons receiving permits for investigations of state archeological landmarks, shall, after completion of the work, restore the lands on which they have worked to their customary condition, to the satisfaction of the Texas Antiquities Committee.

11. If the permittee fails to comply with any of the rules and regulations of the Texas Antiquities Committee or any of the terms of his specific permit, or fails to properly conduct or complete the project, the Antiquities Committee may immediately cancel the permit and notify the permittee of such cancellation by registered letter, mailed to the last address furnished to the Committee by the permittee. Upon notification of cancellation, the permittee shall cease work immediately and vacate the area or site within 24 hours, including removal of all personnel and equipment. Upon cancellation of a permit, permittee forfeits all rights to the specimens and data recovered. A permit which has been cancelled can be reinstated by the Antiquities Committee if good cause is shown within 30 days.

12. Any member or agent of the Texas Antiquities Committee and any officer in charge of land owned or controlled by the State of Texas, may at any time, visit the area or site being investigated under permit. Such a representative of the state may examine the permit as well as the field records, materials, and specimens being recovered.

13. On receipt of an application for a permit to carry out investigation on a state archeological landmark, the Antiquities Committee shall routinely refer such application to the agency or political subdivision having administrative control of the land upon which the site is located, for their review prior to issuance of the permit.

14. No permit issued by the Texas Antiquities Committee may be assigned by the permittee in whole or in part to any other institution, museum, corporation, organization, or individual.

15. Upon publication of the results of an investigation of a state archeological landmark, the permittee will furnish the Texas Antiquities Committee with ten copies of the report at no charge to the Committee.

16. The rules and regulations of the Texas Antiquities Committee may be amended with the approval of a majority of the Committee members.

INYO COUNTY, CALIFORNIA

Inyo County Ordinance No. 146

The Board of Supervisors of the County of Inyo, State of California, do ordain as follows:
SECTION I. Prior to the excavation, digging, exploring or disturbing of any Indian burial ground for the purpose of examination, exhumation, or removal of

human remains therefrom, or for the purpose of collecting human artefacts interned with said remains, by any person whatsoever, application must first be made by written petition, specifically identifying the burial ground desired to be excavated and describing the purpose of said excavation.

SECTION II. Said application shall be made to the Coroner of the County of Inyo, the Board of Trustees of the Owens Valley Paiute-Shoshone Indians and the County Superintendent of Schools. Upon endorsement by a majority of the members of the Board of Trustees above mentioned and by the Coroner of the County of Inyo, and by the County Superintendent of Schools, said petition shall be presented to the Clerk of the Board of Supervisors for consideration by the Board of Supervisors of the County of Inyo who shall affirm or deny permission for such excavation.

SECTION III. No petition shall be approved unless it is stated on said petition that exhumation or the removal of remains and artefacts are necessary in the pursuance of archaeological studies conducted by a professional archaeologist, anthropologist, museum director, or person working under the direction of such a party.

SECTION IV. In no case shall a petition be approved which contemplates or describes the exhumation or disturbance in any way of graveyards or burial grounds still actively or recently used in whole or in part.

SECTION V . Upon the receipt of permission by the Board of Supervisors as aforementioned, and after exhumation or removal of any human part of artefact, an itemized list of all parts and artefacts taken shall be made and returned to the Board of Trustees of the Owens Valley Paiute-Shoshone Indians, the Coroner of the County of Inyo, and the County Superintendent of Schools.

SECTION VI. If any section, sub-section, sentence, clause or phrase of this ordinance is for any reason held to be unconstitutional, or otherwise invalid, said decision shall not affect the validity of the remaining portions of this ordinance. Should any provision, section, sub-section, sentence or clause or phrase of this ordinance be in conflict with state law or cover an area expressly covered by state statute, said statute of the State of California shall prevail in said particulars.

SECTION VII. A violation of this ordinance or any provision thereof is punishable as a misdemeanor by a fine not exceeding Five Hundred Dollars ($500.00) or by imprisonment not exceeding six (6) months or by both such fine and imprisonment.

SECTION VIII. This Ordinance is hereby declared to be urgently required to the immediate preservation of public peace, health and safety and shall take effect immediately upon its publication. The following is a statement of the fact showing its urgency:

Excavation of Indian Burial Grounds has been conducted recently within the bounds of the County of Inyo upon property considered by a substantial number of Indian citizens of the County of Inyo to be burial grounds in which are interred family members of the interested parties. In order to define the rights and duties of all parties concerned and prevent misunderstandings of the conditions upon which said excavation may occur, it is necessary for the immediate public good and welfare that this ordinance and the provisions thereof be immediately effective.

SECTION IX. This Ordinance shall be published with the names of the members of said Board of Supervisors voting for and against prior to the expiration of fifteen (15) days from the passing hereof, in the Inyo Independent, a newspaper of general circulation, printed and published in the County of Inyo, State of California.

PASSED, ADOPTED AND APPROVED this 7th day of August, 1967.

MARIN COUNTY, CALIFORNIA

Marin County Ordinance No. 1589

The Board of Supervisors of the County of Marin Does Ordain as Follows:
SECTION 1. Section 5.32.010 is hereby added to the Marin County Code to read as follows:

5.32.010. In the County of Marin there exist certain deposits of shells and other materials in mounds hereinafter referred to as Indian middens, believed to have been deposited by Indians in the distant past. Said middens may be of inestimable value in formulating the early history of the County and the habits of Indians when said middens are studied under the supervision of qualified archaeologists. Uncontrolled excavations into the aforesaid middens for commercial purposes without regard to their possible historical and archaeological values are destructive to the archaeological integrity of the sites.

SECTION 2. Section 5.32.020 is hereby added to the Marin County Code to read as follows:

5.32.020. It shall be unlawful for any person, firm, corporation or co-partnership to knowingly disturb in any fashion whatsoever, or excavate, or cause to be disturbed or excavated any Indian midden without a permit being issued therefor by the Department of Public Works.

SECTION 3. Section 5.32.030 is hereby added to the Marin County Code to read as follows:

5.32.030. Upon receiving written application therefor, the Board of Supervisors of the County of Marin shall designate an institution of higher learning, or an association having as one of its major purposes the study of Indian relics or sites having archaeological significance, as a liaison agency between the Department of Public Works and institutions of higher learning or associations having as one of their purposes the study of objects of archaeological significance.

SECTION 4. Section 5.32.040 is hereby added to the Marin County Code to read as follows:

5.32.040. Application for a permit to excavate Indian middens shall be in a form acceptable to the Director of Public Works, and may be made by the owner of the middens or a person authorized in writing by the owner, to make such application.

SECTION 5. Section 5.32.050. is hereby added to the Marin County Code to read as follows:

5.32.050. Upon receipt of an application for the excavation of an Indian midden, the Director of Public Works or his designee shall forward the application to the liaison agency designated by the Board of Supervisors pursuant to Section 5.32.030 hereof. Within five (5) days of the receipt of such application the liaison agency so designated shall notify the Director of Public Works whether the midden for which application is made for excavation is of archaeological significance. If the designee certifies that such midden is not of archaeological significance, a permit shall be issued to the applicant upon the receipt of such certificate.

SECTION 6. Section 5.32.060 is hereby added to the Marin County Code to read as follows:

In the event that the liaison agency certifies that the midden for which application for excavation is made is of archaeological significance, the Director of Public Works may issue a permit, but shall subject such permit to conditions, including but not limited to the following:

a. That prior to excavation or removal of materials from such middens the permittee shall not excavate for a period of sixty (60) days.

b. That the permittee or owner of the property be required to grant a license for the excavation, identification and classification of artifacts and proper scientific analysis of materials having historical or archaeological significance to recognized institutions of higher learning or associations having as their major purpose the study of Indian relics and other sites having archaeological value. The terms of such license shall be such as are agreed to by the prospective licensee and property owner.

SECTION 7. Section 5.32.070 is hereby added to the Marin County Code to read as follows:

5.32.070. Any act done under the authority of a written permit issued hereunder shall be in accordance with the terms and conditions of such permit.

SECTION 8. Section 5.32.080 is hereby added to the Marin County Code to read as follows:

5.32.080. Notwithstanding the provisions of Section 5.32.030 hereof, this Chapter shall not be applicable to persons working under the authority of recognized institutions of higher learning or associations having as their major purpose the study of Indian relics and other archaeological matters.

SECTION 9. Section 5.32.090 is hereby added to the Marin County Code to read as follows:

5.32.090. Any person violating the provisions of this Chapter is guilty of a misdemeanor and upon conviction thereof is punishable by a fine of not more than Five Hundred Dollars ($500.00) or by imprisonment in the County Jail for a period not exceeding six (6) months, or by both such fine and imprisonment. In the event of a continuing violation, each day that the violation continues constitutes a separate and distinct offense.

SECTION 10. Section 13.12.050 is hereby added to the Marin County Code to read as follows:

13.12.50. In the event the permittee encounters any Indian middens in doing the work for which a permit was issued hereunder, the permittee shall stop work in the immediate area of said middens and shall not recommence the work until he has fully complied with the provisions of Chapter 5.32 hereof.

SECTION 11. Section 21.48-035 is hereby added to the Marin County Code to read as follows:

In the event the subdivider or contractor encounters any Indian middens in constructing improvements herein, he shall order work halted in the immediate area of said middens and shall not recommence the work until he has fully complied with the provisions of Chapter 5.32 hereof.

SECTION 12. This ordinance shall be and is hereby declared to be in full force and effect as of thirty (30) days after its passage and shall be published once before the expiration of fifteen (15) days after its passage, with the names of the Supervisors voting for and against the same in the Reporter, a newspaper of general circulation, published in the County of Marin.

PASSED AND ADOPTED at a regular meeting of the Board of Supervisors of the County of Marin held on the 20th day of June, 1967.

Principal Federal Legislation Affecting Archeological Preservation

ANTIQUITIES ACT OF 1906

AN ACT For the Preservation of American Antiquities, Approved June 8, 1906 (Public Law 59-209; 34 STAT. 225; 16 U.S.C. 431-433)

Be it enacted by the Senate and House of Representatives of the United States of America in Congress assembled, That any person who shall appropriate, excavate, injure or destroy any historic or prehistoric ruin or monument, or any object of antiquity, situated on lands owned or controlled by the Government of the United States, without the permission of the Secretary of the Department of the Government having jurisdiction over the lands on which said antiquities are situated, shall upon conviction, be fined in a sum of not more than five hundred dollars or be imprisoned for a period of not more than ninety days, or shall suffer both fine and imprisonment, in the discretion of the court.

SECTION 2. That the President of the United States is hereby authorized, in his discretion, to declare by public proclamation historic landmarks, historic and prehistoric structures, and other objects of historic or scientific interest that are situated upon the lands owned or controlled by the Government of the United States to be national monuments, and may reserve as a part thereof parcels of land, the limits of which in all cases shall be confined to the smallest area compatible with the proper care and management of the objects to be protected: *Provided,* That when such objects are situated upon a tract covered by a bona fide unperfected claim or held in private ownership, the tract, or so much thereof as may be necessary for the proper care and management of the object, may be relinquished to the Government, and the Secretary of the Interior is hereby authorized to accept the relinquishment of such tracts in behalf of the Government of the United States.

SECTION 3. That permits for the examination of ruins, the excavation of archaeological sites, and the gathering of objects of antiquity upon the lands under their respective jurisdictions may be granted by the Secretaries of the

Interior, Agriculture, and War to institutions which they may deem properly qualified to conduct such examinations, excavation, or gathering, subject to such rules and regulations as they may prescribe: *Provided,* That the examinations, excavations, and gatherings are undertaken for the benefit of reputable museums, universities, colleges, or other recognized scientific or educational institutions, with a view to increasing the knowledge of such objects, and that the gatherings shall be made for permanent preservation in public museums.

SECTION 4. That the Secretaries of the Departments aforesaid shall make and publish from time to time uniform rules and regulations for the purpose of carrying out the provisions of this Act.

Uniform Rules and Regulations Prescribed by the Secretaries of the Interior, Agriculture, and War To Carry Out the Provisions of the "Act for the Preservation of American Antiquities,"

1. Jurisdiction over ruins, archeological sites, historic, and prehistoric monuments and structures, objects of antiquity, historic landmarks, and other objects of historic or scientific interest, shall be exercised under the act by the respective Departments as follows:

By the Secretary of Agriculture over lands within the exterior limits of forest reserves, by the Secretary of War over lands within the exterior limits of military reservations, by the Secretary of the Interior over all other lands owned or controlled by the Government of the United States, provided the Secretaries of War and Agriculture may by agreement cooperate with the Secretary of the Interior in the supervision of such monuments and objects covered by the act of June 8, 1906, as may be located on lands near or adjacent to forest reserves and military reservations, respectively.

2. No permit for the removal of any ancient monument or structure which can be permanently preserved under the control of the United States *in situ,* and remain an object of interest, shall be granted.

3. Permits for the examination of ruins, the excavation of archeological sites, and the gathering of objects of antiquity will be granted, by the respective Secretaries having jurisdiction, to reputable museums, universities, colleges, or other recognized scientific or educational institutions, or to their duly authorized agents.

4. No exclusive permits shall be granted for a larger area than the applicant can reasonably be expected to explore fully and systematically within the time limit named in the permit.

5. Each application for a permit should be filed with the Secretary having jurisdiction, and must be accompanied by a definite outline of the proposed work, indicating the name of the institution making the request, the date proposed for the beginning the field work, the length of time proposed to be devoted to it, and the person who will have immediate charge of the work. The

application must also contain an exact statement of the character of the work, whether examination, excavation, or gathering, and the public museum in which the collections made under the permit are to be permanently preserved. The application must be accompanied by a sketch plan or description of the particular site or area to be examined, excavated, or searched, so definite that it can be located on the map with reasonable accuracy.

6. No permit will be granted for a period of more than three years, but if the the work has been diligently prosecuted under the permit, the time may be extended for proper cause upon application.

7. Failure to begin work under a permit within six months after it is granted, or failure to diligently prosecute such work after it has been begun, shall make the permit void without any order or proceeding by the Secretary having jurisdiction.

8. Applications for permits shall be referred to the Smithsonian Institution for recommendation.

9. Every permit shall be in writing and copies shall be transmitted to the Smithsonian Institution and the field officer in charge of the land involved. The permittee will be furnished with a copy of these rules and regulations.

10. At the close of each season's field work the permittee shall report in duplicate to the Smithsonian Institution, in such form as its secretary may prescribe, and shall prepare in duplicate a catalogue of the collections and the photographs made during the season, indicating therein such material, if any, as may be available for exchange.

11. Institutions and persons receiving permits for excavation shall, after the completion of the work, restore the lands upon which they have worked to their customary condition, to the satisfaction of the field officer in charge.

12. All permits shall be terminable at the discretion of the Secretary having jurisdiction.

13. The field officer in charge of land owned or controlled by the Government of the United States shall, from time to time, inquire and report as to the existence, on or near such lands, of ruins and archeological sites, historic or prehistoric ruins or monuments, objects or antiquity, historic landmarks, historic and prehistoric structures, and other objects of historic or scientific interest.

14. The field officer in charge may at all times examine the permit of any person or institution claiming privileges granted in accordance with the act and these rules and regulations, and may fully examine all work done under such permit.

15. All persons duly authorized by the Secretaries of Agriculture, War, and Interior may apprehend or cause to be arrested, as provided in the act of February 6, 1905 (33 Stat. 700), any person or persons who appropriate, excavate, injure, or destroy any historic or prehistoric ruin or monument, or any

object of antiquity on lands under the supervision of the secretaries of Agriculture, War, and Interior, respectively.

16. Any object of antiquity taken, or collection made, on lands owned or controlled by the·United States, without a permit, as prescribed by the act and these rules and regulations, or there taken or made, contrary to the terms of the permit, or contrary to the act and these rules and regulations, may be seized whenever found and at any time, by the proper field officer or by any person duly authorized by the Secretary having jurisdiction, and disposed of as the Secretary shall determine, by deposit in the proper national depository or otherwise.

17. Every collection made under the authority of the act and of these rules and regulations shall be preserved in the public museum designated in the permit and shall be accessible to the public. No such collection shall be removed from such public museum without the written authority of the Secretary of the Smithsonian Institution, and then only to another public museum, where it shall be accessible to the public; and when any public museum, which is a depository of any collection made under the provisions of the act and these rules and regulations, shall cease to exist, every such collection in such public museum shall thereupon revert to the national collections and be placed in the proper national depository.

Washington, D. C., *December 28, 1906.*

The foregoing rules and regulations are hereby approved in triplicate and, under authority conferred by law on the Secretaries of the Interior, Agriculture, and War, are hereby made and established, to take effect immediately. *E. A. Hitchcock, Secretary of the Interior. James Wilson, Secretary of Agriculture. William H. Taft, Secretary of War.*

HISTORIC SITES ACT OF 1935

AN ACT To Provide for the Preservation of Historic American Sites, Buildings, Objects, and Antiquities of National Significance, and for Other Purposes, Approved August 21, 1935 (Public Law 74-292; 49 STAT. 666; 16 U.S.C. 461-467)

Be it enacted by the Senate and House of Representatives of the United States of America in Congress assembled, That it is hereby declared that it is a national policy to preserve for public use historic sites, buildings and objects of national significance for the inspiration and benefit of the people of the United States. (16 U.S.C. sec. 461.)

SECTION 2. The Secretary of the Interior (hereinafter referred to as the Secretary), through the National Park Service, for the purpose of effectuating the policy expressed in section 1 hereof, shall have the following powers and perform the following duties and functions:

(a) Secure, collate, and preserve drawings, plans, photographs, and other data of historic and archaeologic sites, buildings and objects.

(b) Make a survey of historic and archaeologic sites, buildings, and objects for the purpose of determining which possess exceptional value as commemorating or illustrating the history of the United States.

(c) Make necessary investigations and researches in the United States relating to particular sites, buildings, or objects to obtain true and accurate historical and archaeological facts and information concerning the same.

(d) For the purpose of this Act, acquire in the name of the United States by gift, purchase, or otherwise any property, personal or real, or any interest or estate therein, title to any real property to be satisfactory to the Secretary: *Provided,* That no such property which is owned by any religious or educational institution, or which is owned or administered for the benefit of the public shall be so acquired without the consent of the owner: *Provided further,* That no such property shall be acquired or contract or agreement for the acquisition thereof made which will obligate the general fund of the Treasury for the payment of such property, unless or until Congress has appropriated money which is available for that purpose.

(e) Contract and make cooperative agreements with States, municipal subdivisions, corporations, associations, or individuals, with proper bond where deemed advisable, to protect, preserve, maintain, or operate any historic or archaeologic building, site, object, or property used in connection therewith for public use, regardless as to whether the title thereto is in the United States: *Provided,* That no contract or cooperative agreement shall be made or entered into which will obligate the general fund of the Treasury unless or until Congress has appropriated money for such purpose.

(f) Restore, reconstruct, rehabilitate, preserve, and maintain historic or prehistoric sites, buildings, objects, and properties of national historical or archaeological significance and where deemed desirable establish and maintain museums in connection therewith.

(g) Erect and maintain tablets to mark or commemorate historic or prehistoric places and events of national historical or archaeological significance.

(h) Operate and manage historic and archaeologic sites, buildings, and properties acquired under the provisions of this Act together with lands and subordinate buildings for the benefit of the public, such authority to include the power to charge reasonable visitation fees and grant concessions, leases, or permits for the use of land, building space, roads, or trails when necessary or desirable either to accommmodate the public or to facilitate administration: *Provided,* That such concessions, leases, or permits, shall be let at competitive bidding, to the person making the highest and best bid.

(i) When the Secretary determines that it would be administratively burdensome to restore, reconstruct, operate, or maintain any particular historic or archaeologic site, building, or property donated to the United States through the National Park Service, he may cause the same to be done by organizing a corporation for that purpose under the laws of the District of Columbia or any State.

(j) Develop an education program and service for the purpose of making available to the public facts and information pertaining to American historic and archaeologic sites, buildings, and properties of national significance. Reasonable charges may be made for the dissemination of any such facts or information.

(k) Perform any and all acts, and make such rules and regulations not inconsistent with this Act as may be necessary and proper to carry out the provisions thereof. Any person violating any of the rules and regulations authorized by this Act shall be punished by a fine of not more than $500 and be adjudged to pay all cost of the proceedings. (16 U.S.C. sec. 462.)

SECTION 3. A general advisory board to be known as the "Advisory Board on National Parks, Historic Sites, Buildings, and Monuments" is hereby established, to be composed of not to exceed eleven persons, citizens of the United States, to include representatives competent in the fields of history, archaeology, architecture, and human geography, who shall be appointed by the Secretary and serve at his pleasure. The members of such board shall receive no salary but may be paid expenses incidental to travel engaged in discharging their duties as members.

It shall be the duty of such board to advise on any matters relating to national parks and to the administration of this Act submitted to it for consideration by the Secretary. It may also recommend policies to the Secretary from time to time pertaining to national parks and to the restoration, reconstruction, conservation, and general administration of historic and archaeologic sites, buildings, and properties. (16 U.S.C. sec. 463.)

SECTION 4. The Secretary, in administering this Act, is authorized to cooperate with and may seek and accept the assistance of any Federal, State, or municipal department or agency, or any educational or scientific institution, or any patriotic association, or any individual.

(b) When deemed necessary, technical advisory committees may be established to act in an advisory capacity in connection with the restoration or reconstruction of any historic or prehistoric building or structure.

(c) Such professional and technical assistance may be employed without regard to the civil-service laws, and such service may be established as may be required to accomplish the purposes of this Act and for which money may be appropriated by Congress or made available by gifts for such purpose. (16 U.S.C. sec. 464.)

SECTION 5. Nothing in this Act shall be held to deprive any State, or political subdivision thereof, of its civil and criminal jurisdiction in and over lands acquired by the United States under this Act. (16 U.S.C. sec. 465.)

SECTION 6. There is authorized to be appropriated for carrying out the purposes of this Act such sums as the Congress may from time to time determine. (16 U.S.C. sec. 466.)

SECTION 7. The provisions of this Act shall control if any of them are in conflict with any other Act or Acts relating to the same subject matter. (16 U.S.C. sec. 467.)

HISTORIC PRESERVATION ACT OF 1966

AN ACT To Establish a Program for the Preservation of Additional Historic Properties Throughout the Nation, and for Other Purposes, Approved October 15, 1966 (Public Law 89-665; 80 STAT. 915; 16 U.S.C. 470)

Be it enacted by the Senate and House of Representatives of the United States of America in Congress assembled, That Congress finds and declares—

(a) That the spirit and direction of the Nation are founded upon and reflected in its historic past;

(b) That the historical and cultural foundations of the Nation should be preserved as a living part of our community life and development in order to give a sense of orientation to the American people;

(c) That, in the face of ever-increasing extensions of urban centers, highways, and residential, commercial, and industrial developments, the present governmental and nongovernmental historic preservation programs and activities are inadequate to insure future generations a genuine opportunity to appreciate and enjoy the rich heritage of our Nation; and

(d) That, although the major burdens of historic preservation have been borne and major efforts initiated by private agencies and individuals, and both should continue to play a vital role it is nevertheless necessary and appropriate for the Federal Government to accelerate its historic preservation programs and activities, to give maximum encouragement to agencies and individuals undertaking preservation by private means, and to assist State and local governments and the National Trust for Historic Preservation in the United States to expand and accelerate their historic preservation programs and activities.

Title I

Section 101

(a) The Secretary of the Interior is authorized—

(1) to expand and maintain a national register of districts, sites, buildings, structures, and objects significant in American history, architecture, archeology, and culture, hereinafter referred to as the National Register, and to grant funds

to States for the purpose of preparing comprehensive statewide historic surveys and plans, in accordance with criteria established by the Secretary, for the preservation, acquisition, and development of such properties;

(2) to establish a program of matching grants-in-aid to States for projects having as their purpose the preservation for public benefit of properties that are significant in American history, architecture, archeology, and culture; and

(3) to establish a program of matching grant-in-aid to the National Trust for Historic Preservation in the United States, chartered by act of Congress approved October 26, 1949 (63 Stat. 927), as amended, for the purpose of carrying out the responsibilities of the National Trust.

(b) As used in this Act—

(1) The term "State" includes, in addition to the several States of the Union, the District of Columbia, the Commonwealth of Puerto Rico, the Virgin Islands, Guam, and American Samoa.

(2) The term "project" means programs of State and local governments and other public bodies and private organizations and individuals for the acquisition of title or interests in, and for the development of, any district, site, building, structure, or object that is significant in American history, architecture, archeology, and culture, or property used in connection therewith, and for its development in order to assure the preservation for public benefit of any such historical properties.

(3) The term "historic preservation" includes the protection, rehabilitation, restoration, and reconstruction of districts, sites, buildings, structures, and objects significant in American history, architecture, archeology, or culture.

(4) The term "Secretary" means the Secretary of the Interior.

Section 102

(a) No grant may be made under this Act—

(1) unless application therefor is submitted to the Secretary in accordance with regulations and procedures prescribed by him;

(2) unless the application is in accordance with the comprehensive statewide historic preservation plan which has been approved by the Secretary after considering its relationship to the comprehensive statewide outdoor recreation plan prepared pursuant to the Land and Water Conservation Fund Act of 1965 (78 Stat. 897);

(3) for more than 50 per centum of the total cost involved, as determined by the Secretary and his determination shall be final;

(4) unless the grantee has agreed to make such reports, in such form and containing such information as the Secretary may from time to time require;

(5) unless the grantee has agreed to assume, after completion of the project, the total cost of the continued maintenance, repair, and administration of the property in a manner satisfactory to the Secretary; and

(6) until the grantee has complied with such further terms and conditions as the Secretary may deem necessary or advisable.

(b) The Secretary may in his discretion waive the requirements of subsection (a), paragraphs (2) and (5) of this section for any grant under this Act to the National Trust for Historic Preservation in the United States, in which case a grant to the National Trust may include funds for the maintenance, repair,and administration of the property in a manner satisfactory to the Secretary.

(c) No State shall be permitted to utilize the value of real property obtained before the date of approval of this Act in meeting the remaining cost of a project for which a grant is made under this Act.

Section 103

(a) The amounts appropriated and made available for grants to the State for comprehensive statewide historic surveys and plans under this Act shall be apportioned among the States by the Secretary on the basis of needs as determined by him: *Provided, however,* That the amount granted to any one State shall not exceed 50 per centum of the total cost of the comprehensive statewide historic survey and plan for that State, as determined by the Secretary.

(b) The amounts appropriated and made available for grants to the States for projects under this Act for each fiscal year shall be apportioned among the States by the Secretary in accordance with needs as disclosed in approved statewide historic preservation plans.

The Secretary shall notify each State of its apportionment, and the amounts thereof shall be available thereafter for payment to such State for projects in accordance with the provisions of this Act. Any amount of any apportionment that has not been paid or obligated by the Secretary during the fiscal year in which such notification is given, and for two fiscal years thereafter, shall be reapportioned by the Secretary in accordance with this subsection.

Section 104

(a) No grant may be made by the Secretary for or on account of any survey or project under this Act with respect to which financial assistance has been given or promised under any other Federal program or activity, and no financial assistance may be given under any other Federal program or activity for or on account of any survey or project with respect to which assistance has been given or promised under this Act.

(b) In order to assure consistency in policies and actions under this Act with other related Federal programs and activities, and to assure coordination of the planning, acquisition, and development assistance to States under this Act with other related Federal programs and activities, the President may issue such regulations with respect thereto as he deems desirable, and such assistance may be provided only in accordance with such regulations.

Section 105

The beneficiary of assistance under this Act shall keep such records as the Secretary shall prescribe, including records which fully disclose the disposition by the beneficiary of the proceeds of such assistance, the total cost of the project or undertaking in connection with which such assistance is given or used, and the amount and nature of that portion of the cost of the project or undertaking supplied by other sources, and such other records as will facilitate an effective audit.

Section 106

The head of any Federal Agency having direct or indirect jurisdiction over a proposed Federal or federally assisted undertaking in any State and the head of any Federal department or independent agency having authority to license any undertaking shall prior to the approval of the expenditure of any Federal funds on the undertaking or prior to the issuance of any license, as the case may be, take into account the effect of the undertaking on any district, site, building structure, or object that is included in the National Register. The head of any such Federal agency shall afford the Advisory Council on Historic Preservation established under title II of this Act a reasonable opportunity to comment with regard to such undertaking.

Section 107

Nothing in this Act shall be construed to be applicable to the White House and its grounds, the Supreme Court building and its grounds, or the United States Capitol and its related buildings and grounds.

Section 108

There are authorized to be appropriated not to exceed $2,000,000 to carry out the provisions of this Act for the fiscal year 1967, and not more than $10,000,000 for each of the three succeeding fiscal years. Such appropriations shall be available for the financial assistance authorized by this title and for the administrative expenses of the Secretary in connection therewith, and shall remain available until expended.

Title II

Section 201

(a) There is established an Advisory Council on Historic Preservation (hereinafter referred to as the "Council") which shall be composed of seventeen members as follows:

(1) The Secretary of the Interior.

(2) The Secretary of Housing and Urban Development.

(3) The Secretary of Commerce.

(4) The Administrator of the General Services Administration.

(5) The Secretary of the Treasury.

(6) The Attorney General.

(7) The Chairman of the National Trust for Historic Preservation.

(8) Ten appointed by the President from outside the Federal Government. In making these appointments, the President shall give due consideration to the selection of officers of State and local governments and individuals who are significantly interested and experienced in the matters to be considered by the Council.

(b) Each member of the Council specified in paragraphs (1) through (6) of subsection (a) may designate another officer of his department or agency to serve on the Council in his stead.

(c) Each member of the Council appointed under paragraph (8) of subsection (a) shall serve for a term of five years from the expiration of his predecessor's term; except that the members first appointed under that paragraph shall serve for terms of from one to five years, as designated by the President at the time of appointment, in such manner as to insure that the terms of not less than one nor more than two of them will expire in any one year.

(d) A vacancy in the Council shall not affect its powers, but shall be filled in the same manner as the original appointment (and for the balance of the unexpired term).

(e) The Chairman of the Council shall be designated by the President.

(f) Eight members of the Council shall constitute a quorum.

Section 202

(a) The Council shall—

(1) advise the President and the Congress on matters relating to historic preservation; recommend measures to coordinate activities of Federal, State, and local agencies and private institutions and individuals relating to historic preservation; and advise on the dissemination of information pertaining to such activities;

(2) encourage, in cooperation with the National Trust for Historic Preservation and appropriate private agencies, public interest and participation in historic preservation;

(3) recommend the conduct of studies in such areas as the adequacy of legislative and administrative statutes and regulations pertaining to historic preservation activities of State and local governments and the effects of tax policies at all levels of government on historic preservation;

(4) advise as to guidelines for the assistance of State and local governments in drafting legislation relating to historic preservation; and

(5) encourage, in cooperation with appropriate public and private agencies and institutions, training and education in the field of historic preservation.

(b) The council shall submit annually a comprehensive report of its activities and the results of its studies to the President and the Congress and shall from time to time submit such additional and special reports as it deems advisable. Each report shall propose such legislative enactments and other actions as, in the judgment of the Council, are necessary and appropriate to carry out its recommendations.

Section 203

The Council is authorized to secure directly from any department, bureau, agency, board, commission, office, independent establishment or instrumentality of the executive branch of the Federal Government information, suggestions, estimates, and statistics for the purpose of this title; and each such department, bureau, agency, board, commission, office, independent establishment or instrumentality is authorized to furnish such information, suggestions, estimates, and statistics to the extent permitted by law and within available funds.

Section 204

The members of the Council specified in paragraphs (1) through (7) of section 201 (a) shall serve without additional compensation. The members of the Council appointed under paragraph (8) of section 201 (a) shall receive $100 per diem when engaged in the performances of the duties of the Council. All members of the Council shall receive reimbursement for necessary traveling and subsistence expenses incurred by them in the performance of the duties of the Council.

Section 205

(a) The Director of the National Park Service or his designee shall be the Executive Director of the Council. Financial and administrative services (including those related to budgeting, accounting, financial reporting, personnel and procurement) shall be provided the Council by the Department of the Interior, for which payments shall be made in advance, or by reimbursement, from funds of the Council in such amounts as may be agreed upon by the Chairman of the Council and the Secretary of the Interior: *Provided,* That the regulations of the Department of the Interior for the collection of indebtedness of personnel resulting from erroneous payments (5 U.S.C. 46e) shall apply to the collection of erroneous payments made to or on behalf of a Council employee, and regulations of said Secretary for the administrative control of funds (31

U.S.C. 665.(g)) shall apply to appropriations of the Council: *And provided further,* That the Council shall not be required to prescribe such regulations.

(b) The Council shall have power to appoint and fix the compensation of such additional personnel as may be necessary to carry out its duties, without regard to the provisions of the civil service laws and the Classification Act of 1949.

(c) The Council may also procure, without regard to the civil service laws and the Classification Act of 1949, temporary and intermittent services to the same extent as is authorized for the executive departments by section 15 of the Administrative Expenses Act of 1946 (5 U.S.C. 55a), but at rates not to exceed $50 per diem for individuals.

(d) The members of the Council specified in paragraphs (1) through (6) of section 210 (a) shall provide the Council, on a reimbursable basis, with such facilities and services under their jurisdiction and control as may be needed by the Council to carry out its duties, to the extent that such facilities and services are requested by the Council and are otherwise available for that purpose. To the extent of available appropriations, the Council may obtain, by purchase, rental, donation, or otherwise, such additional property, facilities, and services as may be needed to carry out its duties.

RESERVOIR SALVAGE ACT OF 1960

An ACT to Provide for the Preservation of Historical and Archaeological Data (including Relics and Specimens) which might Otherwise be Lost as the Result of the Construction of a Dam, Approved June 27, 1960 (Public Law 86-523; 74 STAT. 220; 16 U.S.C. 469-469c)

Be it enacted by the Senate and House of Representatives of the United States of America in Congress assembled, That it is the purpose of this Act to further the policy set forth in the Act entitled "An Act to provide for the preservation of historic American sites, buildings, objects, and antiquities of national significance, and for other purposes," approved August 21, 1935 (16 U.S.C. 461-467) by specifically providing for the preservation of historical and archaeological data (including relics and specimens) which might otherwise be irreparably lost or destroyed as the result of flooding, the building of access roads, the erection of workmen's communities, the relocation of railroads and highways, and other alterations of the terrain caused by the construction of a dam by an agency of the United States, or by any private person or corporation holding a license issued by any such agency.

Section 2.

(a) Before any agency of the United States shall undertake the construction of a dam, or issue a license to any private individual or corporation for the construction of a dam, it shall give written notice to the Secretary of the Interior setting forth the site of the proposed dam and the approximate area to be flooded and otherwise changed if such construction is undertaken; *Provided,* with respect to any floodwater retarding dam which provides less than five thousand acre-feet of detention capacity and with respect to any other type of dam which creates a reservoir of less than forty surface acres the provisions of this section shall apply only when the constructing agency, in his preliminary surveys, finds, or is presented with evidence that historical or archaeological materials exist or may be present in the proposed reservoir area.

(b) Upon receipt of any notice, as provided in subsection (a), the Secretary of the Interior (hereinafter referred to as the "Secretary"), shall cause a survey to be made of the area proposed to be flooded to ascertain whether such area contains historical and archaeological data (including relics and specimens) which should be preserved in the public interest. Any such survey shall be conducted as expeditiously as possible. If, as a result of any such survey, the Secretary shall determine (1) that such data exists in such area, (2) that such data has exceptional historical or archaeological significance, and should be collected and preserved in the public interest, and (3) that it is feasible to collect and preserve such data, he shall cause the necessary work to be performed in such area to collect and preserve such data. All such work shall be performed as expeditiously as possible.

(c) The Secretary shall keep the instigating agency notified at all times of the progress of any survey made under this Act, or of any work undertaken as a result of such survey, in order that there will be as little disruption or delay as possible in the carrying out of the functions of such agency.

(d) A survey similar to that provided for by section (b) of this section and the work required to be performed as a result thereof shall so far as practicable also be undertaken in connection with any dam the construction of which has been heretofore authorized by any agency of the United States, or by any such private person or corporation holding a license issued by any such agency.

(e) The Secretary shall consult with any interested Federal and State agencies, educational and scientific organizations, and private institutions and qualified individuals, with a view to determining the ownership of and the most appropriate repository for any relics and specimens recovered as a result of any work performed as provided for in this section.

Section 3

In the administration of this Act, the Secretary may—

(1) enter into contracts or make cooperative agreements with any Federal or State agency, any educational or scientific organization, or any institution, corporation, association, or qualified individual; and

(2) procure the temporary or intermittent services of experts or consultants or organizations thereof as provided in Section 15 of the Act of August 2, 1946 (5 U.S.C. 55a); and

(3) accept and utilize funds made available for salvage archaeological purposes by any private person or corporations holding a license issued by an agency of the United States for the construction of a dam or other type of water or power control project.

Section 4

There are hereby authorized to be appropriated such sums as may be necessary to carry out the purposes of this Act.

PROPOSED AMENDMENT TO
RESERVOIR SALVAGE ACT OF 1960

Introduced into the 92nd Session of Congress by Senator Moss of Utah (S.1245) and Congressman Bennett of Florida (H.R. 6257) To Amend the Act of June 27, 1960 (74 Stat. 220), relating to the preservation of historical and archeological data.

Be it enacted by the Senate and House of Representatives of the United States of America in Congress assembled, "That it is the purpose of this Act to further the policy set forth in the Act entitled 'An Act to provide for the preservation of historic American sites, buildings, objects, and antiquities of national significance, and for other purposes,' approved August 21, 1935 (16 U.S.C. 461-467), and the Act entitled 'An Act to establish a program for the preservation of additional historic properties throughout the Nation, and for other purposes,' approved October 15, 1966 (80 Stat. 915), by specifically providing for the preservation of scientific, prehistorical, historical, and archeological data (including relics and specimens) which might otherwise be irreparably lost or destroyed as the result of (1) flooding, the building of access roads, the erection of workmen's communities, the relocation of railroads and highways, and other alterations of the terrain caused by the construction of a dam by any agency of the United States, or by any private person or corporation holding a license issued by any such agency; or (2) any alteration of the terrain caused as a result of any Federal, federally assisted, or federally licensed activity or program.

SECTION 2. Before any agency of the United States shall undertake the construction of a dam, or issue a license to any private individual or corporation for the construction of a dam it shall give written notice to the Secretary of the Interior (hereinafter referred to as the 'secretary') setting forth the site of the proposed dam and the approximate area to be flooded and otherwise changed if such construction is undertaken: *Provided,* That with respect to any floodwater retarding dam which provides less than five thousand acre-feet of detention capacity and with respect to any other type of dam which creates a reservoir of less than forty surface acres the provisions of this section shall apply only when the construction agency, in its preliminary surveys, finds, or is presented with evidence that scientific, prehistorical, historical, or archeological data exist or may be present in the proposed reservoir area.

SECTION 3. (a) When any Federal agency finds, or is made aware by an appropriate historical or archeological authority, that its operation in connection with any Federal, federally assisted, or federally licensed project, activity, or program adversely affects or may adversely affect significant scientific, prehistorical, historical, or archeological data, such agency shall notify the Secretary, in writing, and shall provide the Secretary with appropriate information concerning the project, program, or activity. Such agency (1) may request the Secretary to undertake the recovery, protection, and preservation of such data (including preliminary survey, or other investigation as needed, and analysis and publication of the reports resulting from such investigation), or (2) may, with funds appropriated for such project, program, or activity, undertake the activities referred to in clause (1). Copies of reports of any investigations made pursuant to clause (2) shall be made available to the Secretary.

(b) The Secretary, upon notification by any such agency or by any other Federal or State agency or appropriate historical or archeological authority that scientific, prehistorical, historical, or archeological data is or may be adversely affected by any Federal, federally assisted, or federally, licensed project, activity, or program, shall, if he determines that such data is being or may be adversely affected, and after reasonable notice to the agency responsible for such project, activity, or program, conduct or cause to be conducted a survey and other investigation of the areas which are or may be affected and recover and preserve such data (including analysis and publication) which, in his opinion are not being but should be recovered and preserved in the public interest. The Secretary shall initiate action within sixty days of notification to him by an agency pursuant to subsection (a), and within such time as may be agreed upon with the head of the responsible agency in all other cases. The responsible agency upon request of the Secretary is hereby authorized to assist the Secretary and to transfer to the Secretary such funds as may be necessary, in an amount not to exceed one per centum of the total amount appropriated for such project, activity, or program, to enable the Secretary to conduct such survey or other investigation and recover and preserve such data (including analysis and publication) or, in the case of small projects which cause extensive scientific, prehistorical, historical, or archeological damage, such larger amount as may be mutually agreed upon by the Secretary and the responsible Federal agency as being necessary to effect adequate protection and recovery; *Provided,* That the costs of such survey, recovery, analysis and publication shall be considered project costs allocated to the several project purposes. An appropriate share, as determined by the responsible Federal agency, of the costs of survey, recovery, analysis, and publication shall be borne by the grantee in the case of projects, activities, or programs funded under Federal grant-in-aid programs.

(c) The Secretary shall keep the responsible agency notified at all times of the progress of any survey or other investigation made under this Act, or of any work undertaken as a result of such survey, in order that there will be as little disruption or delay as possible in the carrying out of the functions of such agency.

(d) A survey or other investigation similar to that provided for by subsection (b) of this section and the work required to be performed as a result thereof shall so far as practicable also be undertaken in connection with any dam, project, activity, or program which has been heretofore authorized by any agency of the United States, by any private person or corporation holding a license issued by any such agency, or by Federal law.

(e) The Secretary shall consult with any interested Federal and State agencies, educational and scientific organizations, and private institutions and qualified individuals, with a view to determining the ownership of and the most appropriate repository for any relics and specimens recovered as a result of any work performed as provided for in this section.

SECTION 4. In the administration of this Act, the Secretary may—

(1) accept and utilize funds transferred to him by any Federal agency pursuant to this Act;

(2) enter into contracts or make cooperative agreements with any Federal or State agency, any educational or scientific organization, or any institution, corporation, associations, or qualified individual;

(3) obtain the services of experts and consultants or organizations thereof in accordance with section 3109 of title 5, United States Code; and

(4) accept and utilize funds made available for salvage archeological purposes by any private person or corporation.

SECTION 5. There are hereby authorized to be appropriated such sums as may be necessary to carry out the purposes of this Act.

NATIONAL ENVIRONMENTAL POLICY ACT OF 1969

AN ACT To establish a National policy for the environment, to provide for the establishment of a Council on Environmental Quality, and for other purposes, Approved January 1, 1970 (Public Law 91-190; 91 STAT. 852; 42 U.S.C. 4321-4347)

Be it enacted by the Senate and House of Representatives of the United States of America in Congress assembled, That this Act may be cited as the "National Environmental Policy Act of 1969".

Purpose

SECTION 2. The purposes of this Act are: to declare a national policy which will encourage production and enjoyable harmony between man and his environment; to promote efforts which will prevent or eliminate damage to the environment and biosphere and stimulate the health and welfare of man; to enrich the understanding of the ecological systems and natural resources important to the Nation; and to establish a Council on Environmental Quality.

Title I

Declaration of National Environmental Policy

SECTION 101. (a) The Congress, recognizing the profound impact of man's activity on the interrelations of all components of the natural environment, particularly the profound influences of population growth, high-density urbanization, industrial expansion, resource exploitation, and new expanding technological advances and recognizing further the critical importance of restoring and maintaining environmental quality to the overall welfare and development of man, declares that it is the continuing policy of the Federal Government, in cooperation with State and local governments, and other concerned public and private organizations, to use all practicable means and measures, including financial and technical assistance, in a manner calculated to foster and promote the general welfare, to create and maintain conditions under which man and nature can exist in productive harmony, and fulfill the social, economic, and other requirements of present and future generations of Americans.

(b) In order to carry out the policy set forth in this Act, it is the continuing responsibility of the Federal Government to use all practicable means, consistent with other essential considerations of national policy, to improve and coordinate Federal plans, functions, programs, and resources to the end that the Nation may—

(1) fulfill the responsibilities of each generation as trustee of the environment for succeeding generations;

(2) assure for all Americans safe, healthful, productive, and esthetically and culturally pleasing surroundings;

(3) attain the widest range of beneficial uses of the environment without degradation, risk to health or safety, or other undesirable and unintended consequences;

(4) preserve important historic, cultural, and natural aspects of our national

heritage, and maintain, wherever possible, an environment which supports diversity and variety of individual choice;

(5) achieve a balance between population and resource use which will permit high standards of living and a wide sharing of life's amenities; and

(6) enhance the quality of renewable resources and approach the maximum attainable recycling of depletable resources.

(c) The Congress recognizes that each person should enjoy a healthful environment and that each person has a responsibility to contribute to the preservation and enhancement of the environment.

SECTION 102. The Congress authorizes and directs that, to the fullest extent possible: (1) the policies, regulations, and public laws of the United States shall be interpreted and administered in accordance with the policies set forth in this Act, and (2) all agencies of the Federal Government shall—

(A) utilize a systematic, interdisciplinary approach which will insure the integrated use of the natural and social sciences and the environmental design arts in planning and in decisionmaking which may have an impact on man's environment;

(B) identify and develop methods and procedures, in consultations with the Council on Environmental Quality established by title II of this Act, which will insure that presently unquantified environmental amenities and values may be given appropriate consideration in decisionmaking along with economic and technical considerations;

(C) include in every recommendation or report on proposals for legislation and other major Federal actions significantly affecting the quality of the human environment, a detailed statement by the responsible official on—

(i) the environmental impact of the proposed action,

(ii) any adverse environmental effects which cannot be avoided should the proposal be implemented,

(iii) alternatives to the proposed action,

(iv) the relationship between local short-term uses of man's environment and the maintenance and enhancement of long-term productivity, and

(v) any irreversible and irretrievable commitments of resources which would be involved in the proposed action should it be implemented. Prior to making any detailed statement, the responsible Federal official shall consult with and obtain the comments of any Federal agency which has jurisdiction by law or special expertise with respect to any environmental impact involved. Copies of such statement and the comments and views of the appropriate Federal, State, and local agencies, which are authorized to develop and enforce environmental standards, shall be made available to the President, the Council on Environmental Quality and to the public as provided by section 552 of title 5. United States Code, and shall accompany the proposal through the existing agency review processes;

(D) study, develop, and describe appropriate alternatives to recommended courses of action in any proposal which involves unresolved conflicts concerning alternative uses of available resources;

(E) recognize the worldwide and long-range character of environmental problems and, where consistent with the foreign policy of the United States, lend appropriate support to initiatives, resolutions, and programs designed to maximize international cooperation in anticipating and preventing a decline in the quality of mankind's world environment;

(F) make available to States, counties, municipalities, institutions, and individuals, advice and information useful in restoring, maintaining, and enhancing the quality of the environment;

(G) initiate and utilize ecological information in the planning and development of resource-oriented projects; and

(H) assist the Council on Environmental Quality established by title II of this Act.

SECTION 103. All agencies of the Federal Government shall review their present statutory authority, administrative regulations, and current policies and procedures for the purpose of determining whether there are any deficiencies or inconsistencies therein which prohibit full compliance with the purposes and provisions of this Act and shall propose to the President not later than July 1, 1971, such measures as may be necessary to bring their authority and policies into conformity with the intent, purposes, and procedures set forth in this Act.

SECTION 104. Nothing in Section 102 or 103 shall in any way affect the specific statutory obligations of any Federal agency (1) to comply with criteria or standards of environmental quality, (2) to coordinate or consult with any other Federal or State agency, or (3) to act, or refrain from acting contingent upon the recommendations or certification of any other Federal or State agency.

SECTION 105. The policies and goals set forth in this Act are supplementary to those set forth in existing authorizations of Federal agencies.

Title II

Council On Environmental Quality

SECTION 201. The President shall transmit to the Congress annually beginning July 1, 1970, an Environmental Quality Report (hereinafter referred to as the "report") which shall set forth (1) the status and condition of the major natural, manmade, or altered environmental classes of the Nation, including, but not limited to, the air, the aquatic, including marine, estuarine, and fresh water, and the terrestrial environment, including, but not limited to, the forest, dryland, wetland, range, urban, suburban, and rural environment; (2)

current and foreseeable trends in the quality, management and utilization of such environments and the effects of those trends on the social, economic, and other requirements of the Nation; (3) the adequacy of available natural resources for fulfilling human and economic requirements of the Nation in the light of expected population pressures; (4) a review of the programs and activities (including regulatory activities) of the Federal Government, the State and local governments, and nongovernmental entities or individuals, with particular reference to their effect on the environment and on the conservation, development and utilization of natural resources; and (5) a program for remedying the deficiencies of existing programs and activities, together with recommendations for legislation.

SECTION 202. There is created in the Executive Office of the President a Council on Environmental Quality (hereinafter referred to as the "Council"). The Council shall be composed of three members who shall be appointed by the President to serve at his pleasure, by and with the advice and consent of the Senate. The President shall designate one of the members of the Council to serve as Chairman. Each member shall be a person who, as a result of his training, experience, and attainments, is exceptionally well qualified to analyze and interpret environmental trends and information of all kinds; to appraise programs and activities of the Federal Government in the light of the policy set forth in title I of this Act; to be conscious of and responsive to the scientific, economic, social, esthetic, and cultural needs and interests of the Nation; and to formulate and recommend national policies to promote the improvement of the quality of the environment.

SECTION 203. The Council may employ such officers and employees as may be necessary for the carrying out of its functions under this Act, in accordance may employ and fix the compensation of such experts and consultants as may be necessary for the carrying out of its functions under this Act, in accordance with section 3109 of title 5, United States Code (but without regard to the last sentence thereof).

SECTION 204. It shall be the duty and function of the Council—

(1) to assist and advise the President in the preparation of the Environmental Quality Report required by section 201;

(2) to gather timely and authoritative information concerning the conditions and trends in the quality of the environment both current and prospective, to analyze and interpret such information for the purpose of determining whether such conditions and trends are interfering, or are likely to interfere, with the achievement of the policy set forth in title I of this Act, and to compile and submit to the President studies relating to such conditions and trends;

(3) to review and appraise the various programs and activities of the Federal Government in the light of the policy set forth in title I of this Act for the purpose of determining the extent to which such programs and activities are

contributing to the achievement of such policy, and to make recommendations to the President with respect thereto;

(4) to develop and recommend to the President national policies to foster and promote the improvement of environmental quality to meet the conservation, social, economic, health, and other requirements and goals of the Nation;

(5) to conduct investigations, studies, surveys, research, and analysis relating to ecological systems and environmental quality;

(6) to document and define changes in the natural environment, including the plant and animal systems, and to accumulate necessary data and other information for a continuing analysis of these changes or trends and an interpretation of their underlying causes;

(7) to report at least once each year to the President on the state and condition of the environment; and

(8) to make and furnish such studies, reports thereon, and recommendations with respect to matters of policy and legislation as the President may request.

SECTION 205. In exercising its powers, functions, and duties under this Act, the Council shall

(1) consult with the Citizens' Advisory Committee on Environmental Quality established by Executive Order numbered 11472, dated May 29, 1969, and with such representatives of science, industry, agriculture, labor, conservation organizations, State and local governments and other groups, as it deems advisable; and

(2) utilize, to the fullest extent possible, the services, facilities, and information (including statistical information) of public and private agencies and organizations, and individuals, in order that duplication of effort and expense may be avoided, thus assuring that the Council's activities will not unnecessarily overlap or conflict with similar activities authorized by law and performed by established agencies.

SECTION 206. Members of the Council shall serve full time and the Chairman of the Council shall be compensated at the rate provided for Level II of the Executive Schedule Pay Rates (5 U.S.C. 5313). The other members of the Council shall be compensated at the rate provided for Level IV of the Executive Schedule Pay Rates (5 U.S.C. 5315).

SECTION 207. There are authorized to be appropriated to carry out the provisions of this Act not to exceed $300,000 for fiscal year 1970, $700,000 for fiscal year 1971, and $1,000,000 for each fiscal year thereafter.

EXCERPTS FROM DEPARTMENT OF TRANSPORTATION LEGISLATION

49 U.S.C. 1651. Congressional Declaration of Purpose

(a) The Congress hereby declares that the general welfare, the economic growth and stability of the Nation and its security require the development of national transportation policies and programs conducive to the provision of fast, safe, efficient, and convenient transportation at the lowest cost consistent therewith and with other national objectives, including the efficient utilization and conservation of the Nation's resources.

(b) (1) The Congress therefore finds that the establishment of a Department of Transportation is necessary in the public interest and to assure the coordinated, effective administration of the transportation program to the Federal Government; to facilitate the development and improvement of coordinated transportation service, to be provided by private enterprise to the maximum extent feasible; to encourage cooperation of Federal, State, and local governments, carriers, labor, and other interested parties toward the achievement of national transportation objectives; to stimulate technological advances in transportation; to provide general leadership in the identification and solution of transportation problems; and to develop and recommend to the President and the Congress for approval of national transportation policies and programs to accomplish these objectives with full and appropriate consideration of the needs of the public, users, carriers, industry, labor, and the national defense.

(2) It is hereby declared to be the national policy that special effort should be made to preserve the natural beauty of the countryside and public park and recreational lands, wildlife and waterfowl refuges, and historic sites.

23 U.S.C. 138. Preservation of Park Lands

It is hereby declared to be the national policy that special effort should be made to preserve the natural beauty of the countryside and public park and recreation lands, wildlife and waterfowl refuges, and historic sites. The Secretary of Transportation shall cooperate and consult with the Secretaries of the Interior, Housing and Urban Development, and Agriculture, and with the States in developing transportation plans and programs that include measures to maintain or enhance the natural beauty of the lands traversed. After the effective date of the Federal-Aid Highway Act of 1968 [August 23, 1968], the Secretary shall not approve any program or project which requires the use of any publicly owned land from a public park, recreation area, or wildlife or waterfowl refuge of national, State, or local significance as determined by the Federal, State, or local officials having jurisdiction thereof, or any land and historic site of national, state, or local significance as so determined by such officials unless (1) there is no feasible and prudent alternative to the use of such lands, and (2) such program includes all possible planning to minimize harm to such park, recreational area, wildlife, and waterfowl refuge, or historic site resulting from such use.

23 U.S.C. 305. Archeological and Paleontological Salvage

Funds authorized to be appropriated to carry out this title to the extent approved as necessary by the highway department of any State, may be used for

archeological and paleontological salvage in that State in compliance with the
Act entitled "An Act for the preservation of American antiquities," approved
June 8, 1906 (34 Stat. 225), and State laws where applicable.

EXCERPTS FROM DEPARTMENT
OF HOUSING AND URBAN DEVELOPMENT LEGISLATION

40 U.S.C. 461 Comprehensive planning

. . . .

(h) Grants for Surveys of historic structures. In addition to the other grants
authorized by this section, the Secretary is authorized to make grants to assist
any city, other municipality, or county in making a survey of the structures and
sites in such locality which are determined by its appropriate authorities to be of
historic or architectural value. Any such survey shall be designed to identify the
historic structures and sites in the locality, determine the cost of their
rehabilitation or restoration, and provide such other information as may be
necessary or appropriate to serve as a foundation for a balanced and effective
program of historic preservation in such locality. The aspects of any such survey
which relate to the identification of historic and architectural values shall be
conducted in accordance with criteria found by the Secretary to be comparable
to those used in establishing the national register maintained by the Secretary of
the Interior under other provisions of law; and the results of each such survey
shall be made available to the Secretary of the Interior. A grant under this
subsection shall not exceed two-thirds of the cost of the survey for which it is
made, and shall be made to the appropriate agency or entity specified in
paragraphs (1) through (11) of subsection (a) [basically, those listed are federal,
state, regional, and certain local planning and development agencies] for [sic], if
there is no such agency or entity which is qualified and willing to receive the
grant and provide for its utilization in accordance with this subsection, directly
to the city, other municipality, or county involved.

42 U.S.C. 1460. Definitions

. . . .

(c) "Urban renewal project" or "project" may include undertakings and
activities of a local public agency in an urban renewal area for the elimination
and for the prevention of the development of spread of slums and blight, and
may involve slum clearance and redevelopment in an urban renewal area, or
rehabilitation or conservation in an urban renewal area, or any combination or
part thereof, in accordance with such urban renewal plan. Such undertakings and
activities may include— . . . (6) acquisition of any other real property in the

urban renewal area where necessary to eliminate unhealthful, insanitary or unsafe conditions, lessen density, eliminate obsolete or other uses detrimental to the public welfare, or otherwise to remove or prevent the spread of blight or deterioration, to promote historic and architectural preservation, or to provide land for needed public facilities; . . . (9) relocation within or outside the project area of structures which will be restored and maintained for architectural or historic purposes; and . . . (10) restoration of acquired properties of historic or architectural value.

Notwithstanding any other provision of this subchapter, (A) no contract shall be entered into for any law or capital grant under this subchapter for any project which provides for demolition and removal of buildings and improvements unless the Secretary determines that the objectives of the urban renewal plan could not be achieved through rehabilitation of the project area, ...

. . . .

(d) "Local grants-in-aids" shall mean assistance by a State, municipality, or other public body, or (in the case of cash grants or donation of land or other real property) any other entity, in connection with any project on which a contract for capital grant has been made under this subchapter, in the form of (1) cash grants to defray expenditures within the purview of subsection (e) (1) of this section; (2) donation, at cash value, of land or other real property (exclusive of land in streets, alleys, and other public rights-of-way which may be vacated in connection with the project, or of air rights over streets, alleys, and other public rights-of-way) in the urban renewal area, and demolition, removal, or other work or improvements in the urban renewal area, at the cost thereof, of the types described in clauses (2), (3), (7), (9), and (10) of the second sentence of subsection (c) of this section; . . . . [See above.]

42 U.S.C. 1500. Congressional Declaration of Findings and Purpose

[As it would appear to be amended by the Housing and Urban Development Act of 1970, Public Law 91-609, 84 Stat. 1770, Title VII, Section 701 (c) and (d)].

. . . .

(c) The Congress further finds that there is a need for timely action to preserve and restore areas, sites, and structures of historic or architectural value in order that these remaining evidences of our history and heritage shall not be lost or destroyed through the expansion and development of the Nation's urban areas.

(d) It is the purpose of this chapter to help curb urban sprawl and prevent the spread of urban blight and deterioration, to encourage more economic and desirable urban development, to assist in preserving areas and properties of historic or architectural value, and to help provide necessary recreational, conservation, and scenic areas by assisting State and local public bodies in taking prompt action to (1) provide, preserve, and develop open-space land in a manner consistent with the planned long-range development of the Nation's urban areas, (2) acquire, improve, and restore areas, sites, and structures of historic or architectural value, and (3) develop and improve open-space and other public urban land, in accordance with programs to encourage and coordinate local public and private efforts toward this end.

42 U.S.C. 1500a. Grants to States and Local Public Bodies

[As it would appear to be amended by the Housing and Urban Development Act of 1970, Public Law 91-609, 84 Stat. 1770, Title VII Sections 702 (a) and (b)].

(a) Authorization. The Secretary is authorized to make grants to States and local public bodies to help finance (1) the acquisition of title to, or other interest in, open-space land in urban areas and (2) the development of open-space or other land in urban areas for open-space uses. The amount of any such grant shall not exceed 50 per centum of the eligible project cost, as approved by the Secretary of such acquisition or development. Not more than 50 per centum of the non-Federal share of such eligible project cost may, to the extent authorized in regulations established by the Secretary, be made up by donations of land or materials.

. . . .

(c) Restrictions on use of grants. No grants under this title shall be made to (1) defray ordinary State or local governmental expenses, (2) help finance the acquisition by a public body of land located outside the urban area for which it exercises (or participates in the exercise of) responsibilities consistent with the purpose of this title, (3) acquire and clear developed land in built-up urban areas unless the local governing body determines that adequate open-space land cannot be effectively provided through the use of existing undeveloped land, or (4) provide assistance for historic and architectural preservation purposes, except for districts, sites, buildings, structures, and objects which the Secretary of the Interior determines meet the criteria used in establishing the National Register.

(d) Determination of further terms and conditions for assistance. The Secretary may set such further terms and conditions for assistance under this chapter as he determines to be desirable.

(e) Review of applications; consultation with the Secretary of the Interior;

exchange of information. The Secretary shall consult with the Secretary of the Interior on the general policies to be followed in reviewing applications for grants under this chapter. To assist the Secretary in such review, the Secretary of the Interior shall furnish him (1) appropriate information on the status of national and statewide recreation and historic preservation planning as it affects the areas to be assisted with such grants, and (2) the current listing of any districts, sites, buildings, structures, and objects significant in American history, architecture, archeology, and culture which may be contained on a National Register maintained by the Secretary of the Interior pursuant to other provisions of law. The Secretary shall provide current information to the Secretary of the Interior from time to time on significant program developments.

42 U.S.C. 1500b. Planning Requirements

(As it would appear to be amended by the Housing and Urban Development Act of 1970, Public Law 91-609, 84 Stat. 1770, Title VII, Section 703.)

The Secretary shall make grants under section 1500a and 1500c-1 of this title only if he finds that such assistance is needed for carrying out a unified or officially coordinated program, meeting criteria established by him, for the provision and development of open-space land which is a part of, or is consistent with, the comprehensively planned development of the urban area.

42 U.S.C. 1500c. Conversions to Other Uses

(As it would appear to be amended by the Housing and Urban Development Act of 1970, Public Law 91-609, 84 Stat. 1770, Title VII, Section 704.)

No open-space land for the acquisition of which a grant has been made under this chapter shall be converted to uses not originally approved by the Secretary without his prior approval. Prior approval will be granted only upon satisfactory compliance with regulations established by the Secretary. Such regulations shall require findings that (1) there is adequate assurance of the substitution of other open-space land of as nearly as feasible equivalent usefulness, location and fair market value at the time of the conversion; (2) the conversion and substitution are needed for orderly growth and development; and (3) the proposed uses of the converted and substituted land are in accord with the then applicable comprehensive plan for the urban area, meeting criteria established by the Secretary.

[Note: Title VII, Section 705 of Public Law 91-609, 84 Stat. 1770, provides additional wording which would appear further to amend this section and this chapter by adding, "No open-space land involving historic or architectural purposes for which assistance has been granted under this title shall be converted to use for any other purpose without the prior approval of the Secretary of the Interior."]

42 U.S.C. 1500d. Technical Assistance, Studies, and Publication of Information

(a) In order to carry out the purpose of this chapter the Secretary is authorized to provide technical assistance to State and local public bodies and to undertake such studies and publish such information, either directly or by contract, as he shall determine to be desirable.

(b) The Secretary is authorized to use during any fiscal year not to exceed $125,000 of the funds available for grants under this chapter to undertake such studies and publish such information. Nothing contained in this section shall limit any authority of the Secretary under any other provision of law.

(c) Notwithstanding any other provision of this chapter, the Secretary may use not to exceed $10,000,000 of the sum authorized for contracts under this chapter for the purpose of entering into contracts to make grants in amounts not to exceed 90 per centum of the cost of activities which he determines have special value in developing and demonstrating new and improved methods and materials for use in carrying out the purposes of this chapter.

42 U.S.C. 1500d-1. Grants for Historic Preservation

The Secretary is authorized to enter into contracts to make grants to States and local public bodies to assist in the acquisition of title to or other permanent interests in areas, sites, and structures of historic or architectural value in urban areas, and in their restoration and improvement for public use and benefit, in accordance with the comprehensively planned development of the locality. The amount of any such grant shall not exceed 50 per centum of the total cost, as approved by the Secretary, of the assisted activities. The remainder of such cost shall be provided from non-Federal sources.

Criteria for Grants for Historic Preservation. Section 605(h) of Public Law 89-754 provided that: "Commencing three years after the date of the enactment of this act [November 3, 1966], no grant shall be made (except pursuant to a contract or commitment entered into less than three years after such date) under Section 709 of the Housing Act of 1961 [this section] or Section 701(h) of the Housing Act of 1954 [Section 461(h) of Title 40], or under Section 103 of the Housing Act of 1949 [Section 1453 of this title] to the extent that it is to be used for historic or architectural preservation, except with respect to districts, sites, buildings, structures, and objects which the Secretary of Housing and

Urban Development finds meet criteria comparable to those used in establishing the National Register maintained by the Secretary of the Interior pursuant to other provisions of law." This annotation may have been superseded by section 1500a (c) as it appears to have been enlarged by Public Law 91-609, 84 Stat. 1770, Title VII, Section 702(b), particularly in regard to the wording having reference to the National Register. (See page 260.)

42 U.S.C. 1500e. Definitions

(As it would appear to be amended by the Housing and Urban Development Act of 1970, Public Law 91-609, 84 Stat. 1770, Title VII, Section 709.) As used in this chapter—

(1) The term 'open-space land' means any land located in an urban area which has value for (A) park and recreational purposes, (B) conservation of land and other natural resources, or (C) historic, architectural, or scenic purposes.

(2) The term 'urban area' means any area which is urban in character, including those surrounding areas which, in the judgment of the Secretary, form an economic and socially related region, taking into consideration such factors as present and future population trends and patterns of urban growth, location of transportation facilities and systems, and distribution of industrial, commercial, residential, governmental, institutional, and other activities

(3) The term 'State' means any of the several States, the District of Columbia, and Commonwealth of Puerto Rico, the territories and possessions of the United States.

(4) The term 'local public body' means any public body (including a political subdivision) created by or under the laws of a State or two or more States, or a combination of such bodies and includes Indian tribes, bands, groups, and nations (including Alaska Indians, Aleuts, and Eskimos) of the United States.

(5) The term 'open-space uses' means any use of open-space land for (A) park and recreational purposes, (B) conservation of land and other natural resources, or (C) historic, architectural or scenic purposes.

42 U.S.C. 3303. Eligibility for Assistance; Implementation of Programs, ...

(a) A comprehensive city demonstration program is eligible for assistance under sections 3305 and 3307 of this title only if—

(1) physical and social problems in the area of the city covered by the program are such that a comprehensive city demonstration program is necessary to carry out the policy of the Congress as expressed in section 3301 of this title;

(2) the program is of sufficient magnitude to make a substantial impact on the

physical and social problems and to remove or arrest blight and decay in entire sections or neighborhoods; to contribute to the sound development of the entire city; to make marked progress in reducing social and educational disadvantages, ill health, underemployment, and enforced idleness; and to provide educational, health, and social services necessary to serve the poor and disadvantaged in the area, widespread citizen participation in the program, maximum opportunities for employing residents of the area in all phases of the program, and enlarged opportunities for work and training;

(3) the program, including rebuilding or restoration, will contribute to a well-balanced city with a substantial increase in the supply of standard housing of low and moderate cost, maximum opportunities in the choice of housing accommodations for all citizens of all income levels, adequate public facilities (including those needed for education, health and social services, transportation, and recreation), commercial facilities adequate to serve the residential areas, and ease of access between the residential areas and centers of employment;

(4) the various projects and activities to be undertaken in connection with such programs are scheduled to be initiated within a reasonably short period of time; adequate local resources are, or will be, available for the completion of the program as scheduled, and, in the carrying out of the program, the fullest utilization possible will be made of private initiative and enterprise; administrative machinery is available at the local level for carrying out the program on a consolidated and coordinated basis; substantive local laws, regulations, and other requirements are, or can be expected to be, consistent with the objectives of the program; there exists a relocation plan meeting the requirements of the regulations referred to in section 3307 of this title; the local governing body has approved the program and, where appropriate, applications for assistance under the program; agencies whose cooperation is necessary to the success of the program have indicated their intent to furnish such cooperation; the program is consistent with comprehensive planning for the entire urban or metropolitan area; and the locality will maintain, during the period an approved comprehensive city demonstration program is being carried out, a level of aggregate expenditures for activities similar to those being assisted under this title which is not less than the level of aggregate expenditures for such activities prior to initiation of the comprehensive city demonstration program; and

(5) the program meets such additional requirements as the Secretary may establish to carry out the purposes of this title; *Provided,* That the authority of the Secretary under this paragraph shall not be used to impose criteria or establish requirements except those which are related and essential to the specific provisions of this subchapter.

(b) In implementing this subchapter the Secretary shall—

(1) emphasize local initiative in the planning, development, and implementation of comprehensive city demonstration programs;

(2) insure, in conjunction with other appropriate Federal departments and agencies and at the direction of the President, maximum coordination of Federal assistance provided in connection with this subchapter, prompt response to local initiative, and maximum flexibility in programing, consistent with the requirements of law and sound administrative practice; and

(3) encourage city demonstration agencies to (A) enhance neighborhoods by applying a high standard of design, (B) maintain, as appropriate, natural and historic sites and distinctive neighborhood characteristics, and (C) make maximum possible use of new and improved technology and design, including cost reduction techniques.

About the author . . .

Dr. McGimsey has been associated with the University of Arkansas since 1958. He is presently Chairman of the Anthropology Department and Director of the University of Arkansas Museum. He also serves as Director of the Arkansas Archeological Survey, a State agency employing nine archeologists who are responsible for investigating, recovering, and preserving Arkansas' archeological heritage.

Dr. McGimsey first became concerned with public involvement in archeology when he arrived in Arkansas in 1957 and found a good deal of public interest but no organization or resources to develop and channel that interest. He was responsible for preparing the initial drafts of the Arkansas legislation, and he worked closely with archeological societies and state legislature in making the Arkansas program one of the best publicly-supported archeological programs in the country.

Dr. McGimsey received his B.A. in Anthropology from the University of New Mexico in 1949, and his M.A. and Ph.D. from Harvard in 1954 and 1958, respectively. He has conducted archeological research, not only in Arkansas, but also in New Mexico and the Republic of Panama, and he has received more than 40 research grants from national organizations. He is the author of over 80 articles and has also contributed to or helped to write several books on archeology. He is currently working with Congress to improve federal legislation concerning archeology, and recently served as an advisor to the National Park Service's archeological program. He is also a member of the Arkansas State Review Committee for Historic Preservation and the Executive Committee of the Society for American Archaeology.

Dr. McGimsey is listed in American Men of Science (1962) and Who's Who in the South East (1963) and was nominated to the Council of the American Association of Museums in 1970.